THE GREAT

'Man is in danger of disappearing without having
known where he came from and whether or not
his destiny was controlled by unknown masters
who changed its natural course. He does not
know if in very ancient times superior ancestors
built great civilizations, now unknown, and tried
to conquer the cosmos as we have begun to do.
Fascinating, frustratingly impenetrable
mysteries still challenge our curiosity: the magic
blossoming of Egyptian architecture, the
enigmas of Greek mythology, Hyperborea, the
construction of the Pyramids, the "towers of the
flying men" of Zimbabwe and Peru, levitation,
the Cabala, the Grail, and ancient secret
societies.
Sensing, perhaps, that they are living at the end
of an era, rebellious men now want to take off
their blindfolds and question everything that has
been imposed on them . . .'

Robert Charroux

Also by Robert Charroux in Sphere Books

MASTERS OF THE WORLD

Legacy of the Gods

ROBERT CHARROUX

SPHERE BOOKS LIMITED
30/32 Gray's Inn Road, London WC1X 8JL

This book is dedicated to Jean Cocteau
IN MEMORIAM

Set in Times Roman

Printed in Great Britain by
Hazell Watson & Viney Ltd
Aylesbury, Bucks

CONTENTS

I thank Yvette Charroux for her constant, devoted collaboration; Catherine Krikorian, who revealed the secret of Armenia's primohistory to me; and my companions of the Round Table, who gave me the support of their thought and knowledge in the elaboration of this *Book of Betrayed Secrets*.

I also owe my deepest gratitude to Michel Simkine, a master of dialectics; the learned professors Eugène Falinski and Louis Jacot; the biologist Beltran Garcia; and my friends and colleagues Philippe Bermert, François Couten, S. de Davrichewy. Roger Delorme, Jean-Albert Foex, Jacotte de Grazia, Christiane Le Cossec, Jean Roy, Lola Rofocale, and Hélène Vetter, for the documentation they have given me.

PREFACE

Man is in danger of disappearing without having known where he came from and whether or not his destiny was controlled by unknown masters who changed its natural course. He does not know if in very ancient times superior ancestors built great civilizations, now unknown, and tried to conquer the cosmos as we have begun to do.

Fascinating, frustratingly impenetrable mysteries still challenge our curiosity: the magic blossoming of Egyptian architecture, the enigmas of Greek mythology, Hyperborea, the construction of the Pyramids, the 'towers of the flying men' of Zimbabwe and Peru, levitation, the Cabala, the Grail, and ancient secret societies.

Sensing, perhaps, that they are living at the end of an era, rebellious men now want to take off their blinders and question everything that has been imposed on them.

To help serve that purpose I will offer new explanations of visible and invisible history, presented as hypotheses in the marginal areas of official history and extended by introspective investigations into what are known as parallel universes: the Other World, antitime, the antiuniverse. I will not speak with the arrogance of a pundit certain that he knows the facts, but with the humility of a determined seeker who is certain only that he has taken a few steps forward.

An immense error has warped our understanding of our genesis, and history and prehistory have been distorted at will.

Imagine the width of a pencil mark cutting across a line two hundred million miles long, or a grain of sand in the Sahara: that, in concrete terms, is approximately what our historic and prehistoric eras represent in the concept of space-time.

Is it reasonable to believe that our civilization has been limited to that thin mark, that it has been no more than that grain of sand?

Our ancestral traditions, and obscure yet tenacious intuitions, suggest the hypothesis of a great destiny which man fulfilled in cycles of vanished civilizations, but official science says 'No!' to what is now trying to emerge from the deep abysses of the past. Only one truth seems to have survived: that of mystery. We must believe in it as the sole valid and indestructible reality.

Albert Einstein, one of the greatest geniuses of all time, and the man who was perhaps more capable than any other of understanding all things, gave us the golden key to knowledge: 'The most beautiful feeling that one can have is the sense of mystery. It is the source of all genuine art and real science. Anyone who has never known that emotion, who does not have the gift of wonder and rapture, might as well be dead: his eyes are closed.'

In that same frame of mind, the great poet Jean Cocteau had the courage to express approval of my book *One Hundred Thousand Years of Man's Unknown History*,* even though I advanced some extremely adventurous hypotheses in it. Believing with a faith like Einstein's, he honoured me with a long letter which ended as follows:

Your book . . . should be preserved and consulted; one should meditate on the humility of the procession of evidence that marches beside man's long, terrible foolishness, and of the discoveries that are moving forward on poor roads.

You have explained to me several lines of the *Requiem* that I had misinterpreted, for your texts go beyond exegesis and straighten everything that appears crooked to us.

I must beg Jean Cocteau's pardon: that book, I now realize, was only an awkward, groping effort, unworthy of his concern, since a better truth has now appeared to me after a study of apocryphal writings and ancient texts of

* English translation published by Berkley Publishing Corp., 1971.

great vanished civilizations: the Truth of the West. The world was born in the west, light comes from the west: such is the magic key which, I believe, will truly open, at least partially, the gates of the Mysterious Unknown.

I

PRIMOHISTORY*

* By 'primohistory' I mean that period in the life of the human race which precedes protohistory and is parallel to prehistory but differs from it in that it presupposes the existence of advanced civilizations.

Chapter 1

SUBMERGED CITIES AND DESTROYED LAND

The Bible speaks of the Deluge and the Babylonian clay tablets give an identical but older version: that is the written history, in the literal sense of the term, which is generally regarded as the first record of our civilization.

In my opinion, this view is based on a long-standing error of the Hebrews and Christians, for whom the Old Testament remains an immutable canon of truth. Not one word or letter of it must ever be changed, say the Hebrew texts.

It is true that the world owes a great deal to the Hebrews as well as the Hindus, Egyptians, and Greeks, and there can be no doubt that the Bible is a precious document; but Adam and Eve were not Semites, Hindus, Egyptians, or Greeks. Such an idea fails to take account of discoveries made in the past hundred years, revealing the existence of highly advanced prehistoric civilizations which were unfortunately not known to the writers of Genesis.

When we have eliminated the pseudo-hominids – Australopithecus, Sinanthropus, Pithecanthropus, Fontéchevade Man, Piltdown Man – which are either notorious frauds or absurdities, it seems that the first known human being is Cro-Magnon Man, who lived in the Périgord region of France forty thousand years ago.

Staying within the bounds of prehistory, we must say that civilization comes from west central and southwestern France, because we cannot refuse to attribute civilizations to the people who engraved the stone books in the prehistoric library at Lussac-les-Châteaux, or to the painters of the Montignac-Lascaux caves.

Yet archaeologists, from either religious sectarianism or lack of imagination and combativity, refuse to imagine a real Cro-Magnon or Neanderthal civilization, with towns, commerce, industries, arts, and so on.

If by 'civilization' we mean the expression of a society similar to ours, we must undoubtedly relegate the Cro-Magnons to a primitive limbo. But is there any good reason to believe that the first human civilization was Mediterranean or Oriental, or even terrestrial?

Our history goes back much farther than the Sumerian clay tablets, since geology and oral traditions bring us remote echoes of events outside the world of the ancients. These events are hard to date, but their authenticity is certain.

The world beyond the seas

Celtic traditions speak of another world 'beyond the seas,' to the west, whereas the Bible, enclosed in an egocentric system that has become outmoded, situates the cradle of mankind in the Near East of the Tigris and the Euphrates, though with a possibility of expansion toward God's heaven, which may mean other planets or the stars.

Theologians and historians complacently accept the Biblical postulate and have given it their official stamp of approval. But where does that leave the traditions of Ireland, Wales, France, Spain, and Mexico, and mythologies from all over the world, each with its own version of genesis?

If it is to be honest, our study of probable civilizations must take all traditions into account and make all paths converge in the direction of the logical world to which knowledge leads us.

With this approach, we can see that the geometrical centre of mankind is not in the Orient and that known history does not begin with Sumer or the Deluge, which for orthodox archaeologists mark the intersection of scientific certainty and traditional conjecture.

It is undeniable that the worldwide flood described in Genesis implies much more devastating effects than those that have been detected in the region of the Tigris and the Euphrates. The Breton city of Ys was submerged, and so was the land between France and England: that is a historical certainty which goes back farther than Sumer.

The prehistoric alphabetical writings of Glozel

(France), Newton (Scotland), Alvao (Portugal), Bautzen (Germany), and Costi (Rumania) are thousands of years older than the Babylonian tablets and suggest the existence of cultivated peoples who were the heirs of very ancient vanished civilizations.

Archaeologists stubbornly confine themselves within a cramped rationalism: the smelting of iron began no earlier than thirty-five hundred years ago and bronze thus preceded iron (a foolish notion, since it is based only on the fact that bronze lasts longer than iron); the oldest ruins are the ziggurats (terraced towers) of Babylon and therefore the civilized world was born at Sumer.

All that is false.

Buffon, Laplace, Arago, and Humboldt all agree

Chinese traditions maintain that earthly civilization goes back several hundred thousand years.

The naturalist Buffon stated that in certain regions of the globe, 'pieces of granite, porphyry, jasper and quartz have fallen in rows, mingled with fossil bodies foreign to the earth.'

The famous mathematician Laplace wrote, 'Great peoples whose names are scarcely known to history have disappeared from the lands they inhabited. Their languages and even their cities have ceased to exist; of all the achievements of their knowledge and industry, nothing remains but a vague tradition and a few fragments whose origin is uncertain.'

Alexander Humboldt, the creator of botanical geography, held that a great cataclysm had submerged most of the inhabited world in ancient times.

'It is undeniable,' said the great physicist Arago, 'that floods do not explain the effects noted by geologists.' He believed that there had been a profound disruption of the earth's surface, caused by a cosmic catastrophe.

Jean Sylvain Bailly, the King's Astronomer and a member of the Academy of Sciences, wrote in 1785, 'Traditions and monuments give us abundant evidence that before that general conflagration the earth had a universal civilization of which only vestiges now remain.'

On the basis of these statements by famous men, the writer A. d'Espiard de Colonge summed up the problem as follows: 'Everything seems to be piled up without order on the surface of the globe. It is as though another world, or at least some debris from one, had fallen onto the earth.'

In our time, geologists, ethnologists, archaeologists, and scientists of all other disciplines agree in acknowledging that great earthquakes and floods have ravaged the earth and decimated its population at times which can be approximately placed at 4000 B.C., 10,000 B.C., 16,000 B.C., and so on.

Everyone would accept the reality of vanished civilizations if prehistorians had not shown doubt with their Paleolithic and Neolithic eras and their idea that man descends from the ape. If our ancestors were apes, they certainly could not have developed atomic physics, telesion, and space travel!

But in the past few years two discoveries have opened up the whole question and demolished the theories of prehistorians of the old school:

1. It is unlikely that man descends from the ape.

2. The Paleolithic and Neolithic are inventions, monumental errors, based on nothing but misinterpretations. I will discuss this more fully later; for the moment, I will simply point out that our ancestors never used flint knives, axes, and other tools, except for a few outcasts who lived at a more primitive level. If the use of flint tools had been the general rule, we ought to find billions and billions of them. The fact is that, relatively speaking, practically none have been found: only a few hundred thousand axes (the main tool), *not enough to justify the assumption of more than twenty inhabitants of the globe per generation.*

Evidence still exists to show that cities were buried, whole continents were swallowed up by floods and cosmic cataclysms, and unknown civilizations preceded ours.

Buffon, Laplace, Arago, Humboldt, and dozens of other scientists have believed this. Why not you?

Temples and cities under water and land.

In the Gobi Desert, Soviet archaeologists have discovered immense foundations rising from the sand in various places. In the desert near Marib, Yemen, are the ruins of the ancient capital of the Queen of Sheba, but beneath these ruins are the foundations of a much older city, dating from the time when Arabia was a fertile, well-irrigated land.

Farther north, still in the desert, are the ruins of Palmyra, seventy-five miles west of Homs, Syria. Why was this great ancient city built in a desert? Historians are unable to give a cogent answer, and they are all the more puzzled because they know that hundreds of thousands of inhabitants ate, drank, and lived in Queen Zenobia's capital. Everything is explained, however, if we accept the idea that this desert was once arable land.

Palmyra was built by Solomon, according to Jewish tradition, but there were already ruins at that site before his time. Some chroniclers agree with Baron d'Espiard de Colonge's statement that 'a highly praised king [Solomon] found a great treasure buried in a city that had been destroyed by a horrible catastrophe. This was the source of his famous wealth.'

King Solomon sent expeditions to Ophir, thought to have been in what is now Southern Rhodesia, to bring back gold for building the Temple. But the yield was rather disappointing. In reality, Solomon was originally a poor king who had to accept help from Hiram in building the Temple. D'Espiard de Colonge's assertion is therefore not entirely unreasonable.

According to legend, the ancient city of Copae, in Greece, was destroyed by Hercules. The story, of course, conceals a more rational truth.

As late as the nineteenth century, the remains of a city could still be seen at the bottom of Lake Copias. Five thousand years ago, the city must have been at least a hundred and fifty feet higher. Archaeologists were astonished to discover a network of sewers designed to convey sewage to the sea, but since the city had sunk into the bottom of the valley, the sewers rose away from it, rather than descending. This showed that a great cataclysm had occurred there. The Greeks had lost their memory of it, since they attributed it to Hercules' anger.

Yet Copae was a powerful city. Deep passages, cut into the rock, are connected to fifty branches of the sewers to serve as air shafts. The whole system is a titanic achievement, beyond the capabilities of either ancient or modern Greece.

A refuge for initiates

In Egypt, buried temples are discovered several times in each century and there can be no doubt that the desert still covers vast unknown cities.

The monuments of Thebes, the 'hundred-gated city,' with its rock-cut tombs and underground palaces, have been partially uncovered, and so have those of Karnak, where sixteen hundred colossal sphinxes stand guard along a royal avenue. The Sphinx of Giza and the lower part of the Pyramids have also been exhumed, but ancient Egypt, earlier than the pharaohs and the Deluge, still sleeps beneath millions of cubic yards of sand whose accumulation remains unexplained.

Baron d'Espiard de Colonge, who devoted his life to studying this subject and gathering the traditions of North Africa, wrote in his book *L'Egypte et l'Océanie* (Paris, 1882):

It was said in very ancient times that south of the Great Pyramids and west of the deep ruins of Memphis there are a temple and the remains of an old portico more or less buried in the sand and difficult to find in the maze of the desert. Here, according to legend, are the entrances of long galleries leading to labyrinths and ancient, extraordinary habitations of which the Pyramids are only the thick, massive spires. Vast, interconnected branches gave these structures the appearance of a city engulfed in dry matter, rather than being submerged in water.

Still without giving his sources, he adds that this secret will remain hidden for a long time because groups of initiates held their meetings in the buried city, which had also served as a sanctuary for 'high personages of the West.' There was thus, under the Egyptian desert, a subterranean kingdom similar to the Agartha in Tibet.

Foreseeing long in advance, by 'calculations and lofty, learned observations,' that the earth would undergo a great cataclysm the initiates of Egypt and West had built this refuge where they were able to protect themselves from danger and, at the same time, to save 'precious objects of all kinds, and the archives of the primeval world.'

D'Espiard de Colonge's statements are not very convincing, but it is generally forgotten that the excavations of the famous Egyptologist Auguste Edouard Mariette, in the mid-nineteenth century, tend to accredit a fantastic interpretation.

Under the Sphinx

Sixty feet below the Sphinx, Mariette found cyclopean structures and a magnificent temple comprising a vast aggregate of chambers and galleries, made of granite and alabaster. It bore no inscriptions or bas-reliefs and it had been buried for so many thousands of years that no historian had even suspected its existence.

Tradition says that the Sphinx was erected at a time which defies the memory of men, and the same may be true of the Pyramids. It is quite obvious that they were not built in a desert.

In *One Hundred Thousand Years of Man's Unknown History*, I made an important new contribution to this mysterious subject. I can now add still more to it.

If the Pyramids are what they are believed to be – a kind of beacon capable of resisting earthly cataclysms and burial under shifting sands – it must be acknowledged that they are also a shrine in which the most valuable documents of ancient civilizations were hidden. This means that their builders probably intended to give them measurements, a mass and an inner and outer architecture which would reveal highly advanced knowledge of mathematics and astronomy.

The ancient Egyptian monuments are capable of speaking, but too many noninitiates have tried to force information from them. Despite countless scientific, parascientific, and occult efforts, the Great Pyramids have still not yielded up their secret.

The Pyramids

The date of their construction is still a mystery. Napoleon considered them to be about four thousand years old; Herodotus gives their age as six thousand years. To modern archaeologists the Pyramids are tombs and, like the Sphinx, were built during the fourth dynasty, in about 2900 B.C.

The historian Abu-Zeyd el Balkhy writes that 'the inscription engraved on the Pyramids was translated into Arabic and revealed the time of their construction. It was during the period when Lyra was in the sign of Cancer. Calculation gave a date of twice thirty-six thousand years before the Hegira.'

This seems a bit exaggerated!

Papyruses found an Egyptian mummies by the Arab and Coptic archaeologists Armelius, Abumazar and Murtadi give a more plausible account:

> In that time Sauryd, son of Sahluk, King of Egypt, saw in a dream an enormous planet striking the earth with a horrendous noise and engendering darkness on its surface. The decimated populations did not know where to flee to escape from the falling stones and hot, stinking water that accompanied the cataclysm. These events were to happen when the heart of the Lion reached the first minute of the head of Cancer. King Sauryd then ordered the construction of the Pyramids.

This story is in correlation with the fall of the sky described by traditions all over the world and, in my judgment, it refers to the advent of the planet Venus.

The ancients said that the limestone covering of the Pyramids (which has now entirely disappeared) bore inscriptions in an unknown language. These inscriptions were seen in the thirteenth century by the Arab historian and physician Abdallatif.

Nevertheless, no hypothesis satisfactorily clears up the mystery of the Pyramids: their purpose remains a problem, their writing has not been rediscovered and their inner layout is impenetrable to us.

'It still remains to be explained,' said the archaeologist Jomard, 'why such a prodigious mass of stones was erected. And the reasons for all those galleries; that profusion of chambers; that shaft whose entrance and lower extremity are unknown; those oblique, horizontal and bent passages of different dimensions; those twenty-five mortises in the benches of the upper gallery; that large elevated gallery followed by an extremely low corridor; those three singular bays that precede the central chamber and their form and details, without analogy to anything we know. . . .'

Without analogy to anything we know – that may be one of the keys to the enigma!

It is true that occultists have given answers to these questions, particularly by maintaining that the inside of the Pyramids represented a path of initiation; it is true that other monuments in the world present similar though not identical mysteries: megaliths, the aligned stones and megalithic caverns of Brittany and Great Britain, the temple of Hagar Quim on the island of Malta, the statues of Easter Island, the earthen pyramids of Polynesia. The unknown and the mysterious abound on our globe, but the inner architecture of the Egyptian Pyramids is quite specifically 'without analogy to anything we know.'

Extraterrestrial structures?

This raises a question: Does their meaning, their reason for being, lie in concepts foreign to our earthly mentality?

This conjecture was stated one evening at the Round Table around which the members of a Paris secret society study problems of the fantastic and the Mysterious

Unknown. (The society meets periodically in the back room of a restaurant on the Rue Rodier. Around a table lighted by a kerosene lamp, four men and four women consider enigmas and suggest explanations free of scientific and religious dogma in order to enclose different truths in a space and a time, or in a space-time, that cannot be accepted by minds devoted to traditional rationalism.)

On the hypothesis that people from another planet came to Earth, those superior ancestors, after having lived here for hundreds or thousands of years, must have calculated the exact date of the cataclysm that would cause 'the end of the world.' Wanting to leave any future generations a memorial that would serve to instruct them, they built the Pyramids in Egypt and the Gate of Tiahuanaco in Bolivia.

The science of those extraterrestrials was, of course, conditioned by their nature. Our archaeologists, with their earthly minds, have so far been unable to find the key to it, but higher development will no doubt make it possible to translate the message in the future.

When the orientation of the Great Pyramid coincides with the north it will be the sign of a new era, and the hidden truth will then appear, naked, resplendent – and perhaps terrifying.

In seeking coordinates and standards of measurement in the Great Pyramid's dimensions, which are unquestionably significant, occultists have merely foreseen a truth that is still silent and imperfectly defined.

Although these traditions and archaeological discoveries do not clear up the enigma, they give us the certainty that the substructures of the Pyramids go back much farther in time than the Biblical Deluge.

Refuge cities

It is permissible to suggest that the secret city of Giza – if it exists – may have served as a refuge several times, in the course of *several deluges*, and that it may be used for the same purpose in the next worldwide cataclysm? This hypothesis, accepted by initiates, leads us to think that *antediluvian records are still hidden under the Pyramids.*

Traditions of India, Asia Minor, and North and South America strangely agree in saying that initiates were able to find safe refuges on all continents.

In his book *Beasts, Men and Gods*, Ossendowski writes that a Chinese lama 'told the Bogdo Khan that underground caverns in America are inhabited by the ancient people who disappeared beneath the earth.'

A legend? No. It is certain that the American underground cities are no longer inhabited by the 'people who disappeared beneath the earth,' but they were a few thousand years ago, and in the ruins of Tiahuanaco, Bolivia, the nineteenth-century naturalist Charles d'Orbigny saw the entrances of galleries leading to the secret city.

It is even probable that the open tumuli and covered galleries of Brittany and Ireland also served as shelters 'against the fall of stones from the sky' at the time of the great cosmic cataclysm. At the edge of the Brocéliande forest near Néant, in the Morbihan district of Brittany, is a place called Pertius Néanti which, according to occultists, marks the entrance to a secret Celtic refuge analogous to the Agartha.

The Peruvians of the Xauxa valley, and the Mexicans and Indians of the lakes, also have the tradition of a secret refuge used by initiates who had the mission of beginning the world all over again.

The land of the moon

The Bible explains the causes and exact nature of the cosmic cataclysm by divine wrath, but a more rational approach suggests a perturbation of our solar system.

It was said in ancient times that the tragedy of the Deluge coincided with *a great planetary change*.

Baron d'Espiard de Colonge advanced a theory which, though incredible at first sight, should not be rejected without consideration, since it is partially based on facts that are at least significant, if not conclusive.

He believed that a large part of the animal, plant, and mineral matter on the surface of the moon had fallen onto the earth, burying our ancient valleys, cities, and civilizations, erecting mountains where there had been flat land

and turning green, populated regions into sandy deserts.

We now know that, with its bare, ravaged, dusty surface, the moon has the appearance of a planet whose outer layer has been torn away and deposited elsewhere. It seems to have been 'scalped,' which leads us to suppose that it once underwent a terrible cataclysm. Furthermore it has no atmosphere or oceans; either it never had any or else it lost them, which is more likely. And it has been violently bombarded by meteorites that have left it riddled with craters, like the fields of the Argonne in 1918.

This raises a question: Why that bombardment on the moon and not on the earth? Is the moon a planet that came from elsewhere, was battered in the course of its long journey through space, and then, after colliding with the earth or passing close to it, became its satellite?

D'Espiard de Colonge showed great sagacity when, more than a century in advance, he announced great nuclear wars, natural cataclysms, and perhaps an intervention by extraterrestrials. In doing so, he also put forward an idea that has since become common: that of universal evolution.

His overall theory is fantastic, but it cannot be totally disregarded because everyone (except prehistorians) knows that our globe has undergone great bombardments from space which submerged certain regions and wiped out whole populations. Yet the human race has lost nearly all specific memories of the floods and lethal rains of fire, earth, and stones that have periodically ravaged the planet. It happened as recently as 1500 B.C., and it is only by a miracle that we have lived in cosmic tranquillity since then – a miracle that cannot go on indefinitely!

'Modern Europeans and all other peoples,' writes d'Espiard de Colonge, 'have only a few centuries in which to organize and prepare on Earth to withstand numerous assaults from mysterious space. This ordeal will be only one more stage in celestial progress or transformation.

'It is no longer a question of the end of the world, but of universal evolution, with all due deference to those mediocre people who refuse to venture beyond conventional

platitudes and always bring charges of impiety or wild
scientific speculation against the sensible words of anyone
who tries to broaden their thin, shrunken minds.'

A forgotten fact: the end of the last world

Whatever the merits of d'Espiard de Colonge's theories
may be, it seems undeniable that worldwide cataclysms
have occurred in the past.

In the last ten or eleven thousand years the globe has
several times been devastated by catastrophes whose
effects are comparable to the damage that would be
caused by the explosion of thousands of nuclear bombs.
Oceans have rolled over mountains and into valleys, the
poles have shifted, some continents have been submerged
while others rose from the bottom of the sea; and, each
time, nearly all of the human race has perished.

Our ancestors experienced such upheavals in relatively
recent times. Those lucky enough to survive them transmitted memories of them in traditions and sacred writings.

But, whether from foolish unconcern or in obedience to
mysterious orders, the leading figures of our institutions
and sciences either deny those primordial events or pre-
tend to know nothing about them. According to them,
the engulfment of Atlantis is only a story invented by
Plato. With a condescending smile they decree that the
Land of Mu, vanished civilizations, and buried cities are
nothing but mental aberrations on the part of occultists.

The truth is that our whole civilization has been built
on a vast imposture with arbitrary bases, senseless postulates, and so-called sacred writings that have been censored and distorted.

Denouncing the hoax and reconsidering the whole
problem would be a titanic task, a revolution on a worldwide scale, which our leaders cannot afford to undertake.
Whether they like it or not, they must go on playing the
game with loaded dice, smiling at the 'fables' of tradition,
claiming that civilization was born at Sumer and that the
first human being was engendered by the seed of an Asian
or African ape.

But what different truths emerge from the past for anyone who goes back to it without following the rutted road of official history!

If most of the human race perished four thousand years ago, if continents have been submerged, if – who knows? – other planets have brushed against the earth, pulling up its oceans by their gravity and dropping their mountains and perhaps their cities onto it, should we not revise part of our knowledge to make it fit the data of reconstructed history?

That is what I will try to do, referring to the only sources still accessible to us: oral and written traditions.

Deluge: the world began in Armenia

The reality of the worldwide Deluge (which is scientifically accepted) is attested by all ancient peoples with the same essential points: the destruction of mankind, except for one couple who were saved in a boat and later repopulated the earth.

In the Bible the Deluge, though reconstructed from fragment of traditions, is related with a certain coherence.

God said, 'This race of men whom I have created, I will wipe them off the face of the earth – man and beast, reptiles and birds. I am sorry that I ever made them.'* (Genesis 6:7.)

One might condemn the injustice of the Lord, who, in his wrath, was determined to annihilate the guilty and the innocent, the pure and the impure, men and animals; but is it not a matter of symbols?

God did as he had decided, except that he spared the virtuous Noah, his family, and the animals that entered the Ark. 'Everything died that had the breath of life in its nostrils, everything on dry land.' (Genesis 7:22.) Noah and the other survivors landed on Mount Ararat, in Armenia.

If we are to believe the Bible, our present world was not born at Sumer, but in Armenia, and our civilization is therefore at least the second human civilization.

* All Biblical quotations are from *The New English Bible*, Oxford University Press, 1970. (Translator's note.)

The world's archives are saved

Chaldean traditions correlate rather well with those of the Bible. King Xisuthrus was warned by the god Chronos that the Deluge would soon occur. He buried under Sisparis, the City of the Sun, 'the writings that deal with the beginning, middle and end of all things' (writings that were therefore older than the Bible) and, with his whole court, took refuge in a vessel that, like the Ark, finally landed in Armenia, but on Mount Korkura.

An important note: as soon as his vessel had come to rest on the peak of Mount Korkura, King Xisuthrus, the Noah of the Chaldeans, disembarked with the pilot, his wife, and his daughter, and the four of them were never seen again, even though the only dry land at the time was a small island: they were taken away into the sky, as Enoch had been.

Taken away how? By angels or by a flying machine?

According to apocryphal writings, Noah took the world's oldest book, the *Book of Enoch*, with him in the Ark, and several initiates, notably Enoch and Methuselah, took refuge beyond the earth during the whole Deluge.

All over the world, traditions affirm the reality of that Deluge and that 'end of the world.'

In India, the Vedas and the Ramayana relate a similar story in which the god Brahma gives the legendary Manu the responsibility of repopulating the earth. In the more recent Bhagavata Purana, however, it is the King of Drawida who plays the part of Manu, after having hidden the precious Vedas, perhaps in the sanctuary of the Agartha.

In Egypt, foreseeing the Deluge, Hermes Trismegistus writes the sum of human knowledge on steles so that it will escape destruction.

A Jewish tradition reported by the historian Josephus says that, to preserve human knowledge, the patriarch Seth, 'foreseeing the double destruction by fire and water that Adam had predicted, erected two pillars, one of brick and the other of stone, on which this knowledge was engraved.'

Evidence for the earthly cataclysm

Plato says that when Solon had questioned the Egyptian priests of Sais, one of them said to him, 'There have been, and will be again, many destructions of mankind arising out of many causes; the greatest have been brought about by the agencies of fire and water, and other lesser ones by innumerable other causes.' And concerning Atlantis: 'There occurred violent earthquakes and floods; and in a single day and night of misfortune all your warlike men in a body sank into the earth, and the island of Atlantis in like manner disappeared in the depths of the sea.'

The Greeks spoke of two floods: one during the reign of Ogyges and another in the time of Deucalion, son of Prometheus, which is thought to have occurred about thirty-five hundred years ago.

In Germany the flood was preceded by a scourge of fire strongly resembling a cosmic cataclysm, which is also the case with traditions in most other parts of the world, where water and fire from the sky combined to wipe out the human race.

In Exodus and Joshua, the Bible speaks of strange celestial and terrestrial phenomena taking place after the Deluge. In Exodus 9:23–26 we read: 'The Lord sent thunder and hail, with fire flashing down to the ground. The Lord rained down hail on the land of Egypt, hail and fiery flashes through the hail, so heavy that there had been nothing like it in all Egypt from the time that Egypt became a nation. Throughout Egypt the hail struck everything in the fields, both man and beast; it beat down every growing thing and shattered every tree. Only in the land of Goshen, where the Israelites lived, was there no hail.'

One may, of course, have doubts about that providential protection, especially since traditions known to rabbis say that nearly all of Israel perished.

Dating these events at the time of the Exodus, the Egyptians say that a cosmic upheaval put an end to the period of the Middle Kingdom and that most of the human race was killed.

One may also have doubts on the whole subject of the

Exodus. It was probably only a long, wandering journey by a few tribes. The Egyptians, overwhelmed by the cataclysm, surely did not pursue the Hebrews; in that sense, the crossing of the Red Sea is a fable.

The Ipuwer Papyrus speaks of rivers of blood, a rain of red earth, walls devoured by fire and a double wall of water which swallowed up men.

These stories of postdiluvian upheavals are puzzling to historians. Are they really altered versions of the great worldwide Deluge, or, accepting the Biblical and Egyptian dating, do they refer to localized catastrophes?

In Greek mythology, worldwide cataclysms are represented by the revolt of the Titans, the war of the giants and the struggle between Typhoeus and Zeus.

> The sea and the earth resounded with a hideous noise and the shaken sky groaned. ... The fertile earth burned and quivered, vast forests exploded, everything was seething. ... The earth and the sky were mingled; the former was convulsed in its depths, the latter had tumbled down. (*Mythologie Générale*, by F. Guiraud and A. V. Pierre.)

In his book *Worlds in Collision*, Immanuel Velikovsky extends this thesis by attributing the upheavals to the movements of a comet which touched the earth twice before changing into a planet of our solar system: the radiant Venus.

Velikovsky seems to me very close to the truth and I accept all his theories, though I stress an event which, in my opinion, must have preceded the natural cataclysm: an earthly cataclysm caused by men. Velikovsky alludes to such an event in the last lines of his preface.

To my mind it is so obvious that 'the sky fell on the earth' that I would believe it with unshakable faith even if there were no evidence for it.

For the ancient Celts the memory of the cataclysm left the only fear capable of chilling their hearts: the fear that the sky would fall on their heads.

The Lithuanians believed that only one member of the divine race had survived: the Aryan Mannus, whose name recalls the Indian Manu, the Greek Minos, the Cymric Menw, and the Egyptian Menes.

The Deluge of the Turks, Arabs, and Abyssinian Catholics is copied from that of the Bible. In Africa, traditions say that one day in ancient times the sky fell on the earth.

The Bundahish, a sacred book of the Parsis, describes a war between the sky and the earth, between the stars and the planets.

We know through Ovid that the Caucasus was set ablaze, which must have had some relation to the pertoleum deposits there, particularly in Azerbaijan, the 'Land of Fire.'

In India, the cosmic cataclysm is evoked by the combat between Vishnu or Krishna and the Serpent. The Visuddhi Magga says that the earth was turned upside down and that a cycle of the world was destroyed.

The same terms are used in Chinese traditions and may refer to the flood in the time of Emperor Yau, who saw water rising to the mountaintops and killing people by the millions.

There was also 'the end of an age of the world' in Japan. In Siberia it is said that a sea of fire consumed the whole earth. Traditions of the Eskimos, the Lapps, and particularly the Finns ((in the Kalevala) say that the earth was turned upside down and that a worldwide fire followed by a flood wiped out the human race.

In South America the flood of Bochica, in Colombia, and that of the Mexican Coxcox are similar to Noah's, with a number of survivors that could be counted on one's fingers. In Brazil the sky once fell on the earth. In Polynesia there was a flood and a rain of fire, after which some parts of the land were submerged while others rose from the sea.

It is worth noting that the end of the world has a cosmic nature in all traditions, even those from the most remote parts of Africa and Polynesia, with one exception: the Bible, for which the whole world is concentrated around Jerusalem.

These worldwide floods and cataclysms, attested by traditions and proved by Cuvier and geologists, leave little if any doubt about the reality of vanished civilizations, submerged continents, and a whole invisible history that is fascinating to reconstruct.

Chapter 2

THE WORLD WAS BORN IN THE U.S.A.

Look at a topographical map of the earth for a moment, pretending to know no more about human history than an extraterrestrial newly arrived from Venus or Betelgeuse. You will see that a good part of the planet is divided into deserts, on the one hand, and forests, fertile plains, and grasslands, on the other.

If you have a logical mind, one thought will immediately come to you: civilizations must not have developed in North Africa, Egypt, Mesopotamia, or Afghanistan, since those regions are veritable deserts where it is all but impossible to find such essentials as drinking water, arable land, rivers, abounding in fish, game animals from forests and grassy plains, wood and stone for building. . . . If ancient peoples settled there, they must have been totally lacking in common sense!

They chose the desert
That is what you would have to think if you knew nothing about human history. Yet in spite of everything it was in those barren lands, and only there, that the greatest civilizations of Africa and Asia were developed (just as the greatest European civilization arose in rocky Greece).

Is it not senseless and incredible?

North and south of those areas were forests rich in game, fertile plains irrigated by thousands of brooks and rivers, with land good for growing millet, grapes, wheat, barley, lentils, and all the fruit trees of creation. Hares, rabbits, partridges, wild pigs, and deer could be taken by any bowman, and the rivers teemed with trout, pike, salmon, lampreys, and sturgeon. Yet the prehistoric peoples who invented civilization disdained these green lands and chose the deserts of Africa and Asia; that is, they chose aridity, hunger, and want.

It is incredible but true, a mysterious reality that calls

for rational study but seems to have aroused little interest in archaeologists and philosophers.

It would be futile to object that in the past those lands may not have been deserts as they are today, because ancient writings would refute the objection for the two or three thousand years before Christ. In the Bible, for example, the wandering Hebrews are never shown becoming lost in a forest, travelling by boat on a river, picking daisies in spring, or making hay in the meadows of verdant valleys; instead, they trudged across vast deserts and depended on manna for their survival.

Fracture lines

Another fact deepens the enigma: those Asian and African civilizations were located on a parallel of latitude where earthquakes are frequent, and the same is true, except that the lines are of longitude rather than latitude, of the powerful Incan civilization in the Andes and the Mayan and Aztec civilizations in the mountains of Mexico and Guatemala.

If you draw a map of the areas where there are earthquakes, volcanoes, and fracture lines in the earth's crust, you will have a map of the lands where civilizations were born: Mexico, Guatemala, Peru, Chile, Colombia, Bolivia, North Africa, Spain, France, Italy, Greece, Egypt, Persia, Mesopotamia, Afghanistan, China, India, and so on, as well as the mysterious Hyperborea and the hypothetical Atlantis and Mu, which are wholly or partially submerged.

Not only did our prehistoric ancestors prefer a desert to a green paradise, they also carried masochism to the point of settling in the most dangerous places they could find, the only places where the earth spews out fire and lava and opens to kill, destroy, and send the oceans surging forth in tidal waves and floods.

It is as though man had a compelling unconscious need to draw some sort of radiation or emanation, necessary to his development, from cracks opening into the womb of Mother Earth.

A son of Gaea created from clay and dust, man wants

to live in close contact with the maternal womb, however monstrous it may seem, because he then receives the breath of life from the entrails of the earth and participates in the ceaseless birth of cracks and the fertilizing rhythm of evolution.

The religion of the womb is common to all peoples. Even the Catholic Church observes it, with veneration of the mystic almond of the Virgin and black statues of the Virgin, notably the one at Chartres, known as Our Lady of Under the Earth, in which esotericists see a symbol of the return to matter.

Going still farther, they identify the entrails of Gaea, or Mother Earth, with the labyrinths of mythology and those that are traced out by the floors of certain cathedrals, such as Chartres and Montpellier. In this sense, initiation often takes the path from the womb to the entrails to symbolize the 'reverse path' leading through death to the Beyond of a parallel universe.

Eroticism is the plus sign that signifies genesis; that is, physical laws, electrodynamics, psychology, and, on the human level, the supremely elaborate manifestation of cybernetics.

Near the gaping womb of Gaea, who gave birth to him, man knows that he must not cut the umbilical cord: he knows that he must die there, but he accepts his destiny.

And from that aberrant initial choice, that masochism, came industries utilizing fire; architectural art, and time in motion, marked off by great discoveries and the most prodigious civilizations: that of Egypt, with its temples and pyramids; those of Arabia, Persia, and Afghanistan; that of Mesopotamia, with the amazing Sumer; those of the Incas and the Mayas.

To survive, man had to sharpen his genius to the point of becoming sublime, under penalty of death. He had to imagine, invent, and create in a few generations what the prehistoric golden age, stagnating in millennia without duration, had been unable to give him.

(The existence of a golden age clashes with the principle of universal evolution. In the absolute, there cannot be a golden age, a golden number, or an immutable truth.

Not even in death. The golden age presupposes immortality and therefore an eternally static nature inhabited by people who do not procreate, sexless like the angels of Christian mythology. If a deep truth is hidden in this symbol, it may relate to a universe that is not the one we know.)

But why had earlier prehistoric men not chosen to live dangerously? Why had they not responded to the call of the earth's cracks? Were there so few of them that the need for safety was stronger than the need to evolve? Or did they belong to another race? This hypothesis is not absurd and deserves to be studied.

Either Cro-Magnon and Neanderthal men were native earthlings who had degenerated as the result of radiation set off by their ancestors* and had instinctively rejected evolution and its symbols, fire and iron; or else the people of protohistory – Sumerians, Hebrews, Egyptians, Incas, Mayas – were descendants of races alien to our planet, which would explain their superior intellects and technological creations, but not their singular behaviour.

Someone decided in the invisible

The instinct of self-preservation was manifested in all of them, whether they descended from native earthlings or extraterrestrials, but in some of them it was overshadowed by a miraculous, magic, or inspired foreknowledge.

In this sense, prophets were able to look into the future and see the time when the desert would give birth to civilization, then swallow up outdated cities and people who had accomplished their task and their cycle. Perhaps they saw, under those sterile sands, the rich petroleum deposits that would be the reward of long tribulations or form the infernal charge which would blow up the planet in apocalyptic times.

* In the second chapter of *One Hundred Thousand Years of Man's Unknown History*, I stated the view that superior ancestors brought on a worldwide nuclear disaster, as we may be about to do, and that the tragically impaired survivors had to climb back up the scale of evolution to restructure the human race.

Within the framework of evolution it is believed that in order to reach the sublime heights of which he is capable, man must seek solutions involving unstable systems and reject easy solutions of balance.

Since prehistoric man was perfectly adapted to his way of life he was no longer subject to biological evolution and he obeyed only nature. Then one day he rejected that obedience and opted for free will. He left the golden age by choosing the iron age. This implies a superior awakening of consciousness, a liberation of intelligence against the dictatorship of instinct that has blocked his development. He therefore chose fracture lines and deserts as the places where he would pursue his adventure. He now had to reckon with instability and death, but at the same time he escaped from noncreation and the eternal present.

Whatever explanation we may propose, we must eventually come to the superior cause that guided the choice of dancing on a volcano. And that cause may be called universal law or determinism. It may also be called God or Lucifer, the Prince of Intelligence and man's intellectual guide. Or Satan, if we consider the horrors of civilization. ... It all depends on the meaning given to evolution.

Thus nothing had yet become clear in the genesis of mankind, but a rhythm could be discerned: an expansion of the universe, probably with periods of contraction corresponding to 'Brahma's breath' and conventional theories of the pulsating universe.

One great fracture zone of the globe seems to escape the general law governing vanished civilizations: the territory now occupied by the United States. In this zone, between the thirtieth and fortieth parallels of north latitude, everything should have blossomed and flourished, but instead there was only a vacuum, and what should have been a prodigiously fertile soil remained incomprehensibly barren.

To a mind attuned to the fantastic, this anomaly suggests a paradoxical hypothesis: what if the greatest and oldest civilization developed in precisely the place where there are now no vestiges of ancient civilizations?

Examining the U.S.A. hypothesis

If superior ancestors lived on the site of the present U.S.A. in primohistoric times, and if their civilization was destroyed by a nuclear catastrophe, would it not be normal that nothing should remain of it today?

If a nuclear war wiped out the human race, what would be left of our civilization a million years from now? Nothing, except perhaps for the stone tools of people living in places like Borneo and New Guinea.

And so many changes have taken place in our globe through the millennia! Certain deserts were grassy plains in remote times; the heart of the Sahara was under water; there was dry land between France and the British Isles. ... So anything was possible in the long chain of time. The era of superior ancestors could have unfolded in unknown America before the era of prehistoric men, or parallel with it.

To be given serious consideration, of course, this hypothesis must be supported by discoveries, miraculously preserved documents – in short, a collection of credible evidence, rather than assertions that can only be taken on faith. With a certain amazement, I must confess, I saw the idea grow stronger, take shape, colour, and consistency, cease being a conjecture and become a near-certainty that emerged alive through the world's traditions, science, and visible history.

Light is in the west

It is only by an arbitrary convention that historians generally regard the east as the source of all development. Tradition and historical research show that, on the contrary, the dawn of mankind rose in the west.

Traditionally, it was toward the west the prehistoric men moved; it was in the west that they sought the Other World where millions of suns shone in everlasting daylight; all the great invasions and migrations of peoples converged on the west, the land of desire, or, more precisely, the British Isles, Gaul, and Iberia, the last headland of the great continent.

What were those ancestors seeking in the fabulous west bounded by the ocean? What misty atavism guided them in that direction?

Ignoring that primordial fact is a senseless mistake, yet most historians have not hesitated to make it.

After the prehistoric era and the quest for the initiation that Ulysses sought on the island of the Elysian Fields in the great western ocean, the historic era also regarded the west as the location of wondrous lands and islands that are now thought to be legendary: Brazil Island, San Brandan, the Happy Islands, the Other World or land of the Grail, and Hyperborea. (The Scandinavians, Germans, and Celts considered Hyperborea to be their birthplace. Taking account of geological factors, it seems to have coincided with the present territory of the United States before the cataclysm that caused the axis of our globe to be tilted at an angle of 23° 27'.)

And finally it was toward the west that the ancient Greeks and Egyptians situated Atlantis, whose existence will sooner or later have to be generally accepted.

Thus, for a 'paradoxical' hypothesis, we have a point of departure that can claim a certain orthodoxy!

The United States (I will often call it America for the sake of convenience) comprises a vast area where deserts, vitrified rocks, and the absence of human beings in remote times seem to imply a curse or a taboo which may well have been the result of an atomic cataclysm, whether natural or not.

On a scientific level there is no doubt about the reality of that cataclysm, but the reasons for it are still highly controversial.

The earth is askew

Thousands of years ago, in the time of our unknown ancestors, the earth's axis was not tilted, which meant that there were no seasons. It was then, in the time before the great cataclysm, that there existed what tradition has called the golden age, in the limited sense of the term.

Rotating on a north-south axis inclined at an angle of 23° 27' to the plane of the ecliptic, our globe as it is now

depicted does not intrigue us very much, since it is one of
our oldest childhood companions, with the map of Europe in which, following a secret rite, France is pink, Spain
is yellow, Italy is violet, and Belgium is green.

But from that tilting of the earth's axis flows all of
human history and what ought to be the foundation of our
knowledge. If schoolteachers taught their pupils, even on
the most elementary level, that cosmogony and geology
are the essential base of knowledge, human development
would make a prodigious leap forward. People would then
realize the flimsiness of empirical teachings and they
would have a clearer view of their origin and destiny.

The tilt of our globe shows beyond doubt that it once
underwent a terrible cosmic upheaval which also affected
all the other planets of the solar system in varying degrees. And that brings us straight to the heart of the problem: we earthlings are not unique, privileged creatures
confined within a closed world; we belong to an infinite
system and *all our human history has meaning only if we
integrate it into universal evolution.*

When the cataclysm occurred, the earth tilted and
wavered. The poles slid across the continents and the seas.
Drifting on the furiously churning oceans, ice floes the
size of Corsica or Sicily collided with each other. Mountains trembled on their bases. Towns and cities, with their
swarming masses of horrified people, were drawn into
maelstroms while the oceans, in the grip of centrifugal
force, rushed across the continents and climbed the
highest mountains.

In an instant the population of the earth, millions or billions of people – will we ever know? – what drowned and
crushed, and a whole unknown civilization was reduced to
a shapeless mass in which nothing identifiable remained.

Did a few people survive? We may assume so, but it is
also possible to assume that everyone on earth perished
and that our present human race had an extraterrestrial
origin. The first assumption, however, seems more likely.

Here we have a rational history of the earth mingled
with the hypothesis of a civilization wiped out by a natural

cataclysm which, I believe, was preceded by one or more nuclear explosions whose reality must be demonstrated.

This is a bold view and, of course, it is not accepted by traditional historians. It is supported mainly by geophysical observations, traditions bequeathed to us by ancestors who escaped the cataclysm, and certain evidence that tends to pinpoint nuclear explosions in two centres of vanished civilizations: America and the Gobi Desert.

We will thus see the resurgence of the invisible history of mankind, now lost in the depths of time, the sand of deserts, and certain traditions which may still be preserved among the people of another planet.

Taboo on the U.S.A.

Between the thirtieth and fortieth parallels of north latitude lie the richest and most densely populated lands on earth; it is here, more than anywhere else, that men built their cities. Yet they always showed a mysterious reluctance to live in two places, the Gobi Desert and America, which seem to have been under some sort of taboo.

It can be said that the inhospitable climate and soil of the Gobi Desert discouraged human settlement, but what explanation can be given in the case of America? It is an exceptionally rich territory, with lands well suited to all kinds of farming and herding, and it includes Florida, which produces larger and tastier fruit than any other part of the world. Yet protohistoric men shunned that earthly paradise and prehistoric men were unwilling to settle in it!

Extensive archaeological excavations in America have yielded only meagre results. The remains of some primitive people of Mongoloid type, about eight thousand years old, have been discovered near Santa Barbara, California; they may have been Mexicans from before the great exodus. The bones of mammoths killed by stone-tipped arrows have been unearthed. The 'Minnesota girl' appears to date from twenty thousand years ago, and there are a few carved bones and shells from about that same period.

Altogether, the discoveries are only enough to justify the assumption of passing tribes or a few isolated populations. There are no painted caves, no flint-tool sites, no clay tablets. ... Practically speaking, it can be said that except for a few individuals who probably came from Asia by way of the Bering Strait, prehistoric human life was absent from North America. Even in the sixteenth century there were only a few Indian tribes who had never developed an advanced civilization.

After its discovery by Christopher Columbus, North America was so empty of inhabitants that the main problem of the colonists was to populate it by massive immigrations from England, Italy, France, Germany, and Scandinavia. And, to the shame of mankind, the African slave trade was organised to remedy the lack of manpower.

No other region of the globe, except for the Gobi Desert, has even been found with such a sparse native population. Why?

Mexicans lived in the U.S.A.

This fantastic enigma was partially answered only by traditions of the Mayas in nearby Mexico. They believed that North America was the land of death, that only souls which would never be reincarnated went to it, but that it had been inhabited in the remote past by the ancient human race.

The latter idea has been supported by specialists in Mexican history. They point out that for thousands of years oral traditions, transmitted from generation to generation, attributed a northern origin to the peoples of Mexico, and that the accuracy of these traditions is confirmed not only by nineteenth-century discoveries of ancient structures in California and Mississippi, but even more strongly by comparative study of a large family of American languages.

What the Popul Vuh says

Other stories give specific details of the cataclysm that annihilated the ancestors of the Mexicans and was undoubtedly the cause of their emigration.

Many moons ago the peoples of the Third Age [the

men of wood*] were condemned to death by the gods. A great deluge of fire and torrents of resin [flame] came down from the sky. Finally violent hurricanes† finished destroying the creatures of wood. Their eyes were torn from their heads, their flesh was gnawed, their entrails were bitten, their nerves and bones were chewed by the votaries of the God of Death.

And the men began running two by two like ears of corn, one behind another, and they climbed up on houses but when they reached the eaves they fell. They tried to climb trees but the trees collapsed beneath their weight. They tried to take refuge in caves but the caves repulsed them when they approached.

The above is from the Popul Vuh, the sacred book of the Mayas, which according to ethnologists is the oldest document of human history, older than the Bible of the Hebrews, the Rig-Veda of the Hindus, or the Zend-Avesta of the ancient Iranians.

It is interesting to note that this cataclysm – deluge, fire from the sky, earthquakes – has disturbing similarities to the atomic war described by Hindu sacred writings:

The fire from the terrible weapon destroyed cities by producing a light brighter than a hundred thousand suns. . . .

This fire made men's hair and nails fall out, whitened the feathers of birds, coloured their feet red and turned them into tortoises.

* This actually means men made of wood. It may be a symbolism stressing the primacy of the soul or intellect over the body, whose function was regarded, comparatively, as much more passive.

The ages described by the Popul Vuh belong to the cycles of the Five Suns: the Sun of the Tiger, the Sun of the Great Wind, the Sun of the Fire of the Sky, the Sun of the Deluge, and the present Sun, which will last till the end of the world.

† Traditionalists believe that at this time the Yucatan was joined to North America by land that is now under the Gulf of Mexico. The regions where the violent hurricanes occurred may have been either the southwestern United States or Florida, where such storms are still frequent.

To ward off the fire, soldiers ran and jumped into rivers to wash themselves and everything they had to touch.

—From the Ramayana and the Drona Parva

The mutations and radiation effects clearly reported by the Sanskrit books are described in almost the same terms by the Mexican sacred writings: fire that comes from the sky, tears out eyes, gnaws flesh and entrails.

Finally the men of the Third Age underwent physical mutations, exactly as if they had been exposed to radiation by an atomic explosion, since their race disappeared and was replaced by the 'Race of the Fourth Age.'

'Nothing remains of the men of the Third Age but the monkeys of the forests. These [mutated] monkeys are descendants of men. That is why the monkey resembles man.' (From the Popul Vuh. Unlike conventional prehistorians, the ancient Mexicans believed that the monkey descended from man, by mutation and deterioration of the species.)

We can thus conclude that according to the written traditions of two peoples living twelve thousand miles apart, the atomic cataclysm struck two parts of the globe: Asia and America; or, more precisely, referring to geophysical data, the Gobi Desert and the United States.

Did the ancient Americans and Hindus try to play the part of gods? Did they fight an atomic war against invaders who may have come from another planet? Or were those atomic explosions caused by a natural cataclysm?

It would be hazardous to make a choice among those explanations, but the reality of the fact itself seems well established.

Venus and the fabulous West

In any case, the extraordinary scientific knowledge attributed to the people of that time seems to indicate an intervention by extraterrestrials, before or during the atomic cataclysm. This idea is supported by a great deal of evidence, particularly in Mexico, where it is quite obvious to an alert archaeologist, and in ancient Peru (which included Bolivia), with its traditions, the unparalleled implements of the Incas, and the carvings of Tiahuanaco.

Quetzalcoatl, the white god of the Toltecs, both a serpent and a bird, was a great friend of human beings. He brought them civilization and knowledge of the arts, fire and metallurgy, just as Prometheus and Oannes did. The Toltecs and Aztecs said that he had come from the 'bright planet' (Venus) and that his skin was white, a detail which showed that he did not belong to the red race.

He withdrew to 'the old land of Tlapallan' after flooding, suffocation, and poisoning had ruined his city of Tulla, which may have been a twin of Thule, in Hyperborea. He 'set off across the eastern sea, preceded by his servants transformed into birds with gay plumage, promising to return.'

It is significant that most of the great initiators of the ancient world are mysteriously attached to the land of the west and the planet Venus, and that they set off eastward toward an unknown destination.

The Incan god Viracocha 'went eastward and disappeared in the waters.' He was a kind of Prometheus of alien origin – like Orejona the Venusian who, according to Andes tradition, was the mother of mankind. She came from Venus in a spacecraft 'brighter than the sun' and landed at Tiahuanaco, Bolivia, near Lake Titicaca. She looked like a modern woman except that she had a long, pointed head and hands with four webbed fingers. Before the cataclysm that destroyed his race, one of her Venusian descendants from Tiahuanaco went off, like Prometheus, to reveal the main secrets of scientific knowledge to mankind, particularly in Egypt, Sumer, and India. (See the third chapter of *One Hundred Thousand Years of Man's Unknown History.*)

The Yucatec god Cukulcan 'came from the west with nineteen companions. He stayed ten years in the Yucatan, established wise laws there and disappeared in the direction of the rising sun.'

The mysterious god Ptah (his name means 'worker') was either an extraterrestrial or a monstrous mutant. He was married to the goddess Bast, who was both a lioness and a cat. Reputed to have 'opened the primordial egg,' he was said to be the master of the world. Like Prometheus, he brought fire from the sky and was the elder brother of mankind.

The Tiahuanacan or Atlantan who brought forth Egyptian civilization was surely the prototype of Prometheus. His image was adopted and adapted by the Greeks, but they kept his ties with America and the planet Venus through his mother 'the ocean nymph with marvellous feet,' a relative of Orejona, and through his saviour Hercules, hero of the initiation in the Garden of the Hesperides, situated 'at the westernmost limit of the earth, beyond the ocean river.'

The Atlantan and Prometheus, like the other initiators with whom they are identified, went off to finish their tormented lives in the east.

The many faces of Lucifer

It is obvious to me that all those heroes – Quetzalcoatl, Viracocha, Cukulcan, Ptah, Oannes, the Atlantan, Prometheus, and Lucifer the Venusian, the 'light-bearer' of the men of the Bible – were the same superior being, probably of Venusian origin, with a personality transfigured by different peoples. They were also the same as Amitabha, the Hindu 'god of the west,' and the god of the western 'other world' of the Polynesians and the European Celts.

Traditions are disturbingly convergent on this point and the convergence is accentuated by the fact that such widely separated peoples as the Hindus, Celts, Mayas, and Incas had stories of fire that came from the sky (an atomic explosion, in my opinion) and destroyed a cycle of civilization at a time *before the Biblical Deluge.*

How can anyone reject such correlations? How can anyone refuse to grant that they probably represent a primohistoric reality?

According to Mexican traditions, Quetzalcoatl one day went off to the east – which no doubt referred to the land of the Atlantans, far beyond the present Yucatan Penin-

sula – and 'made himself perish in a great fire.' This story
may mean that he left in a flying machine similar to the
chariots of fire that took Enoch, Xisuthrus, Noah, Moses,
and Elijah into the sky.

But the traditions added that Quetzalcoatl would return, which would prove that he had actually not perished, but had only gone elsewhere.

After his departure, which was a real event, the Mexicans posted sentries on the east coast to watch for his return. When Cortez and his men landed in the sixteenth
century, the Indians believed that Quetzalcoatl had come
back, and therefore received the Spaniards with great
honours.

The extraterrestrial god

Since that time, the memory of the flying god has been
perpetuated by the strange ceremonies of the 'wheels of
flying men,' by the *voadors* who perform acrobatic feats a
hundred feet above the ground, attached to ropes hanging
from a high mast, and also, no doubt, by the mysterious
heads of stone giants, wearing helmets like those of modern astronauts, which the Olmecs erected in Mexico.

What more do skeptics need to make them at least
grant the probability of an intervention by extraterrestrials, and therefore the existence of an unknown civilization, in primohistoric times.

The Popul Vuh explicitly mentions that civilization of
the men of the Mexican Third Age (and of the Third
Sun: a rain of fire) when it describes 'cities having great
populations and houses with rain gutters.'

Other traditions tell of the vast emigration of the ancient Mexicans from the northern land (that is, the
United States), where they had encountered catastrophe
and death: 'On the advice of their priests, they went
southward, fleeing the land of death. They would know
they had reached the promised land when they saw an
eagle on a cactus, holding a snake with its talons.'

Here is one more indication of a primohistoric civilization in North America, before the time of Sumerian civilization.

It remains to be seen whether physical evidence will prove the accuracy of these stories and show beyond question that the United States is 'the land where the world began.'

Nineteenth-century ethnologists were aware of 'ancient structures in California and Mississippi,' but since these structures had not been dated it was difficult to determine whether or not they might be older than the ziggurats of Sumer.

Vitrified prehistoric cities

In the nineteenth century Captain Ives William Walker made some archaeological discoveries in the western United States which, in my opinion, leave no doubt on the subject.

The whole area between the Gila and San Juan, he said, was covered with ruins. In one place he found the remains of a city that had been about a mile long. Vitrified stones showed that a terrible cataclysm had occurred there. At the centre of the city was a huge rock, twenty to thirty feet high, on which the wreckage of an immense structure could still be seen. The south end of it seemed to have been melted in a furnace, and the rock on which it rested also showed signs of having been melted. The lines of the streets and the positions of the houses were still visible. There were many similar ruins nearby. The local Indians had no traditions about the people who had lived there. They had a religious fear of the ruins, but knew nothing of their history.

The Americans are so overawed by the pronouncements of European prehistorians that they consider it unthinkable even to entertain the hypothesis that their country, with its cities of concrete buildings and its plains ploughed by tractors that will soon be automated, could have been the birthplace of the oldest known civilization. But the curse that hung over this land for thousands of years is an enigma that calls for explanation.

The number-one American mystery

Another important fact should have alerted critical

minds: the total absence of horses in North and South America at the time of the Spanish conquest. It is well known that the Aztecs and Incas were astounded when they saw the soldiers of Cortez and Pizarro riding animals that were unknown to them: horses.

In Europe, Asia, Africa, and even Oceania, the horse belonged to a very old prehistoric family and had always played a part in social evolution. In America it was totally absent, just as remains of prehistoric people, sites, and civilization were absent.

This was too unusual to be true, especially since the United States has now become a fertile breeding ground for horses. They thrive there, particularly in Texas, where there are vast herds numbering in the thousands, and in some places there are even herds of wild horses.

Only a few years ago the truth came to light with the discovery of some bones of the oldest known horse, much older than the prehistoric horses of France, Tartary, and the Arab countries.

That discovery was made in the United States.

Paleontologists are now unanimous on this point: the horse did not originate in Europe, Asia, Africa, or Oceania: it originated in America and, more specifically, in the United States. From there it spread to South America by way of the Isthmus of Panama and to the rest of the world by way of the Bering Strait.

This fact gives our unknown history a vast extension which prehistorians have carefully refrained from exploiting. (To safeguard their conventionally accepted system, they have denied the authenticity of the Altamira cave paintings, discredited Glozel, sequestered the prehistoric library of Lussac-les-Châteaux, and so on. Altamira has already been cleared; the rest will follow. See the second chapter of *One Hundred Thousand Years of Man's Unknown History*.)

It has thus been proved that long before Sumer, perhaps ten to fifteen thousand years earlier, the horses lived in the United States, its birthplace, and then suddenly, for no known reason, totally disappeared!

Only a great cataclysm could have caused that total

disappearance, a cataclysm which obviously must have wiped out other animal species and also, no doubt, human civilizations much older than those of Europe and Asia.

Prehistoric man lived, evolved, and developed advanced civilizations in the United States, then completely vanished, like the horse, as the result of an accident that we have reason to identify as an atomic explosion.

We now have an explanation for the mysterious statue of a horse that could still be seen in the fifteenth century on a promontory in the eastern Azores, facing the open sea – facing the America that was unknown to Europeans.

We also know why the sea horse became the god Poseidon of Atlantis and Greece.

Ten questions in search of an answer

An atomic explosion, accredited by our interpretation of the Popul Vuh, gives a satisfactory solution to the enigmas that have been raised. They can be formulated as follows:

1. Probability of a civilization on a fracture line naturally favourable to development.
2. Likelihood of an atomic cataclysm.
3. Valleys of death and vitrified cities.
4. A natural cataclysm responsible for the earth's inclination of 23°27'.
5. Exodus of the ancient Mexicans.
6. Reasons for the disappearance of the horse from the land where it originated.
7. Taboo on North America and men's refusal to live there.
8. Civilization in the United States before Sumer.
9. Stories of a land of 'white ancestors' and quests for the Happy Isles, Brazil Island, Hyperborea, and Thule.
10. Light came from the west.

And we now understand why ancient peoples were unwilling to live in the 'Land of Death,' where Captain Walker saw vitrified cities in places that have kept evocative names: Death Valley and Fire Valley, thirty-five miles from Las Vegas.

Chapter 3

THE ENIGMA OF THE GOBI DESERT

The area in America where the nuclear explosion seems to have taken place lies between approximately 30° and 40° north latitude and 90° and 110° west longitude.

On the other side of the earth, the second epicentre is in the Gobi Desert, between 36° and 50° north latitude and 80° and 120° east longitude.

The Gobi Desert (also known as Shamo) is a vast territory in Outer Mongolia, twice as large as France. Because of its barrenness, its sand storms, its harsh climate, and the hostility of its tribes, it is almost unknown to archaeologists and geographers.

Legends – but are they really only legends? – attribute the title of Master of the World to the enigmatic great religious leader who rules the people of the desert.

The fact is that a mystery emanates from that region, whose reputation for magic surpasses that of Tibet.

Mr. Molotov's pilgrimage to Ulan Bator

When the American ethnologist W.S. Lewis came back from a trip to Mongolia in 1962 he stated that V. M. Molotov, Stalin's former right-hand man and Khrushchev's main adversary, owed the special favours he enjoyed to the aid given him by the Bodgo-Gegen, leader of the lamas of central Asia and a reincarnation of the living Buddha in the same way as the Dalai Lama of Tibet.

It is impossible to verify this statement, but it is certain that Molotov benefited from an immunity that intrigued political circles: it was as if an unknown force were able to control the will and conduct of his powerful enemy Khrushchev.

In the nineteenth century Czar Alexander I obtained similar aid from the Bodgo-Gegen of Ulan Bator, and this was partly responsible for the fall of Napoleon.

The death of Alexander I was very mysterious. There

were rumours which convinced the Russian people that for a long time after the official date of his death in 1825 he travelled around his empire under the name of Feodor Kusmich.

In the Kremlin archives there were records of that strange affair dating from the Romanovs; it is not unreasonable to suppose that Molotov may have consulted them and used them to his own advantage.

Sacred books and a magic ring

Does the 'Master of the World' in Mongolia influence the world's political destiny? I am tempted to think so, and in any case historical facts give the idea a certain credibility, at least in the minds of occultists.

But who is that Master of the World?

His name is Jebtsung and he is inhabited by the soul of Amitabha, the god of the west and the merciful spirit of the four mountains that surround the holy city of Ulan Bator (formerly Urga).

Jebtsung is not officially recognized by the rulers of the People's Republic of Mongolia, who are politically hostile to 'superstition,' but as the Bodgo-Gegen he is the spiritual ruler of a hundred thousand lamas and a million subjects.

He no longer resides in the sacred Bodgo Ol, the Vatican of his eight predecessors, which the Communist Scientific Committee has 'nationalized.' He wanders over the steppes, followed by an impressive court of lamas and shamans. The idea of an itinerant Master of the World is not very conducive to believing that he and his shamans have supranormal powers, but it would be hard to disprove those powers.

Ferdinant Ossendowski, an eminent Polish scholar, escaped from grave dangers by means of a magic ring given to him by the Bodgo-Gegan of Nabaranchi. Lamas predicted within an hour the death of General Ungern von Sterberg, an adversary of the Bolsheviks. In 1933 Dr. Maurice Percheron, a French scientist, had unquestionable proof of a mysterious force which was apparently used for the advantage of certain powerful Mongols.

'And how are we to explain without magic,' writes Charles Correga, 'the fact that Genghis Khan, an untutored herdsman aided by a handful of nomads, was able to subjugate a succession of peoples and empires a thousand times more highly advanced than he was?'

Kublai Khan, who held sway over Mongolia, China, India, Afghanistan, Persia, and half of Europe, adopted the Buddhist religion when he saw the wonders worked by Turjo Ghamba before representatives of all religions.

Hitler tried to use the magic of the Mongols to conquer the world, but he was betrayed by shamans who never gave him the secrets of domination.

Those secrets, enclosed in enormous chests guarded by the Shabinari monks in the service of the present Bodgo-Gegen, are written in sacred books: the two hundred and twenty-six volumes of the Panjur and the one hundred and eight volumes of the Ganjur. Their magic power is materialized in religious objects, principally a prodigious ruby set in a ring which Genghis Khan and his successor Kublai Khan constantly wore on the right index finger.

(The Maha Chohan, the false Master of the World and genuine adventurer who came to France in 1947 and was first the teacher, then the friend and finally the enemy of Michael Ivanoff, the 'magus' of Sévres, wore on his right index finger an emerald ring which he claimed had belonged to Genghis Khan. It contained, said the charlatan, 'a hydrogen atom capable of blowing up the world.')

Such is the strange land, the terrible desert – the worst of all deserts – whose ancient history is all but unknown, despite its importance in the destiny of our planet.

We can conjecture some of the primohistory of the Gobi Desert by using a key provided for us by the traditionalistic historian Jean Roy:

In the valley of the Indus the high civilization of an archaic people, the Dravidians, blossomed thirty-five hundred years ago and then, a few centuries later, absorbed the light-skinned Veddides and the dark-skinned Melanides.

The Melanides came from the Tarim basin in the

region of Lop Nor (the present Sinkiang).* Entering the high valleys of the Indus through the Karakoram Pass, they brought the Dravidians knowledge of the ten-digit numerical system now known as the 'Arabic system,' which was transmitted to the West much later, at the time of the Arab invasions.

The Dravidians gave the Melanides the name of Naachals, which means 'high brothers.' Exoterically, this name might be explained by the fact that they came from the mountainous regions of Karakoram, where there are peaks from twenty-three to twenty-eight thousand feet high.

Among the Naacahals, only the 'Knowers' had the secret of the ten-digit system. They did not claim to have invented it, but they said it had been entrusted to them.

In that case, who had taught them, on those desolate plateaus twice as high as Mont Blanc, the prodigious secret of our present numerical system?

The White Island

Certain traditions, which I will later describe in detail, state that the knowledge of the Melanides was revealed to them by men who came from the sky in a spacecraft and landed on the White Island in the Gobi Sea.

That island is said to exist today in the form of Mount Atis, four hundred miles northeast of Lop Nor. It is here, twelve thousand miles away, that we find the counterpart of the American mystery in Nevada.

A taboo hangs over the Gobi Desert. Here, too after sand storms, cities emerge from the ground, cities whose origin is lost in the depths of time; here, too, there were once floods, tidal waves, and fire from the sky.

* If we are to believe specialists in unidentified flying objects, the Sinkiang region is still the centre of a mystery. In any case it is partly a forbidden military zone and it may be the supply base of the 'Black Knight,' the enigmatic satellite that has been orbiting the earth since 1957.

Soviet aviators flying over the Gobi Desert have photographed the ruins of large cities, recognizable by their foundations. In the near future the sands of the Gobi will speak, and then all of conventional protohistory will be placed in question.

In the great deluge described by the Vedas (the Catapatha Brahmana, one of the oldest Indian texts), the legendary Manu built an Ark which an enormous fish 'caused to pass over the Mountain of the North;' that is, the Ark landed in what is now the Gobi Desert, perhaps on the White Island. The India specialist A. Weber saw this story as an obscure memory of the immigration of the Aryans who went to India, and probably also to Japan, when they were driven from their homeland by a deluge or an earthly catastrophe.

Into the region of the Gobi Desert came peoples who had revolutionary knowledge unknown to other men. We must assume that their exodus, similar to that of the ancient Mexicans fleeing from the California-Nevada region, was motivated by powerful imperatives; and the transformation of fertile lands into barren desert and bleak steppes seems to indicate the occurrence of a terrible cataclysm.

We can now understand why, for thousands of years, men refused to go back to those cursed places where their ancestors had been 'struck down by the wrath of God.'

Special attention should be given to a statement by Jean Roy concerning 'men who came from the sky' and landed on the White Island.

The Mongolian name of the Gobi Desert is Shamo, which may be related to the name of the god Shamos who, according to the Talmud, was worshipped in the form of a black star. Shamos was also the 'evil luminary' of the Arabs, probably Saturn or some other heavenly body from which a danger to the earthly human race had come (again the idea of a cosmic tragedy or an extraterrestrial invasion).

Now that we have conjecturally located the two centres of the ancient atomic explosions, it will be interesting to see whether features common to the United States and the Gobi Desert have extensions into the present. And it is here, no doubt, that we will make the most startling discoveries, as if everything were only an eternal recurrence, from glimpsed primohistory to the invisible history of the twenty-first century.

Ancient Indian writings (Ramayana, Drona Parva, Mahavira) explicitly tell of an atomic war on earth; since the Popul Vuh (irradiation of the peoples of the Third Age, according to Recinos and Villacosta) and the Bible (destruction of Sodom and Gomorrah) support this idea, it is permissible to believe that the ancient Americans and Mongols tried to play the part of gods, like the atomic scientists of 1945.

Did they use nuclear weapons against invaders from the sky, or did they exterminate each other? It is hard to answer that question.

The secret history of our time

Since 1945 the idea of a humanly provoked atomic destruction has seemed more probable than that of a divine vengeance to inhabitants of Hiroshima and Nagasaki, but for certain Americans and Russians this opinion is strengthened by exaggerated coincidences, because it is precisely in ancient California and Mongolia that many American and Russian rockets are stored and tested.

March, 1963; February-March, 1964 – on those dates, in California, American Nike-Hercules missiles were ready to take off from underground bases. The technicians assigned to control them in case of war were under the surveillance of policemen with orders to shoot any of them who might go insane, commit an obvious act of treason, or try to set off the launching mechanism without an explicit order, which would mean the partial destruction of at least one nation.

Yet several missiles, fortunately without their nuclear warheads, exploded *for no known reason, even though all humanly conceivable precautions had been taken to guard against such an accident.*

Nuclear explosions in Mongolia

February, 1960. In a desert similar to that of Nevada, near the Mongolian border, at the same latitude and at an almost diametrically opposed longitude, the Soviets had also stockpiled nuclear bombs. What an amazing predestination of places!

In February, 1960, Western secret services learned that two Russian generals had died; then the whole truth gradually leaked out and it became known that several H-bombs had exploded *for no known reason, even though all humanly conceivable precautions had been taken to guard against such an accident.* Many Russians were killed and thousands were wounded. The earth's gamma-ray radioactivity rose to four times the critical level, but this was carefully concealed by the secret services of all governments.

It is certain that people in the vicinity of Lake Balkhash were evacuated toward the Caspian Sea. American detectors and seismographs registered two explosions corresponding to the detonation of two hundred to two hundred and fifty A-bombs. Two stocks of bombs had blown up within a few seconds of each other; the second explosion was more violent than the first.

A few days after the catastrophe, radioactivity reached the critical level in Paris and made the most sensitive photographic emulsions unusable.

A year later there was a proliferation of birth defects that is still remembered all over the world, particularly in the Soviet Union, China, and Japan. Mrs. Khrushchev, who knew the hidden reason for it, had pangs of conscience that prompted her to say publicly, 'Let us throw all atom bombs into the sea!'

So there were two very strange accidents, both at latitude 36° north, with one at longitude 112° west and the other at 90° east; that is, they were in the two areas where, more than ever, there is reason to believe that atomic cataclysms occurred in the remote past.

Where bombs once exploded, they will explode again

Nuclear explosions thousands of years ago, nuclear

explosions in recent years – probability theory opposes
the idea that such extremely rare events could happen in
the same parts of the world without a specific reason.

And we must assume, with horror, that some day, soon
or in the distant future, but inevitably, the American nuclear stockpiles in Nevada and the Russian or Chinese nuclear stockpiles in central Asia will again explode *for no
known reason, even though all humanly conceivable precautions have been taken to guard against such an accident.* (The American stockpile at Fort Richardson,
Alaska, nearly exploded during the 1964 earthquake. The
missiles were moved and some of the safety locks were
broken.)

Once again, ninety to ninety-five per cent of the human
race may be destroyed. Future generations will then wonder *again* why Nevada and Mongolia seem to arouse a
kind of atavistic repugnance in people. . . .

Nevada and Mongolia: two poles of human destiny
where reflections of remote events may still exist. In the
vast area now studded with such cities as Las Vegas, Los
Angeles, Salt Lake City, Kansas City, Saint Louis, Memphis, Little Rock, Dallas, New Orleans, and Houston,
*there were once the proud cities of superior ancestors who
had achieved space travel, cybernetics, television, and
atomic fission.*

Chapter 4

THE STONE AGE: AN INVENTION OF PREHISTORIANS

It is hard to find any explanation for man's genesis other than evolution from a branch of the animal kingdom. Subjectively, of course, we are inclined to rebel against the idea of simian ancestors; rightly or wrongly, we consider it unflattering. A miraculous genesis would suit us better!

Was man created spontaneously, as a special privilege?

Are we children of God, creatures of God? Yes, certainly, if we identify God with universal intelligence; no, without a doubt, if we regard God as a creator who modelled in clay and made the first woman from a rib of the first man.

The earth has a privileged orbit

There seems to be no privilege for any link in the chain of universal evolution. No privilege for the Himalayas, which might be a warm Eden without eternal snows; no privilege for the Pacific Ocean, whose water might not be salty; no privilege enabling an ant to have the size of an elephant, or an elephant the size of an ant; no privilege for any of the billions of suns being consumed in the vastness of the sky.

Yet the question can be raised with regard to man. Our tendency to consider ourselves the centre of the universe, as the Bible says, is foolish; but it is still true that our spaceship, the earth, is better made and equipped for cosmic travel than the other planets.

We are not very well informed on this subject, but Mars is arid, Venus is foggy, the moon is airless, and it is undeniable that Earth offers the best conditions for life as we know it, probably because of its exceptional orbital position in relation to the sun.

From the laws of universal expansion we believe we

know that every day the planets move a little farther away from the centre of the solar system; that is, they move in widening spirals.* This implies that they originally left from the centre, probably at different times (Louis Jacot's theories) and that Mercury and Venus will some day occupy Earth's present orbit, while Mars, Jupiter, etc., have occupied it in the past. There thus seems to be a time and a point at which planets are either too young or too old, the ideal situation being that of Earth.

An exodus from planet to planet

But the older planets were once in that same situation and they must have benefited from the privilege it confers, with the same possibilities of plant, animal, and human development. This enables us to formulate a fascinating hypothesis.

When the inhabitants of the planet that immediately precedes ours in age (not necessarily Mars, since there have been great cosmic upheavals) found themselves in conditions unfavourable to life, they began making preparations for an exodus to Earth, where all branches of life had already begun their evolution.

Like Noah in the Ark, the first astronauts from the endangered planet must have carried out a reconnaissance mission, taking with them plant seeds and selected animal specimens. Will our own astronauts not have the same kind of mission when they go to Mars or Venus?

The primohistoric astronauts had the responsibility of beginning the adaptation of various species before the arrival of colonists who, perhaps for major reasons, were unable to make the journey sooner.

* All sorts of nonsense has been written about the Great Pyramid; its measurements are said to give the number *pi*, the circumference of the earth, the distance from the earth to the sun, and so on. But if the Great Pyramid now gives the *exact* distance from the earth to the sun, there was an initial error because the earth, by virtue of the laws of universal expansion, is constantly moving away from the centre of our system, so that it is now farther from the sun than it was in the time of the ancient Egyptians. The correct figure then would be false now, and vice versa.

Inhabitants of other planets had done the same in earlier times, forming a series of relays from planet to planet, always in the same direction and toward the same privileged orbit: the one we now occupy.

Man's origin thus goes back very far in time, but his birthplace has always been about ninety million miles from the sun.

This hypothesis does not rule out the natural appearance of native human beings on Earth; it simply assumes that if there were such natives, they were joined by extra-terrestrials. It even seems to have strange affinities with the theory of the seven heavens in spiritualistic doctrines, the concentric celestial spheres imagined by the ancients and the secret teachings of the Rosicrucians, the last holders of knowledge of 'the beginning, the middle and the end.'

We have no incontestable proof of the existence of human beings on Earth more than twenty or thirty thousand years ago, because we have no remains of civilizations or human bones older than that. The first links that prehistorians date at half a million or even a million years ago are completely arbitrary.

The earthly human race, whatever its age and origin may be, must have disappeared several times in the course of great cataclysms. No material evidence has survived, but the memory of the primohistoric civilizations of recent millennia has remained in traditions.

Despite our signals, radio calls, and rockets, no response has come to us from other planets; but in the vast space of our galaxy it is possible that one planet, even more privileged than ours, has witnessed the advent of a superior human race and constitutes the real cosmic Eden, the nonearthly paradise from which Adam was not expelled.

CTA-102

This hypothesis, once called insane by orthodox defenders of the established order, became respectable on April 13, 1965, when Russian astronomers announced that in collaboration with American astronomers they were studying modulated signals from space which might have been emitted by 'supercivilized' beings.

Skeptics reacted immediately. The astronomer Davies, of the Jodrell Bank Observatory, said that the signals resembled those coming from quasers and that there was no need to resort to the idea of a faraway civilization to account for the regular phases of their emission, since it might be a natural oscillation, like the cycle of sunspots.

This was also the opinion of the Belgian Professor Raymond Coutrez and Sir Bernard Lovell, director of the Jodrell Bank Observatory. Most astronomers, however, accepted the possibility of highly civilized creatures living in unknown regions of space.

A source of radio emission known as CTA-102 we detected in the United States in 1960, along with a number of other sources – CTA-21, 3C-444, 3C-455 – whose emissions were in the thirty-centimeter band and had radio-frequency spectra of an unusual shape.

The internationally known Russian astronomer Iosef Shklovsky said on April 12, 1963, at the Sternberg Astronomical Institute in Moscow:

The American Mount Palomar Observatory has established that at the point from which CTA-102 emits its waves there is a very small star whose magnitude of 17.3 is that of the smallest known stars. This star has great energy; that is all we can say about it so far.

Study of these unusual matters began with a well-founded idea of young Dr. Kardashev: assuming the possible existence of civilizations far superior to ours, they ought to be capable of altering their whole planetary system and, for example, emitting signals as powerful as those received from CTA-102, tens of thousands of times more powerful than all the energy now produced in our world. These signals ought to be emitted on a wavelength providing the best conditions for preventing them from being jammed by the natural 'noise' in the universe; that is, a wavelength on the order of tens of centimetres.

The Soviet observations were carried out by the astronomer Sholomitsky, who described their results as follows: 'CTA-102 does not seem to be more than five million light-years from Earth. Monitoring of emissions on the 32-centimeter band clearly shows a periodicity of 100 to 102 days in the signal. During this period it increases and decreases, with very steady maximums.'

The probability of the existence of cosmic beings is thus recognized by scientists. This is a great step forward in knowledge of a reality whose certainty will be established in the future.

Were the mysterious 'men' of CTA-102 once in contact with Earth? It would be adventurous to say so, but it is interesting to note that their emissions seem to be directed toward our planet at a frequency which astronomers consider particularly favourable.

As for the present distance of the star – three to five million light-years – it is only an apparent obstacle, since our notions of time and space are probably different from those of the inhabitants of CTA-102

Will we some day see astronauts from that civilization land on Earth and proclaim themselves our superior ancestors?

The most fantastic conjectures are permissible on the scale of the universe, but in the absence of any absolute proof it is necessary to study the viewpoint of conventional prehistorians (however outdated it may be) concerning what they have called Stone-Age man, or the cave man; that is, our ancestor, 'prehistoric' man.

Eve's brilliant disobedience

Whether he is terrestrial or extraterrestrial, man is bound up with matter and seems to be at least a logical phase in the process of evolution, if not its final product.

But in his case evolution has become exceptionally rapid: his intellectual development, his awareness, and his free will have been sharpened and manifested in a mathematical progression which opens the ascending spiral to an angle of nearly 180°. His advent can thus be regarded as approaching the limit at which evolution merges with the infinite or, as spiritualists would say, with God.

If he is an animal, man is undeniably superior to all others because he thinks, distinguishes between good and evil according to his standards, rebels against nature and even tries to subjugate it. With him begins the era of Lucifer, the prince of intellectuals and the heavenly angel who was not afraid, at least in appearance, to thwart God's plans. This can be interpreted to mean that man identifies himself with Lucifer and wants to make himself the master of his world.

Using the symbol of the earthly paradise, Genesis describes man's attainment of awareness and free will. God forbids Adam and Eve to touch the fruit of the tree of knowledge, and of course they eat it.

I say 'of course' because it is obvious that the episode was inevitable and *intended*. God knew that his order would be disobeyed and he had no doubt already decided that it would be thus, as in Lucifer's rebellion, but by the sinners' own will.

In this way Adam and Eve attained awareness and free will, and God, by relinquishing part of his power to them, gave all mankind the most precious of gifts.

The episode of the earthly paradise might be described as the French Revolution of Biblical times!

Moreover, how could the Creator have placed his creatures in command of the sky and its stars, and the earth and its prodigious nature, if they had not had the power of ruling, deciding, and knowing? What meaning would creation have had if human evolution had not been possible and assumed from the beginning?

If we imagine passive obedience on the part of our two Biblical ancestors, we reach a nonsensical conclusion. Adam and Eve resolved their situation in the most intelligent way possible.

If we want to give the episode its true value we must broaden its interpretation and, at the same time, give another meaning to Lucifer's rebellion.

This mythology must be placed within the context of

human evolution as we have conceived it ever since we were nourished by Eve's apple.

Man's destiny

Biologists feel that we are at the end of our adventure. In particular, this is Jean Rostand's view.

The approaching end of the human race is attributed to free will and liberated man's rejection of the laws of nature, but it may actually fall within the framework of foreseen evolution.

Our evolution seems to have brought us to the extreme permissible limit of our proud knowledge. With one more leap forward, Lucifer would identify himself with God, and man, now the master of the earth, would extend his dominion to the cosmos.

This is only a hypothesis, but we may logically assume that the cycle is nearing its end, and our biological conditioning supports that view.

Men want to subjugate the atom and conquer the sky, in a new version of the war of the Titans against the gods, but the Titans may, like apprentice sorcerers, bring on their own downfall if radiation deteriorates their power of procreation.

According to the scientists of the Institute of Life, which since 1962 has grouped eminent biologists from all over the world for the declared purpose of defending *Homo sapiens* (see *One Hundred Thousands Years of Man's Unknown History*), in three more generations, by about the year 2035, the whole human race may be unable to have children that will not be afflicted with serious birth defects.

Would this be the end of the world? Not necessarily. 'Science has always given more than was expected of it,' says Jean Rostand, which may mean that man would find a way to perpetuate his species without procreation.

Sterile mankind would then return to the original characteristics of creation: an asexual species, as in one-celled organisms. Reproduction would be artificial. Or perhaps men would continue their efforts toward the elimination of physical death until they achieved immortality and began reliving the golden age which, according to tradition, existed in the past.

Would our species then dissolve into sublimity to the point of becoming identified with God, as Teilhard de Chardin would like? Or, since its eternity would be only illusory, would it return to plasma-matter before beginning a new ascending cycle?

The laws of evolution can scarcely teach us anything about our destiny, for the fact is that evolution has no scientific rigor and cannot even be proved. Many species – earthworms, bacteria, algae, and so on, not to mention the famous coelacanth – have been living since very remote eras without having undergone any notable alterations; that is, without having evolved.

Six basic errors

Man's origin and final destiny are mysteries which are all the harder to solve because history and prehistory often contain gaps and even monumental errors.

As prehistorians present it, man's distant past was divided into specific periods known as the Paleolithic and the Neolithic, or the Old Stone Age and the New Stone Age. This is a great help to orthodox concepts of prehistory. They would be very shaky without that convenient invention. It is the cornerstone of the whole system.

It is now clear that the main assumptions of prehistory are so unjustified that they cannot be accepted even as possibilities because they contain at least six basic errors.

1. There is no proof that man descends from the ape. The two species are so different that a blood transfusion between a man and a gibbon, chimpanzee, or orangutang has the same risks as between categorically different animal species.

No real links connecting man and the ape have ever been found. All the alleged links, such as Sinanthropus, Australopithecus, Pithecanthropus, Atlanthropus, and Anthropopithecus, are frauds on the same level as 'Piltdown Man.'

Using that method of establishing our family tree, one could just as easily prove 'that the stick is the ancestor of the bed, passing by way of the hunting seat, the folding chair, the stool, the armchair and the sofa.' (Jean Servier, *L'Homme et l'Invisible*.)

2. Prehistoric men did not live in caves, except in such rare cases as still occur today. There are no caves near most flint sites: no caves at Saint-Acheul (Acheulean), Levallois-Perret (Levalloisian), Chelles (Chellean), Le Grand-Pressigny (Pressignian). ... The prehistoric men who lived in those regions certainly did not go to sleep at Eyzies every night! They lived in huts or, more probably, since they were so skilled in working with stone, in houses.

3. Prehistoric men dressed as we do: hats, jackets, trousers, shoes. This is undeniable because it is proved by the drawings engraved on the stone tablets from the prehistoric library of Lussac-les-Châteaux, which are not sequestered in the Musée de l'Homme in Paris. Only the innocuous drawings are shown there. Those that prove the existence of an advanced civilization in the Magdallenian period always happen to be 'put away somewhere,' but no one knows where.

After I had reported this in *One Hundred Thousand Years of Man's Unknown History*, Constantin Brive, a journalist of *L'Auto-Journal*, decided to see whether or not I was lying when I affirmed the existence of those engraved stone tablets. He had to break through insidious barriers and overcome obvious attempts at evasion, but he eventually became certain that the tablets were exactly as I had described them and that they showed prehistoric men wearing hats, jackets, trousers, and shoes. His article in *L'Auto-Journal* of August 8, 1963, timidly revealed the machinations of those who had tried to thwart his investigation, but he was either afraid or unable to say, as he had explicitly told me he would, *who was lying in that affair*.

4. Prehistoric men had writing, as is proved by the engraved tablets of Glozel. They are unquestionably genuine and were recognized as such after the spectacular trials in which prehistorians bit the dust, vanquished by the light of the facts and the good faith of the discoverer of the tablets, Emile Fradin. (The museum at Glozel, ten miles

from Vichy, France, is still open to the public. In my opinion it is one of the three wonders of the ancient world, the others being the caves of Lascaux and the pre-historic library of Lusac-les-Châteaux.)

5. Prehistoric men did not live in the precarious state described by conventional textbooks. On the contrary, they lived in a kind of materialistic golden age whose re-sources were numerous, inexhaustible, and easy to exploit.

The fact is obvious: in our time, thousands of people live, or could live, solely by food-gathering, hunting, and fishing, even though our forests are vanishing and the fish in our rivers are being killed off by detergents and other chemicals. In prehistoric times fish and game were abundant and there can be no doubt that people had vast supplies of food all around them.

6. Prehistoric men were not the crude, dim-witted crea-tures they are presented as having been. They were painters, potters, and brilliant artists, as is shown by the discoveries at Glozal and the painted caves of Lascaux and Altamira. Caves were used as workshops only by the simple-minded members of society. The others knew how to work with glass, coal, and, in all probability, metals.

Iron and electroplating thirty thousand years ago

'But iron was unknown in the Paleolithic!' prehistor-ians will object.

Iron was unknown? Then how are we to explain that in regions particularly rich in iron ore, such as Alsace-Lorraine, there is no trace of a culture using stone tools?

Those regions were certainly inhabited by prehistoric men, mainly in the sixth and seventh millennia B.C., but we find no flint tools there because it was more conven-ient, more rational, even for the lowest classes of society, to make and use iron objects. And it is probable that civ-ilizations using steel, aviation, and atomic science flour-ished on all continents thousands and thousands of years ago.

By the nineteenth century there were already scientists who had reached this conclusion but did not dare to express it This was true of the Egyptologist Auguste Edouard Mariette, who discovered the Serapeum of Memphis and the tombs of Apis.

Excavating at a depth of sixty feet under the Sphinx of Giza, in a hard, compact soil mingled with stones, Mariette found enormous structures containing works of art that showed exquisite workmanship. The origin of the Sphinx is lost in the depths of time, and those structures, under a layer of hard soil built up through the millennia, were even older!

But that is not all. Among the objects buried so deeply in that primohistoric ground there were, to quote an account dating from the middle of the nineteenth century, contained in the *Grand Dictionaire Universel du XIXe Siècle*, 'pieces of gold jewellery whose thinness and lightness might make one believe that they had been produced by electroplating in the round, an industrial technique that we have been using for only two or three years.'

This discovery is, of course, highly embarrassing to those who are determined to maintain the view that civilization began in Sumer no more than six thousand years ago!

Similar discoveries have been made in other places. On many objects from Memphis and Thebes – vases, cups, spearheads, etc. – there is a thin layer of metal on which it is impossible to find any trace of brazing or manual work. This layer is so uniform, and its crystalline structure is so similar to that of products obtained by electroplating, that some scientists have not hesitated to say that electroplating was known to the ancient Egyptians.

As for the use of iron, it goes back eight thousand years among the Haddads of Africa, and much farther elsewhere.

According to careful calculations made by engineers, the iron mines on the island of Elba, Italy, were in use at a time 'at least ten times older than the one known to us.' Considering that the Greeks in the time of Homer already knew that island, which they called Aethalia because smoke from forges was always rising above it, we reach the conclusion that the exploitation of its mines must go back *more than thirty thousand years.*

After that, how can anyone dare to talk about the 'Stone Ages,' the Neolithic and the Paleolithic?

The Paelolithic and the Neolithic: inventions of prehistorians

The Paleolithic and the Neolithic: that is the rigid cornerstone of outdated prehistory!

But I do not hesitate to say that *the Paleolithic and the Neolithic have never existed except in the imagination of prehistorians.*

It is true that some prehistoric men used flint tools, but their number was so small as to be insignificant. Prehistoric men used flint tools as twentieth-century men eat caviar or chew gum; that is, in a proportion of one in a thousand, or one in ten thousand.

I have presented this view to specialists and their reactions fall into two categories: orthodox prehistorians shrug their shoulders and avoid all discussion, but are completely unable to refute anything in my view; unorthodox prehistorians judge it to be perfectly accurate.

I will now give a condensed version of the reasoning behind my view.

The population of a nation or a region can be approximately calculated on the basis of the number of houses or automobiles, or necessary tools such as knives in the case of nontechnological societies. We may arrive at a figure of ten million inhabitants for France, or a hundred million; at ten thousand for the Sahara, or eight hundred thousand. But our result will seldom be more than twice as great as the actual figure and never more than five times as great.

If we could know the number of knives that existed in the Middle Ages, we would know about how many people lived at that time. But most medieval knives have been completely destroyed by rust.

If men of the Paleolithic and the Neolithic had only chipped or polished flint tools and no metal at all, as prehistorians claim, it should be possible to recover the 'knives' of that time, however long ago it may have been, because flint does not disintegrate. It can easily last a million years without the slightest deterioration visible to the naked eye. A million years is about how long man is said to have lived on earth.

In my view, prehistoric men necessarily used tools for cutting, carving, and self-defence. Men have always needed such tools as knives, axes, files, and chisel.

Let us classify as objects useful to prehistoric man everything that resembles a knife in shape or function: axes, scrapers, gravers; in short, nearly all flint objects of acceptable size used by men. A normal man, even in our time, needs a certain number of tools in the course of his life: axes, saws, chisels, pliers, picks, and so on. The whole collection amounts to about a hundred objects.

Therefore prehistoric man, who could make a stone axe in about ten minutes (this is the time taken by M. Borde, of Bordeaux, for making a crude axe), and found abundant flint at the sites known to us, must have made and used at least a hundred tools in his life, since they wore out, broke, or became lost. But in any case they have not disappeared or disintegrated.

It is known that in ordinary loose soil stones, and therefore flint tools, are forced upward by upheavals of the earth, combined with centrifugal force. This explains why stones can be taken from a garden every year without ever clearing the soil of them permanently. Similarly, artillery shells and fragments of them still rise in the battlefields of World War I. Every year children find such shells in gardens, forests, and cultivated fields, and are the victims of accidents.

My study began at a site that I know well: Charroux, in the Vienne district of France. It is one of the most important sites for axes, which were an essential tool.

One to two thousand axes have been found there, but the site was nearly exhausted in a few years. The number of axes still buried can be estimated at between two and five thousand, the latter figure being *wildly optimistic*.

Except for Le Grand-Pressigny, Charroux is one of the

largest sites in France. It is on the Prehistoric Highway halfway between Le Grand-Pressigny and Les Eyzies, on the bank of the Charents, four miles from the famous Chaffaud cave. (The Prehistoric Highway of France runs parallel to the road between Paris and Bordeaux, passing through picturesque localities and beautiful landscapes. Its exact course is as follows: Le Grand-Pressigny, La Roche-Posay, Angles-sur-l'Anglin, Saint-Savin, Lussac-les-Châteaux, L'Isle-Jourdain, Charroux, Civray, Angoulême, Nontron, Périgueux, Les Eyzies.) There are forty-nine caves in the region, but one of them seems ever to have been inhabited.

Flint is particularly abundant at Charroux and the figure of a hundred axes per man per twenty-five-year generation is an extremely low estimate. Actually, the average prehistoric man must have made much more than a hundred axes in his lifetime, whether out of necessity, as a form of recreation, or as gifts.

Knowing this, we can make an approximate calculation without going back to the earliest periods of prehistory.

In fifty thousand years, two thousand generations of men lived at Charroux. According to our estimate, they used about ten thousand flint axes. Assuming that a hundred axes were necessary for one lifetime, how many men lived at Charroux per generation?

$$\frac{10,000 \text{ axes}}{100 \times 200 \text{ generations}} = 0.50 \text{ man}$$

Or, with a hundred axes per man over a period of only ten thousand years; i.e., four hundred generations:

$$\frac{10,000}{100 \times 400} = 0.25 \text{ man}$$

If you feel that a hundred axes is an exaggerated figure, bring it down to ten and you will obtain, for two thousand generations:

$$\frac{10,000}{10 \times 2000} = 0.5 \text{ man}$$

And for only four hundred generation:

$$\frac{10,000}{10 \times 400} = 2.5 \text{ men}$$

Try other possibilities; calculate, for example, for a million years (forty thousand generations) with ten axes per man:

$$\frac{10,000}{10 \times 40,000} = 0.025 \text{ man}$$

Or with one axe per man over two thousand generations:

$$\frac{10,000}{1 \times 2000} = 5 \text{ men}$$

In these calculations I have taken the figures *most unfavourable to my view*: there are not ten thousand axes at Charroux; that is about the number of tools and unformed chips which might possibly have been used.

No matter how we calculate, we obtain absurd results! And the results are equally absurd in the case of Le Grand-Pressigny, Les Eyzies, the Chambes plateau, or Saint-Acheul.

We cannot have an accurate idea of the population of France in prehistoric times, but certain limits come to mind: thirty thousand, perhaps three hundred thousand? In my judgment, the truth must lie somewhere between those two extremes.

Assuming the figures of thirty thousand men, fifty thousand years and a hundred various tools necessary for each man per generation, we should find or be able to unearth *six billion* flint tools in France. But there are fewer than a million in our museums and private collections, and it would be ridiculous to believe that six billion still remain buried.

Our heritage of flint tools amounts to about six hundred thousand, which would give the following population for France per generation, using figures stated above:

$$\frac{600,000}{100 \times 2000} = 3 \text{ men}$$

That would mean only fifty to a hundred men per generation for the whole earth, since France was the greatest population centre in prehistoric times.

These results are absurd and the conclusion is obvious: *the number of flint tools does not indicate the number of men who lived in France.* It indicates only the number of retarded individuals. Such individuals occur in any population and, along with Piltdown Man and the nonexistent skull of Sinanthropus, they have provided the models on which prehistorians have built their pseudo-science.

Therefore prehistoric men – who numbered more than fifty per generation all over the world! – used something other than flint for their tools, something that has disappeared by natural disintegration. In all likelihood it was iron and alloys of other metals.

In any case the terms 'Paleolithic' and 'Neolithic,' which prehistorians apply to the so-called Stone Age, are extremely misleading. Ten, fifty, or even a hundred men per generation, all over the world, may have used flint axes, but there is no justification for defining a whole period by that insignificant percentage of the total population.

By the same logic, we could say that the twentieth century is part of the Stone Age, since people in New Guinea and Borneo still use flint tools; or the Caviar Age or the Chewing Gum Age, since a few people eat caviar or chew gum.

From all this we can see that our direct ancestors were not as obtuse as we have been led to believe and that all of conventional prehistory is unsubstantial and based on errors.

But what seems much more important to me is that the collapse of conventional prehistory, with its idea of prehistoric man living in caves and using stone tools, opens a door into man's unknown past. Now that we have swept aside false theories, we can imagine that past as awesome and fantastic – as it undoubtedly was!

Chapter 5

THE UNIVERSE AND THE ARK-ROCKET

The zero point where everything exists in the uncreated

It is impossible to conceive of nothingness, preceding creation. How can we imagine a silent, empty 'universe' without time, space, motion, light, heat, or intelligence? Sophists, moreover, would not fail to point out that although nothingness is only an abstraction it is a phenomenon in itself, and therefore a created reality!

The human mind can speculate only within the limits of a bounded, visible universe in which even abstraction has concrete properties.

The mystery of creation is still forbidden to us, but since two of its phases, the present and the future, are not closed in time, it offers a relatively accessible mental landscape.

In the theory of a biconic universe expanding and contracting (imagine a series of cones arranged in a line and paired so that the point of one touches the point of another) the geometric centre of the whole is the zero point of junction at which contraction ends and expansion begins. It is thus a point of immobility, equilibrum, and nothingness, but is existence is only theoretical.

This process in which cones succeed one another seems miraculous because the human mind cannot conceive or accept indefinitely repeated expansion and contraction, or the zero point of nonexistence, or spontaneous creation after that point.

Yet it corresponds to Brahmanic cosmogony (Brahma's inhalation and exhalation), the theory of the expanding universe, the theory of the necessary cycles of life, death and rebirth, and Lavoisier's law: nothing is lost, nothing is created, everything is transformed.

Escaping a little from our small three-dimensional universe, we can try to accept as a working hypothesis the coexistence of nothingness and plenitude, the uncreated and the created. This is assumed, moreover, in the classical theory of creation from noncreation, with the original cell containing the whole universe, in mass as well as volume.

The zero point, which some people identify with God, also permits the coexistence of time and antitime. What has not yet been created therefore exists in the nonexistent, which contains the preconceived plan of creation. There is then a passage from the idea to its realization, from the immaterial to the material.

However we may conceive of the universe, our thinking cannot go beyond the stage of adventurous theory, because we constantly come up against incompatibilities and mysteries.

If some day man consciously moves in five, six, or seven dimensions, perhaps he will then understand what now escapes him or seems unrelated to the data he possesses.

The problem of creation is always studied within our three-dimensional concepts, without taking account of other parallel or interacting worlds whose existence is possible if not probable. In dreams, man has the power to create and annihilate, but it seems that the phenomena occur only in either thought or a different universe. If there were actually materialization, it could either feed the potential of our invisible world or participate in the creation of another universe.

As for materialization in the supranormal, it has never been proven. Does this mean that it is impossible, that the supranormal, the Beyond, and other invisible worlds are nonexistent?

If they exist and can be penetrated by thought or in some other way, it follows that our universe loses some of its mass in favour of the different universe into which our thought penetrates and brings its substance. This hypothesis works in both directions: it implies that matter can be brought into our universe by creatures or thoughts from other worlds.

In the genuine miracle of germination, the preconceived plan exists even before the seed is formed, and therefore in nothingness or the present, which is only the existent that has not yet been created. In this sense the future is always contained in the present, as matter and time are always contained in nothingness.

Mystery, always mystery!

It is therefore as absurd to ask the question, 'How was the world created?' as it is to give it an answer that calls forth a senseless series of other questions resembling a children's game: If there was a time when the universe did not exist, what preceded it? Nothingness. Who made nothingness? God. Who made God? And so on.

One great difficulty for man in his quest for knowledge is being able to situate himself and his perception in relation to what seems to him infinitely great or infinitely small. Despite all the power of his genius, the magic of his mathematics, and the immense complexity of his speculations, he will never reach the end of the chain.

On another level, a Tibetan tradition expresses this idea by saying that in order to write the name of God all men in Creation would have to work together for thousands of years, trying the different possibilities of the alphabet, and even then they would succeed in writing only the first few letters.

More simply, Orthodox Jews are forbidden to say or write the name of God, just as the ancient Egyptians were forbidden to build points on the sacred pyramids.

The universe: a plasma full of emptiness

But to satisfy his Luciferian curiosity, man had to imagine the how and why of things.

He believes that the infinitely small is in the image of the infinitely great and that galaxies, nebulae, and star clusters properly belong to that infinitely great. Starting from this belief, he has forged a 'total' universe with its own mechanism, laws, and principle. It is as if, knowing only the point that marks the apex of the letter A, he had imagined all the letters of the alphabet!

It is probable that our perceptible universe – star clusters, nebulae, planets, etc. – is comparable in relative size to a particle of plasma taken from a human being for study under a microscope. The biologist who studies it can distinguish bacteria, viruses, red corpuscles, lymph, and other microscopic things in an ocean of emptiness. But if he did not know beforehand, could he determine that it was plasma? If so, could he tell whether it came from an animal or a human being? From a flea, a fish, a bear, an elephant? Or from a drunkard, a mentally retarded man living in a cave, an Einstein, a Bergson? Or from a pretty woman's shapely arm, or her leg, or her foot, or her delicate breast?

And even if he succeeded in identifying and analysing the individual, would he then have an insight into the universe? Would he see cities with teeming crowds, roaring traffic, museums containing artistic masterpieces, research laboratories, cathedrals, stadiums, theatres, and brothels? Would he have even a fleeting glimpse of the intelligence of a Descartes, the genius of a Rodin, the beauty of a Balkis?

There is not one chance in a billion that our concept of the universe has a valid basis, because everything we perceive is infinitely diluted. We have an idea of the universal component but we confuse the mechanism of that component with the useful mechanism of the object itself. We have an idea of matter but only a faint glimmer of understanding of its intelligence.

In my opinion, therefore, scientific research should be regarded only as a chivalrous or sporting quest, and when we speak of the universe it should be clearly understood that we mean *our* universe.

Invisible universes

Our means of trying to identify our sublime container, our universal Grail, are insignificant: they are equivalent to the means that Don Quixote had for righting the wrongs of mankind.

However powerful our telescopes may become, and however precise our electronic machines, our research takes place only within a highly inadequate three-dimensional framework.

Is there a universe, or are there universes?

We are so certain that our quest is futile that we cheat from the beginning: we have nested a multitude of nuclei and particles in the atom (which was supposed to be the smallest possible particle) and divided the whole – the universe – into various smaller wholes, so that we now have atoms, worlds, cosmoses, and universes that we explain with tottering laws propped up by other laws that are convenient but arbitrary, all of which does not form a very convincing system!

These laws and this research, in their present state, allow us to assume the existence of new dimensions: the fourth, fifth, sixth, seventh, and so on; not to mention the Mysterious Unknown, the Invisible, which solicits our thought.

In its new meaning, the universe may be composed of billions of galactic universes and, in addition, a number of parallel universes: worlds of thought, worlds of the Beyond, invisible worlds, multidimensional worlds, perhaps even worlds without dimensions.

It is not my intention to analyse, even summarily, the main theories of cosmology, but it seems necessary to present those that crystallize the new spirit and venture into the path of revolution.

The fantastic universe of Louis Jacot

For the Swiss professor Louis Jacot nothing is motionless, nothing is permanent, absolute zero is a gratuitous invention and therefore the universe was not created: it has always existed.

There is nothing particularly unorthodox in this, but two laws serve as springboards for new ideas which, though perhaps not entirely admissible, may contain the germ of tomorrow's truths.

Hubble's Law: The speed of recession of nebulae is proportional to the distance considered (five hundred to a hundred thousand kilometres per second in a constantly expanding universe).

Bode's Law: In our solar system, the distances of the planets from the sun, as far as Uranus, correspond to the following geometric progression: 1, 2, 4, 8, 16, 32, 64, The law holds true seven consecutive times, but there are two exceptions to it. The first consists in the fact that the progression begins not with the sun, but with Mercury; the second concerns planets beyond Uranus, where distances cease to double and become constant. (See *Eléments de Physique Evolutive*, by Louis Jacot.)

To support his ideas, Jacot accepts or rejects certain concepts: the universe is full; universal gravity is an illusion; gravity is explained by concentric pressure of the ether; theories of relativity are a means by which one can justify whatever one wants to prove, using errors, distortions, and variable standards.

A number of physicists have accepted this view but, by adapting it to Bode's Law, Jacot has arrived at an astonishing version of our solar history. It can be briefly stated as follows:

As the sun rotates on its axis it forms a constantly growing bulge at its equator. When this bulge reaches a certain mass, the sun gives birth to a planet fetus which, like a child, first stays close to its mother, then grows and sets off for the frontiers of our little universe. The planets closest to the sun – Mercury, Venus, Earth – are therefore the youngest, while Pluto, Neptune, Uranus, etc., are the oldest.

Our planet also gave birth to a satellite (the moon). It had a slow rotation at first, then semislow, then rapid. Its slow rotation ended with the last ice age of the Quaternary and it did not begin rotating once every twenty-four hours until after a long transition period.

With each slow rotation, ice caps formed on the hemisphere plunged in darkness, while on the other hemisphere, from the equator to the poles, the climate was very warm and vegetation was tropical (which would explain amber, the fossil resin of the Baltic, tropical fossils in coal deposits of the far north, the ice ages of prehistoric times, ancient chronologies and the seemingly implausible ages of the patriarch).

The passage from semislow rotation (about two months) to rapid rotation of twenty-four hours caused the melting of ice and what is known as the Universal Deluge, which Jacot dates at about 3500 B.C.

This cosmology obviously upsets a number of concepts

that were considered well established, particularly the concept of time.

Scientists estimate the age of the earth at somewhere between four and eight billion years, or perhaps as much as ten billion. After studying the various methods of dating (except for that of argon) – radioactivity of rocks, erosion, sedimentation, varves (annual layers of silt), coal formation, physical and astronomical methods, etc. – Jacot concludes that orthodox science has made an enormous error of interpretation. According to him, our planet has existed for only a hundred thousand to a hundred and fifty thousand years!

The land of Mu is on the moon

The idea that the moon was formed of matter torn away from the earth, leaving a scar that became the Pacific Ocean, is an attractive hypothesis that has been upheld many times, but until Louis Jacot no one had been able to imagine a plausible explanation for it.

Since tradition situates the ancient continent of Mu in the middle of the Pacific, we can deduce from these theories that Mu supplied the material for the moon. Our astronauts therefore have a chance, minute but not negligible, of finding vestiges of a very old civilization on the moon – vestiges that came from Earth!

Jacot's evolutional physics also gives rise to extrapolations in the interplanetary domain that are not lacking in interest.

If men from space once landed on our planet, where did they come from? It is highly unlikely that they came from Mercury or Venus, since those are younger planets; but the supposed inhabitants of Jupiter or the asteroids, in the remote past, or of Mars, more recently, had good reason to want to leave their planets before they became uninhabitable.

All this is hypothetical, of course, since evolution may have taken place more rapidly on Venus than on Earth, and the inhabitants of other planets in the cosmos may have created means of escape that we cannot even imagine.

Was Teilhard de Chardin right when he said that 'only the fantastic has any chance of being true?'

Teilhard de Chardin's cosmology

Respectful of dogmas but aware of the revolution that was imposing itself on Christian minds, Father Teilhard de Chardin constructed a cosmology that can be summarized as follows:

The world rises evolutionally from inorganic matter to deliberate thought.

Evolution continues on the individual scale as well as the supraindividual scale, this arrangement always producing more consciousness.

On the biological level, mankind rises toward unification and spiritual concentration in a divine supracentre (or Centre of Centres).

The ideal consummation (terminal or eschatalogical state) of the world occurs at an ideal point: the Omega Point, or 'suprapersonal' centre of personalization.

All evolution takes place around an ultraphysical axis that pre-exists in the world.

The intelligence of matter

In a different hypothesis, though one that takes the classical mother-cell as its point of departure, the evolution of matter includes elements of the fantastic which broaden our conjectural horizon by forming a synthesis of accepted scientific theories, certain more empirical theories and traditional data that have either remained unknown to rationalists or have been unjustly rejected by them.

Evolution is made up of *necessarily unstable* systems which, through birth, life, and death, tend toward steadily increasing complexity and spirituality.

Atheists believe that this mechanism is blind and lacks guiding intelligence.

For nonatheists, if the universe has a goal (finite universe) man's last reign will be identified with the guiding intelligence that believers call God. This intelligence is in everything and man is part of it.

Here, in a highly condensed version, is a possible

process of evolution as it would occur in accordance with my principles:

The basic matter of the universe is made of a kind of 'original plasma' composed of motion, light, and energy. It is uncreated, eternal, alive, and activated by superior intelligence. (In the beginning, according to some scientists, there was a temperature of several billion degrees; everything was radiation or waves, with immense possibilities of transmutation and, perhaps, of intelligence.)

Ascending realms start from this plasma, return to it and begin a new cycle that is richer and more spiritual than the preceding one, and has a superior essence.

This may validate seemingly irrational beliefs in reincarnation and resurrection.

If the universe were finite, it would reach its end only with the sublimation of matter, not of man.

The principle of hylozoism is that life and intelligence are everywhere, from minerals to man. So-called lifeless matter contains as much potential intelligence as a mathematician's brain. It may be, however, that only an infinitesimal amount of it is used. The human brain also uses only a fraction of its potential: ten billion grey cells out of a total of thirty billion. In the case of minerals, the proportion of potential intelligence actually used may be much smaller, and this intelligence may be made imperceptible by the immense forces of inertia that oppose it.

But we may wonder whether the intelligence of minerals is not more obvious than is commonly recognized. Does not the earth close around seeds? Volcanic eruptions, earthquakes, and especially that living force of the Mysterious Unknown called telluric currents may demonstrate the intelligence of the globe, our Mother Earth, from which all thinking human creatures have come.

Furthermore, is it reasonable to deny intelligence to those billions of billions of electrons, neutrons, protons, etc., which undergo mutations and transmutations and are the cause of the fact that our globe, in the Invisible, is a constantly seething mass?

That globe lives as each element of the atom does. It is a component of minerals, plants, and animals. It is Gaea, the mother of man. It is his grave; it recuperates his matter and also, probably, all or part of his psychic potential.

Mysterious DNA

Each realm of nature, from minerals to man, has senses, intelligence, and a soul.

It has been denied that minerals, plants, and lower animals – and even women! – have a soul, but to support that idea one would have to specify the time and the realm in which the soul is suddenly manifested. In reality, however, it never bursts forth spontaneously, which would be inexplicable.

Intelligence, senses, and a soul are therefore attributes of all links in nature, beginning with the one that is believed to be the lowest in the chain of evolution: DNA (deoxyribonucleic acid). It is a mineral in crystallized DNA and a living organism when it is a virus.

Furthemore, we never know very clearly where a realm begins and ends. The sea anemone is an animal, but it resembles a plant so strongly that for centuries it was classified as such. The famous naturalist Réamur, known as 'the Pliny of the eighteenth century,' believed in the correctness of this classification so firmly that for a long time he refused to tell the Paris Academy of Sciences the name of the man who had proved the animal nature of the sea anemone, in order to 'save him from ridicule.'

Plant nerves

The idea of universal intelligence has had growing numbers of supporters in scientific circles since the naturalist Nemec demonstrated the plant nervous system at the ends of the roots of onions, hyacinths, ferns, etc.

If you 'wound' a plant, whether it be a hundred-foot sequoia or a bit of moss, the contents of the cells flow from the opposite side to the wound. If a radicle is corroded, it curls up and writhes like a wounded animal. It has been observed under a microscope that when a leaf or a flower is pulled off a plant, a veritable spasm runs through its cells, over a wide area.

(Despite their ignorance and naïveté, it is easy to

sympathize with vegetarians. They are probably right in thinking that their diet, reasonably applied, is a healthy reaction against excessive meat-eating, but they are mistaken when they think that vegetarianism abolishes 'crime' against animals. They confuse sentimentality with reason and distort the laws of nature, however cruel they may seem to a simplistic mind.)

Professor Halberlandt has proved that the upper side of a leaf is an eye with facets and lenses which concentrates the sun's rays at the centre of each cell.

If an oak should some day begin speaking and solving mathematical equations, would it not have to be classified as a superior animal, even with its branches, acorns, and birds' nests? Unfortunately, of course, oaks do not speak, at least not in the sense defined by men, but as Aristotle said (more or less!) twenty-three centuries ago, they can still think.

The behaviour of certain plants and animals is often perplexing. In New Guinea, for example, the male of the *amblyornis*, a type of swallow, gathers leaves and flowers and makes them into a kind of richly coloured carpet around his mate's nest, with an obvious concern for esthetics.

The clever teasel

All hypotheses of tropisms – geotropism, heliotropism, hydrotropism, nyctotropism, etc – do not explain why convolvulus moves toward a support two out of five times, no matter in which direction it may lie.

Teasel, a thistlelike plant, has an especially well-developed intelligence. At the intersection of each of its leaves with its stalk, it forms a little basin in which rainwater and dew collect. Intelligence? Not yet, perhaps. But it happens that each little basin attracts many insects, including mosquitoes, which fall into the water and drown. They soak in the water for a time, then the teasel eats them by putting out very thin protoplasmic hairs. Many animals do not show that much cleverness – that much imagination, one is tempted to say!

Bacteria will travel great distances, in relation to their size, to reach a potassium salt solution, even one that is enormously diluted, yet they ignore glycerin solutions that would give them excellent nourishment. Bacteria simply prefer the taste of potassium!

And so, from one end of the lower evolutionary chain to the other, there are traces of sensitivity, will, and soul which we are only beginning to perceive.

Everything comes from other planets

Evolution is a universal, irreversible phenomenon, though it has not been clearly proved and is difficult to verify. And in calling it an irreversible phenomenon – that is, one which cannot return to an earlier form – I am stating a conventional view for which there is no conclusive evidence, as is shown by a case observed in Osoka, Japan, by Dr. Ziro Nikuni and a group of other medical experts. On men suffering from a mysterious disease, they saw a growth of cotton fibres that would have been enough to make several suits! It was not a form of parasitism; that would have provided a plausible explanation. The sick men had three distinct natures in them: a mineral nature through their physical constituents, a plant nature, and an animal nature.

For the sake of convenience we often speak of 'links' between two realms, but in reality those links do not exist. And we must admit that 'universal' evolution involves many species which have not evolved since the most remote eras of creation.

On the whole, life appears to us without much coherence. It is as if our planet were a zoo and an experimental installation created by superior beings for their own edification. Or, from the standpoint of Baron d'Espiard de Colonge's theories, it is as if forms of life had once been deposited on Earth from some wandering planet, by collision or interplanetary osmosis.

A third and much more likely hypothesis is that seeds of life accidentally came to Earth through interstellar space, or that life was deliberately brought here and acclimatized by travellers from other planets who came with seeds and selected animals specimens, just as our own astronauts will do when they land on an uninhabited planet.

These possibilities completely change the problem of evolution.

We seek truth, but perhaps we invent it out of whole cloth because we do not know our position on the scale of sizes. The galaxies we see through our telescope, at distances of several million light-years, may be only at the edge of an unfathomable universe.

If so, the laws governing our perceptible world are limited, not general. It is mathematically certain, in fact, that real universal laws have only a remote relation to the circumstantial little laws formulated by our scientists.

What becomes of universal gravity, opacity, and time in the unknown life of the atom? What is the meaning of lengths, width, and thickness in a medium heated to a temperature of a hundred million degrees?

Men have always tried to apprehend the Unknown by measuring it with their known dimensions and localizing it in their earthly adventure. But that adventure is now moving outward and we must be increasingly prepared to consider it likely that life on our planet had a foreign origin, that plants, animals, and human beings were brought to Earth at a time when there was no other life on it. This is not a frightening hypothesis.

In the narrow range of vision left to them by their blinders, prehistorians see our 'ancestral' *Homo sapiens* lifting himself from the level of the anthropoids, making flint tools, and then laboriously climbing the steps of knowledge, but those theories have been forcefully rejected by men in all times and places. Whether they be red in America, brown in Polynesia, black in Africa, yellow in Asia, or white in Europe, men have always maintained that our civilization came from elsewhere, *that it is not terrestrial!*

We can even say that according to the oldest known document, the *Book of Enoch*, the technique of smelting metals and making weapons (shields, daggers, swords), the ancient pharmacopoeia, and the art of makeup, including the use of cosmetics and the practice of plucking or accentuating eyebrows, were taught to us by extraterrestrial beings who came to our globe, attracted by the beauty and sex appeal of earthly women!

A censored version

It is obviously not very flattering to God's noble creatures to admit that their civilization began with a rather sordid affair involving a visit from a group of lecherous astronauts whose only excuse was that they were too hot-blooded.

Such a story could be presented on television only in a censored version, and it is easy to understand the qualms of Biblical scribes when they had to relate it. They handled it skilfully in a few lines (Genesis 6:2–4) whose real meaning should be clear to anyone.

Did the moon spill its continents, seas, and cities onto the earth, as d'Espiard de Colonge said? I do not think so.

Was there interplanetary travel in very ancient times? I answer with a categorical yes, especially since such travel is the only chance of salvation for beings living on a planet where their survival is threatened.

It is *possible* that 'space people' will land on our planet tomorrow or within a few centuries, but it is *certain* that within a few thousand years (and probably much sooner) earthly men will have to settle on the moon, Mars, Venus, or Mercury if they want to go on living.

Man's biological flexibility is prodigious, but it is doubtful, even with accelerated evolution, that he can adapt to the inevitable physical changes that lie in store for our planet: accelerated rotation, lessened density, rarefaction of the atmosphere, drying up of the oceans, severe cold, etc. Escape to another planet will then become a vital necessity.

If we are to believe the physicist Louis Jacot and Bode's Law, and if planets older than Earth, such as Mars, Jupiter, Saturn, and Uranus, were once inhabited, their populations were forced to flee to a more hospitable planet, one that occupied a more favourable position in relation to the sun. There must have been an exodus from Uranus to Saturn, then from Saturn to Jupiter, then from Jupiter to the destroyed planet whose fragments now form the asteroids, then from that planet to Mars, and from Mars to Earth.

An Ark named Venus

On this hypothesis, our origin and our civilization would be directly linked to Mars and, farther back in time, to all the other planets.

Yet we have good reason to agree with traditions and the American scholar Immanuel Velikovsky in believing that our initiators were Venusians, for Venus is unquestionably a vagabond planet that did not become part of our solar system until a relatively recent time.

I will discuss this in more detail later, but for the moment I will say that Venus may be either a stabilized comet or a kind of gigantic spacecraft used by extraterrestrials for the purpose of fleeing from a threatened galaxy.

Prehistorians are hypnotized by the rare and extremely doubtful bones of prehistoric humans and humanoids who were supposedly our ancestors. In place of their ideas, tradition and logic offer the symbolic image of Noah's Ark: fleeing a cataclysm, human couples with selected specimens of animal life set off in a ship to reconstruct a vanished world.

The first human being may have been born on Earth and he may even have had apes for ancestors; it is not an implausible hypothesis. But it is also possible that he was born on another planet and I am convinced that this was the case with some of our ancestors, who were called angels and demigods by ancient peoples.

Is evolution different on other planets than it is on Earth? We do not know, but we will know some day when we too set off in an Ark-rocket to recreate a civilization in another region of space. It will then be up to our distant descendants to believe in our prodigious adventure!

II

PROTOHISTORY

Chapter 6

ANGELS AND THE *BOOK OF ENOCH*

The primohistory that we have just resuscitated differs considerably from what is professed by the Bible and official science.

The Bible is regarded by many as the universal ocean from which rivers of knowledge flow. I must confess, however, that despite my great interest in sacred books I can no longer accept them as anything but distant interpretations of events that were sometimes accurately described, but had become nearly incomprehensible to those who reported them, often with additions of their own. Interpretation must now be enlightened by acquired knowledge and freed of dogmatic restraints.

Seven verses in the Bible

For two thousand years, millions of people have made strenuous efforts either to uphold the Bible against all scientific reasoning or to destroy its essence with narrow-minded, negative sectarianism. And there have been billions of people who have never studied it, because of either laziness or fear of reprisals.

My undertaking may therefore be considered highly adventurous, but I will face the problem honestly and propose solutions in the hope that they may help others who try to understand the Bible.

Since my views will antagonize many people of all religious persuasions and clash with accepted beliefs, opinions, and biases, I want to state clearly that I am not questioning anyone's motives and that I owe allegiance to no political group, but that my respect for the ideas of others cannot prevent me from seeking truth or 'different truths.' Tolerance and the right of free speech are man's most valuable acquisitions and I invoke them in my favour.

Analysed in that frame of mind, the Bible appears as a document in which only seven verses are worth the serious attention of twentieth-century mankind: the first seven verses of the sixth chapter of Genesis.

With few exceptions, the rest only expresses an outdated morality and relates events that have never concerned the Chinese, the Australian aborigines, the Eskimos, the American Indians, and all modern peoples. The story of how two hundred Hebrew warriors exterminated three hundred Moabites no longer interests anyone but specialized historians.

For citizens of the present world, however, there are three important and fascinating points:

1. Shortly after the creation of the world, 'the sons of the gods had intercourse with the daughters of men.' (Genesis 6:4.)

2. Certain events, of which we are told nothing, occurred and made God angry.

3. Regretting that he had created the human race, God destroyed it.

What could be more important to men than the destruction of their world? Compared to such a catastrophe, anything else is insignificant. This ought to be the main story in Genesis, but it is told sketchily, without explanation, in only a few lines: mysterious extraterrestrials arrive, then God decides to annihilate the human race. It is strange and disconcerting. . . .

But first of all, who were those 'sons of gods,' whom the Church Fathers called 'angels'? (In the *Book of Enoch*, these 'angels' are indiscriminately called 'sons of the heavens,' 'sons of the holy angels,' 'watchers,' and sometimes simply 'men.') Were they celestial creatures, from the kingdom of God the Father, who came to the planet Earth to make love with earthly women?

Can people living in the era of nuclear power, television, and space travel believe in such phantasms that have never been seen by anyone alive today, like fairies, goblins, and elves? For those who have faith, there is no problem: the Bible is literally true; but who would dare to believe in it rationally?

Are we to say that angels have never existed? If so, the Bible – along with all other sacred writings, including the

Apocrypha, which unanimously tell similar stories – should be classified as a children's book.

But if those 'angels' represent a hidden truth, a symbol, who are they? Where do they come from?

I will cautiously give the only identification that can be accepted in our era of extraplanetary adventure.

The sons of the gods and the daughters of men

In the first verse of the sixth chapter of Genesis we learn that not long after the creation of Adam and Eve the human race began expanding. The population of the earth was still extremely small, probably no more than a few thousand.

Verse 2: 'The sons of the gods saw that the daughters of men were beautiful; so they took for themselves such women as they chose.'

Verse 4: 'In those days, when the sons of the gods had intercourse with the daughters of men and got children by them, the Nephilim were on earth. They were the heroes of old, men of renown.'

These 'men of renown,' born of the earliest earthly women and the 'sons of the gods,' may very well be identified with leaders of nations or the heroes or demigods of mythology.

But what about the 'sons of the gods'?

If we are to believe authorized commentators on the Bible, angels came down from God's heaven to make love with women and impregnate them. What lechers those angels were!

Without thinking that heaven is a den of rogues, I cannot accept that sacrilegious explanation, especially since it is hard to conceive of angels who not only have carnal desires but are physically equipped to satisfy them.

Are angels material beings who have sexual attributes like ours and are even more strongly gripped by the demon of lust than we are?

Apocryphal texts, such as *The Combat of Adam and Eve*, translated from the Ethiopian, are opposed to such an unreasonable explanation:

'And ancient sages wrote about them and said that the

angels had come down from heaven and that they had joined with the daughters of Cain and begotten giants with them. But they were mistaken in that opinion; it is not true that angels, who are spirits, sinfully mingle with mankind.... But in accordance with their being and their nature, they are neither male nor female, but pure spirits, and since their fall they have become black.'

It should be stressed that this text has an essentially religious orientation and is not intended to be heretical.

But if the 'sons of the gods' were not angels, we can only think of unusually large men, since they had giant children. At that time the descendants of Adam and Eve were easily identifiable because they were grouped together and few in number, so those men were surely not earthlings!

Abandoning for a moment the game imposed by the Bible, I do not believe in a man and a woman who were created from clay and served as the prototypes of our human race, and I can therefore accept the possibility that those giant lechers may have come from another part of the globe: Asia, America, Europe, Oceania, Africa. But the Bible says they were the sons of the gods and the apocryphal texts are unanimous in saying that they were beings from the sky and that they *came down* to the earth.

In the absence of any other plausible explanation, such travellers can only be regarded as having been flying men, aviators or astronauts, probably of a race different from ours, since their physical characteristics gave little reason to believe that they had an earthly origin.

We must go back to ancient writings to find more of the revealing details that abound in an apocryphal text much older than the Bible: the *Book of Enoch.*

In the Bible, it is disturbing to note that only two verses (2 and 4 in the sixth chapter of Genesis) mention the coming of the 'sons of the gods,' and that the whole history of the world from the fantastic landing to the tragedy of the Deluge is then dispatched in a few lines.

But the *Book of Enoch* devotes twenty-two chapters to the story of those 'angels' and the causes of God's anger.

Twenty-two chapters as compared to seven verses in the Bible!

A question naturally comes to mind: *Why has the essential part of the story told in Genesis been concealed?*

The Book of Enoch

The *Book of Enoch*, three copies of which were brought from Abyssinia in about 1772 by the great Scottish scholar James Bruce, was copied from an original written in Hebrew, Chaldean, or Aramaic which many translators consider to be the world's oldest manuscript. Two copies of it are in England and one is in France.

It was tampered with by Catholic scribes who, with pious intentions, added chapters announcing the coming of the Son of Man or the Messiah, but those additions are easy to detect.

(In their desire to accredit the existence of Jesus as the Messiah, scribes and monks of the first sixteen centuries after Christ mutilated or destroyed all documents – manuscripts, engraved stones, books, etc. – capable of raising doubts with regard to the tenets of Christian orthodoxy. This vast work of falsification was also carried on by the priests of other religions, so that there is no longer any ancient manuscript, except perhaps for the Dead Sea Scrolls, whose authenticity and integrity seems unquestionable.)

Enoch was a mysterious personage who was taken over by the tradition of Israel, but his existence actually goes back much farther than Hebrew civilization.

Some scholars maintain that before the Bible, and before the Vedas of the Hindus, the Laws of Manu of the Brahmanists, the Chings of the Chinese, etc., there were manuscripts which served as models for the sacred books that we know.

Moses speaks several times of texts older than the Pentateuch and quotes passages from them, as in Numbers 21:14. They are also mentioned in Joshua 10:13, II Samuel 1:18 and elsewhere. Moses appears to have summarized those books in the first twelve chapters of Genesis.

If we are to believe tradition, Enoch came from Uppe-

Mesopotamia or Armenia, for he is presented as the initiator or father of the legendary King Kayu-Marath or Kayomers, 'King of the Earth' and of Azerbaijan. The connection between Enoch and Armenia is extremely important because it was precisely in Armenia that the first Indo-European civilization was born. It will be interesting to note, later in our account, that according to historians Kayomers instituted the ceremony of *pabus*, or foot-kissing, and that Armenian and Circassian women are regarded as the most beautiful in the world. These details will be directly linked to extraplanetary adventure.

In Moslem manuscripts it is said that Kayomers drew knowledge of the true God from the books of the prophet Edris ('Edris' is the Arabic form of 'Enoch').

All-too-human angels

We thus have an approximate identification of the Armenian Enoch. His book is apocryphal (literally 'hidden,' i.e., meant for initiates) but accepted as authentic; it was even regarded as canonical by the early Church. It begins with this exordium:

'In the name of God, full of mercy and grace, slow to anger, always ready for clemency and mercy, this book is the book of Enoch, the prophet.'

In Chapter 7 the narrator comes to the heart of his subject, without having mentioned Adam and Eve or any dramatic events in heaven.

Chapter 7, Verses 1-2: 'When the children of men had multiplied in those days, it happened that elegant and beautiful daughters were born to them. And when the angels, the children of the heavens, had seen them, they fell in love with them; they said to each other, "Let us choose women from the race of men and have children with them." '

We are already in a climate different from that of the Bible. Women had existed on Earth for only a short time – or at least those who were elegant and beautiful – be-
se they would already have been noticed by
f the heavens.'
celestial beings angels? Yes, in the sense

understood by the Incas when they saw Cortez and his men arrive, or by jungle tribes when they saw aviators for the first time.

Orejona, the Venusian woman who landed near Lake Titicaca according to Andes traditions, perhaps with an initial reconnaissance group, was later deified. (In my view, several extraterrestrial reconnaissance groups landed, notably in Peru, Mongolia, Armenia, and Hyperborea, which is now submerged. If an emigration was being planned, one or more reconnaissance missions were certainly undertaken. There is no reason why a woman should not have taken part in those first landings; on the contrary, it was extremely important to have a woman undergo the test of the journey to see if she would still be able to procreate.)

Is it not perfectly logical for primitive peoples to regard men who come from the sky as supernatural beings?

Enoch specifies that those angels, who behaved like ordinary human beings, were of a race alien to ours.

Let us continue examining the other verses.

Verses 3-7: 'Then Samyaza, their leader, said to them, "I fear that you may not accomplish your intention, and that I alone may bear the penalty of your crime." But they answered, "We swear to you, and we will all bind ourselves by mutual oaths: we will change nothing in our intention, we will carry out what we have resolved." And they swore and bound themselves by mutual oaths. They numbered two hundred, and they came down at Aradis, a place near Mount Armon.' (This name is not in the Bible.)

It must be noted that the conspiracy of the two hundred extraterrestrials – for they are literally extraterrestrials, not being of earthly origin – aroused certain misgivings in Samyaza's conscience. As for the members of the expedition, their way of speaking is consistent with the idea that they were daring, adventurous astronauts who may have been long deprived of carnal pleasure, with which they were apparently well acquainted. Those 'angels' were certainly not beginners in that area!

Verses 9-11: 'These are the names of their leaders: Samyaza, their leader, Urakabarameel, Akibeel, Tamiel,

Ramuel, Danel, Azkeel, Sarakamyal, Asael, Armers, Batraal, Anane, Zavebe, Samsaveel, Ertael, Turel, Yomyael, Arazeal. Such were the leaders of those two hundred angels; and the rest were with them.' (Compare Arazeal and Aruseak, Armenian names for the planet Venus.) 'And each of them chose a woman, and approached her, and cohabited with her; and they taught the women sorcery, enchantments and the properties of roots and trees. And those women conceived and gave birth to giants.'

How are we to accept the idea that 'angels,' ordinarily living in the heavenly bliss of God's kingdom, could express feelings worthy of bawdy troopers and know about things that were naturally unknown in heaven: sorcery, enchantments, and the medicinal or nutritious properties of plants?

Chapter 8, Verse 1: 'Azazyel also taught men to make swords, knives, shields, breastplates and mirrors; he taught them the making of bracelets and ornaments, the use of paint, the art of painting one's eyebrows and using precious stones and all kinds of dyes, so that everyone was corrupted.'

Thus mirrors, weapons, cosmetics, and feminine artifices were not invented on Earth. On another planet, men had a civilization partly the same as ours, and women used beauty products identical or similar to those sold in our stores.

In the following verses, other angels teach 'sorcery, enchantments, the art of observing the stars, signs, astronomy, the movements of the moon,' and so on.

One can teach only what one has learned and experienced; is it possible that in God's heaven 'angels' could have learned to make instruments of war, trinkets, and jewellery, and 'the art of painting one's eyebrows'? Is it possible that to a pure, guileless Earth they brought contamination from heaven?

In all honesty, it is hard not to acknowledge that those 'angels' thought and acted in ways that were typically human and completely irreconcilable with a divine nature. But if we attribute to them the nature of astronauts who had come from another planet, everything falls into place!

If we accept the story in the *Book of Enoch*, the only rational interpretation of it is that it describes the colonization of Earth by astronauts who had come either because they wanted to conquer it or because they had been forced to emigrate from their own planet. If so, the two hundred extraterrestrials were probably only a scouting party who had to report on their mission to general headquarters.

This is a rational hypothesis, supported by our own plans for space exploration. It will become still more plausible as we continue to examine the story and Enoch's function is seen more clearly. Perhaps he was also an extraterrestrial; perhaps he was the scrupulous Samyaza, most likely a delegate from general headquarters, since he disapproved of the scouting party's behaviour, returned to his leaders, and even became a mediator between them and the astronauts who had disobeyed orders.

Chapter 12 (Section 3), Verses 1-2: 'Before the accomplishment of all these things, Enoch was taken away from the earth and no one knew where he had been taken or what had become of him. He spent all his days with the saints and the watchful ones [initiates].'

Like Elijah, who, the Bible tells us, was 'carried up in the whirlwind to heaven,' Enoch became an astronaut or an aviator and went to make his report to his superiors. (In Armenian-Caucasian mythology, according to Professor Joseph Karst of the University of Strasbourg, the genie Karapet is identified with Enoch. The name 'Karapet' comes from the Georgian *kari*, 'gate' or 'master of the gate,' or *karvosani*, 'master of the camp,' with the general meaning of 'messenger,' which can obviously be applied to the Armenian Enoch.)

I realize how strongly this fantastic interpretation clashes with our bourgeois complacency and atavistic credulity, but unless we are to resort to an interpretation that is even more fantastic and unacceptable in our time – that of a sinister revolt by perverse angels who fled from an agitated heaven – there is no other way to give meaning to the events in question.

The first fathers of Hyperborea

With the words and mentality of his time, the narrator describes 'heaven,' with its 'wall made of crystal stones,' which strangely recalls the Hyperborea of tradition, enclosed by high walls of ice. The similarity is worth noting because it tallies with certain stories in the Norse Sagas.

In Norse and Celtic tradition, Hyperborea is located near Greenland; that is, in the north and the west. This is the direction in which Enoch situates the base established as the headquarters of the extraterrestrials. He visits various western regions of the earth, then the dwelling of the Eternal King in the northern part of the earth.

Chapter 69 (Section 12), Verses 3-4: 'Since then, I have no longer gone among the children of men, but he placed me between two spirits, between the north and the west, where the angels had received ropes to measure the place reserved for the righteous and the chosen. There I saw the first fathers, the saints who lived in that beautiful place for all eternity.'

It should be noted that Enoch easily identifies heaven with the earth; and he states that 'the holy place' – the Eden where the sweet-smelling tree of the righteous grows – is in the west, at the limit of our globe, where the sky itself begins.'

Chapter 33, Verses 1-3: 'Then I went northward to the limit of the earth, and there, at the confines of the world, I saw a great and splendid wonder. I saw the open gates of heaven. There were three of them, distinct from one another.'

He does not say that he left our globe and rose into the sky. He seems to know nothing of the south and the east. He meets the 'first fathers,' the superior men whom I see as the supreme leaders of the scouting party sent to Armenia.

Sometimes, however, Enoch dissociates heaven and earth. With regard to the rebels he writes as follows:

Chapter 68, Verses 3-4: 'Here are the names of the leaders of their hundreds, their fifties and their tens. The name of the first is Yekum; it was he who beguiled all the sons of the holy angels, who incited them to go down to earth to beget children with human beings.' (So the holy angels have children in heaven!) Verses 6-7: 'The name of the third is Gadrel; it was he who revealed the means of killing to the sons of men. It was he who seduced Eve.'

This is one of the few passages where Eve's name appears. There is never any mention of Adam, who, according to this story, was the world's first deceived husband!

The end of the Apocalypse is extremely confused because it comes back to the creation and finally relates the Deluge, the just punishment of the wrongdoing of those I assume to have been astronauts.

The guilty angels are hurled into the Valleys of Fire, which may refer to the Land of Fire (Azerbaijan) near which Noah's Ark landed.

A Slavic text called the *Book of the Secrets of Enoch* gives a curious description of men who visited the narrator: 'Two men appeared to me. They were very tall, taller than anyone else I had ever seen on earth. Their faces were like the shining sun, their eyes were like lighted lamps. Fire came from their mouths. Their clothes were like a spray of foam and their arms were like golden wings at the head of my bed.'

This description deals not with angels, but with *men*. They seem to be dressed as we ordinarily think of astronauts, with transparent helmets and plastic suits.

Near the Ferghana uranium mines in Uzbekistan, U.S.S.R., between Afghanistan and the Aral Sea, the Soviet archaeologist Georgi Shatski recently found some rock carvings of figures that appear to be wearing space suits and helmets and give the impression of being genuine astronauts. He believes that the carvings are from the period known as the Paleolithic.

In Mexico, the giant stone heads left by the mysterious Olmec people also seem related to an interplanetary adventure.

The Russian scientific journalist Agrest, studying texts of the Dead Sea Scrolls, discovered the following: 'Men came from the sky and other men were taken from the earth and carried into the sky. The men who came from the sky remained on earth for a long time.'

A good believer will, of course, limit himself to the literal meaning; but in the twentieth century intransigent critics cannot help thinking of a conspiracy to stifle a dangerous secret.

Careful study of the *Book of Enoch* reveals disturbing details and makes one nearly certain that Enoch is not describing a vision, but an actual journey. It is true that he says he had several visions, but he strangely mixes up heaven and earth, as if he could not separate them very clearly in his mind; he seems as confused as, for example, a sixteenth-century Indian would have been if he had travelled to China in a helicopter or a jet.

He is 'transported over the earth and put down before the door of his house' (Chapter 80, Verse 7). But if he had only had a vision without actually going anywhere, he would have had no need to be brought home!

And in Chapter 64, Section II-2, the truth seems to come out when he says that Noah 'set off and went toward the limits of the earth, toward the dwelling of his ancestor Enoch.'

Is this the uncovering of the secret? It is clear to the writer of the story that the patriarch Enoch, 'taken away alive to go into heaven,' actually withdrew 'to the limits of the earth,' between the north and the west; that is, to Hyperborea or Florida, where he had his secret earthly dwelling near his superiors.

Noah (Chapter 64, Section III-1) sees 'the earth tilt and threaten ruin.' That, too, is very strange! Was Noah, as the Bible of the Egyptian Gnostics says, 'taken alive into heaven,' to escape from the Deluge? Perhaps by the mysterious ancestors who lived 'between the north and the west'? Ancestors who had flying machines? Or did Noah see the earth 'tilt' exactly as one has that impression when one takes off in an airplane?

All this strongly suggests that Enoch actually made a journey through the air and did not merely see it in a dream.

The *Book of Enoch* and the *Book of the Secrets of Enoch* thus give testimony which sheds fantastic light on mankind's forbidden past.

What credence can we give to those manuscripts which, despite their implausibilities and confusions, are the first documents of our history and also present a truth that has undoubtedly been deformed by misunderstanding and copying errors?

In the Zohar, the oldest account in the Cabala, the *Book of Enoch* is mentioned several times as a work 'preserved from generation to generation and piously handed down.' It was rejected from the Jewish canon and finally proscribed by the Christians, but not until the third century, and its prestige has remained very great because it is regarded as the only antediluvian manuscript.

This belief is strengthened by the fact that Enoch described the movements of the sun and the moon in a very scientific way, yet made certain errors which, as Hoffmann says, can be explained only by the supposition that he was describing a system that existed before the order of nature was changed by the worldwide Deluge.

Tradition states that the *Book of Enoch* escaped destruction because Noah took it with him in the Ark. It is therefore not without reason that this work is considered to be the true Bible of men.

Allowing for the displacement of the poles that occurred later, at the time of the Deluge, the astronomical data in the *Book of Enoch* lead us to believe that its author lived in ancient Armenia, near the source of the Euphrates, where astronauts in love with the beautiful daughters of men made their landing. And this idea is given further support by geological considerations.

Chapter 7

A PRIMORDIAL SECRET AND
A DANGEROUS WORD

The mystery of human genesis and vanished civilizations may be cleared up if we can correctly identify the 'angels, sons of the gods.' This is not a gratuitous hypothesis.

Atheists and most so-called sensible people simply reject the sacred texts as fables, legends, or nonsense. This sectarian attitude overlooks the real value of our traditional heritage, despite its uncertainties and alterations.

It seems absolutely certain to me that the Bible and the Apocrypha represent a truth that may have been overstated or mutilated, but rests on authentic foundations.

What, then, are we to believe?

If the 'angels' came from the heavenly kingdom, if they are nonhuman creatures serving as links between God and us, our interpretations are completely useless.

In our created, material universe, however, the heavenly kingdom has few able supporters! And angels, whether good or bad, guardians or singers, have no more been identified, photographed, seen, or verified than have elves, fairies, gnomes, and goblins.

If the Bible deserves to be taken seriously, though not always literally, we must accept the idea that the 'angels' in it were intelligent, flesh-and-blood creatures like us, which amounts to saying that those angels, sons of the gods, were *men*.

I must admit that identifying them as extraterrestrials – for I will soon draw that conclusion definitively – is a little disconcerting to our faint-hearted conventionalism.

Even in the twentieth century it is unconventional to say that men from another planet have already come to ours, though there are a number of people who accept that idea; they realize the deep meaning of our efforts to conquer space and the consequences they will inevitably have in the future. But then there are the others!

They are divided into two groups. First, those gullible souls who see extraterrestrials every morning on their way to work and never let a year go by without spotting two or three flying saucers. And second, there are the sceptics and disbelievers who take their stand on known facts, which undeniably places them in a strong position.

'You deny the existence of angels, ghosts, and fairies,' they may say, 'because they correspond to no proven, perceptible, physical reality, and yet you believe in extraterrestrials! Have you even seen them?'

I must confess in good faith that I have never seen any extraterrestrials, but I *have* seen astronauts, satellites, and rockets, and I know that in recent years spacecraft have been going farther and farther away from Earth, toward the stars. Some have landed on the moon, others have passed close to Mars and Venus. Men from Earth will undoubtedly set foot on another planet before the year 2000. It would be foolish to deny it.

I think it would be equally foolish to believe that what will be done tomorrow could not have been done yesterday.

I freely admit that we have no tangible proof that extraterrestrials came to our planet in ancient times, and that as long as we lack such proof the idea will be only a hypothesis; but it would be irrational to refuse to grant the *possibility* of its being true.

Before identifying the angels in the Bible and the *Book of Enoch* as men from another planet, I will try to show that we can learn something about these mysterious visitors through the strange adventures in which they were involved.

Was Noah a Hyperborean?

After the worldwide Deluge, according to the Biblical tradition, all of mankind perished except the eight passengers of Noah's Ark. When they had landed in Armenia, they had the heavy task of repopulating the world. So if we are to believe this story, everyone on earth is a descendant of Noah.

But this point is not entirely clear, since, by the

admission of his putative father Lamech, Noah's ancestry is open to question. Lamech was not at all convinced that his wife Bat-Enosh was faithful to him, though she may actually have been innocent of adultery.

In Chapters 106-107 of the *Book of Enoch* we read: 'And after a time my son Methuselah took a wife for his son Lamech and she conceived and gave birth to a son. And his skin was white as snow and red as a rose, and the hair on his head was white as wool; and his eyes were beautiful.' Then Lamech says to his father Methuselah, 'I have brought into the world a child different from others; he is not like men, but resembles a child of the angels of heaven.'

In a scroll known as the *Apocrypha of Genesis*, Lamech questions his wife Bat-Enosh about the strange child to whom she has just given birth, and she justifies herself with touching nobility. (In the following quotation, words between parentheses are illegible in manuscript; they have been reconstructed by Professor Biberkrant of the University of Jerusalem.)

'Then she controlled her anger and spoke with me, and said to me, "Oh, my lord, oh (my husband, remember) my pleasure! Would I have sworn to you by the Great Saint, by the King of Heaven (and all of Earth) that that seed was from you, and that pregnancy by you, and (that) fruit was planted by you and not by any stranger and not by any 'watchers' and not by any son of heaven. . . ." '

The great fear of jealous husbands

Lamech obviously felt that Noah's physical characteristics were not those of his race. To me, the description of Noah irresistibly suggests the Hyperboreans, with their snow-white skin and light, golden hair.

The passage quoted above shows that long after the coming of the 'sons of the gods' – or angels, according to the Fathers of the Church – those lecherous, vigorous beings had left a vivid and extremely disturbing memory. The incident, rather comical from a distance of several thousand years, gives the impression that for a long time human beings were terribly mistrustful of those strongly sexed 'angels' who seem to have been obsessed with love-making.

Lamech was not at all overjoyed at the thought that he might have been deceived by an angel from heaven. Since he and his wife were firm believers, they would presumably have considered it a great favour if heaven had given them the gift with which Joseph's wife Mary was honoured. But they were not pleased. It is clear that, to them, the supposed angels were only unscrupulous seducers, from which we may conclude that the extraterrestrials had lost their prestige and were no longer regarded as divine. They were still called 'angels from heaven,' but it was understood that they were women-chasers and that although they had great knowledge they were learned above all in the art of cuckolding husbands.

Yet that unreasoning fear on the part of jealous husbands in ancient times, which degenerated into a psychosis for several centuries, probably had an honourable explanation.

Only Joseph believed the angel who gave this account of his wife's pregnancy: 'It is by the Holy Spirit that she has conceived this child.' (Matthew 1:20.)

Russian commentators, who are not afraid of being sacrilegious, since they are atheists, have concluded from these angelic adventures that Jesus was the son of an extraterrestrial. It is a tenable view despite its lack of orthodoxy.

However, we must allow for an undeniable bias on the part of the Russians. They have given three different opinions on Jesus:

1. Jesus is a myth, since no historian in the time when he is supposed to have lived ever mentioned his existence. This would explain the systematic destruction, during the Middle Ages, of all historical works from the first century and the first half of the second century.

2. Jesus and the Apostles were extraterrestrials on a mission to Earth.

3. Joseph neglected his pretty wife Mary and the inevitable finally happened: she became pregnant by another man. There was nothing very reprehensible in all that, but

it is wrong that a satanic conspiracy should have presented that love-child as the son of God and even as God himself.

I feel that these eminently subversive opinions are worth citing because they parallel a Soviet political tendency which, in October, 1963, lashed out against 'bourgeois Jews.'

Moses was an Egyptian

It is true that my analysis questions the very foundations of the Jewish and Christian religions, but in our time can anyone believe all the stories in the Old Testament?

Biblical history is not the history of the Hebrews: it is the history of the West, all the peoples from Scandinavia to Egypt, from France to eastern Russia.

At first the Bible was intended to be only the logbook of a nomadic desert tribe, but, through a mysterious force, its destiny became bound up with that of Europe and the most highly civilized nations in the world.

For two thousand years the Bible was the Bible; that is, the sacred monument of the One God and eternal truth. Changing, doubting, or interpreting it was a crime, a sacrilege. Our cities, inventions, and cathedrals are magnificent exaltations of a thought born in the mind of a humble Hebrew shepherd.

Men of the West cannot forget that; it binds them permanently to their spiritual brothers, through their flesh, hearts, and genius. But a new time has come with the advent of science. We need to 'recycle ourselves,' to use Leprince-Ringuet's expression; despite all our affection for our good old ancestral Bible, if we are to survive and evolve we must close it forever on the naïve and charming chapter that we had not finished reading.

The great neurologist Sigmund Freud (and many others before him) was struck by the incredibility of certain things in the Bible, and although he recognized how painful it was for him to refute them, he had the courage to present his interpretations respectfully but firmly.

He made an especially careful study of the mystery of Moses and drew this conclusion: the great patriarch, reformer, and lawgiver of the Hebrews could only have been an Egyptian, and the Law of Moses, like circumcision, was Egyptian in origin.

Like Sargon, King of Akkad, Moses was placed in a waterproof rush basket and set adrift on a river. Pharaoh's daughter found the child, adopted him, and named him Moses. That is what legend tells us.

According to learned historians, the name Moses comes from the Hebrew *mosheh*, 'drawn out,' because he was drawn out of the water.

How could such an absurdity have been believed for so many centuries?

At the time when Moses is supposed to have lived (I must point out that his real existence has by no means been proved), the Hebrews, a nation of nomadic shepherds, were to the Egyptians what the Gypsies now are to sedentary, bourgeois people. Still worse, they were a hated race whose multiplication was judged to be so pernicious that Pharaoh had ordered the killing of all Hebrew male children at birth.

Can we imagine a daughter of the President of the French Republic adopting a child during World War I and giving him a German name such as Siegfreid or Wilhelm? Yet, in relation to her own time, that is what Pharaoh's daughter is said to have done. It is completely incredible, especially when we know that the Egyptian word for 'child' was *mose*, a much more plausible etymology than the Hebrew *mosheh*.

Moses was therefore very probably an Egyptian. He was brought up at the royal court, and the historian Flavius Josephus gives a long description of his lofty situation.

In Acts 7:22 we read that he was 'trained in all the wisdom of the Egyptians'; that is, he was given the scientific education reserved for the priestly class. He is said to have commanded Pharoah's armies and to have fought in Ethiopia. He was a man of high position who had a great destiny and died under very suspicious circumstances.

The mysterious Melchizedek, master of the world
In our study of angels in relation to the identity of the
beings who came from the sky, another personage demands our attention: the mysterious Melchizedek. The
Bible gives us very few details about him, yet he must
have been extremely important because we read in
Genesis 14:18-20, 'Then Melchizedek king of Salem
brought food and wine. He was priest of God Most High,
and he pronounced his blessing on Abram: "Blessed be
Abram by God Most High, creator of heaven, and earth.
And blessed be God Most High, who has delivered your
enemies into your power" Abram gave him a tithe of all
the booty.'

Except for a brief mention in Psalm 110, this is the only
reference to Melchizedek in the Old Testament, and it is
too little not to arouse a legitimate suspicion. Fortunately
there are apocryphal writings that tell us more about him.

The twenty-third chapter of the *Book of the Secrets of
Enoch* relates the birth of Melchizedek (whose name
means 'king of righteousness' in Hebrew). Here is a summary of what it says:

Sophonium, wife of Nir, was sterile and yet one day
she found herself pregnant. She died before her child was
born, however; he came out of her dead body and immediately began speaking in praise of the Lord. Nir and
Noah named him Melchizedek. The Lord had Saint
Michael take him away from the earth and place him in
Eden, so that he would escape the Deluge. He was later
placed at the head of the priests of his people. When
mankind has been purified, he will be the Master of the
World.

A truly strange priest, especially since the ancient
chroniclers did their best to obscure his biography, as if
they wanted to cast a veil over *a secret that no one should
know.*

According to some writers, he was Noah's son; the
Fathers of the Church declared him to be 'a figure of
Jesus and an eternal pontiff.'

The sect of the Melchizedekians, supporting their view
with the fact that Saint Paul said Melchizedek had 'no

father, no mother, no lineage' (Hebrews 7:3), maintained that he was not a human being, but a heavenly virtue superior even to Jesus Christ, a mediator between God and the angels.

(In certain esoteric circles it is believed that Melchizedek's dynasty has been perpetuated through the millennia in sanctuaries placed under the care of initiated rabbis, in a way similar to the eternal survival of the Tibetan Buddha. When the right time has come, the last descendant of Melchizedek will make himself known and will become the King of Righteousness, or the Master of the World, or the Messiah of the Hebrews.)

And so, after an extraterrestial incursion, the 'angels' reappear, and the mystery is deepened by an opinion stated by Dom Augustin Calmet in *Discours et dissertations sur le Nouveau Testament* (1705): that Melchizedek was Enoch himself – yes, Enoch, the mediator between the scouting party in Armenia and the extraterrestrials of Hyperborea; or, if you prefer, between the angels and God. Dom Calmet even saw him as one of the three kings who followed the strange star to Bethlehem. According to Dom Calmet, those kings were Enoch, Melchizedek, and Elijah.

What strange coincidences in the association of those three: Enoch, who was taken alive from the earth and went up to heaven; Melchizedek, who was taken alive from the earth and went to Eden; Elijah, who was taken alive from the earth and went up to heaven after having worked miracles much greater than those attributed to Jesus!

Their actions strongly suggest that they knew the secrets of aviation or space travel.

And they knew many other secrets, if we are to believe tradition. Elijah revived the dead, kindled a fire at a distance, caused lightning and rain, burned up enemy soldiers with 'fire from the sky,' divided the waters of the Jordan and crossed it on dry ground.

What scientific truths are hidden behind those legends? And if they are scientific truths, where could they have come from, if not from an advanced civilization that is now unknown?

Can we not discern a prodigious mystery here, enveloped in symbols and circumlocutions?

A dangerous word

In the past, hidden truths that had escaped censorship still showed through in certain teachings. The Egyptian Gnostics maintained that Noah did not build an Ark and float above the flooded earth, but that he took refuge in the sky by leaving on 'a luminous cloud.' (*Les Livres secrets des Gnostiques d'Egypte*, by Jean Doresse.)

In 1621, Jacques Auzoles Lapeire wrote concerning Melchizedek: 'He was procreated either by a new creation or in some extraordinary manner unknown and uninterpretable to us. This patriarch was Enoch, who had left the earthly paradise and changed his name. He was created before Adam and belonged to a celestial race far superior to that of men.'

And we are amazed to discover that the key figures in the Holy Scriptures – Enoch, Noah, the lofty and powerful Melchizedek, Moses, Elijah, Jesus – *were all born of unknown fathers*, and that nearly all of them had a story involving angels in their origin.

Furthermore, *they were all taken alive from the earth and transported elsewhere* – as if they were able to go to a mysterious place in some sort of mysterious craft. Moses was also taken away, according to *The Assumption of Moses*. His 'face-to-face' interview with God on Mount Sinai, which lasted forty days and forty nights, permits us to suppose many things, especially since *no one was allowed to come near the mountain*. It should also be noted that Moses went off alone to die, and that 'to this day no one knows his burial-place.' (Deuteronomy 34:6.)

It is hard to ignore such a mystery. In my opinion it conceals the truth about our genesis.

It would take only a word to make everything become comprehensible and logical, a magic, abhorred word, *a dangerous word that would change the face of history!*

But it is a word which orthodox thinkers, who owe allegiance to terrible conspiracies, must say only with a condescending smile, even if their hearts and imaginations respond to the call of the strangled truth.

As early as A.D. 366, at the Laodician Council, whether from qualms of conscience or as a practical measure for helping to keep secrecy, it was forbidden to speak of angels by name. (Angel worship is a heresy.) It was important to set up a barrier around something that might have 'let the cat out of the bag.'

In short, it is dangerous to talk about angels – or rather those beings made like us who set up their headquarters in the Hyperborea of tradition.

Centuries have passed, blurring and jumbling facts, names and dates; men have added to the deterioration by effacing the original writing of manuscripts and turning them into palimpsests. Yet we have kept a miraculously intact memory of superior ancestors whose country lay in the direction of America, beyond the ocean; an indestructible memory which for two thousand years in historical times drove the Celts and Scandinavians, direct descendants of Enoch, Noah, and Melchizedek, in a nostalgic quest for Hyperborea and Atlantis.

Chapter 8

VENUS, THE PLANET OF OUR ANCESTORS

The greatest fear of ancient peoples, whose awareness of being an integral part of the universal order was clearer than ours, was that the sky might fall. They were still close to the time when great cosmic upheavals had disrupted the planet. Those events are now so remote that most of us either do not know they ever happened or have no desire to learn anything about them.

I can readily imagine the indifferent or incredulous shrug that will greet the idea of such a fear! Yet some day, perhaps tomorrow, a little comet will appear on the horizon as one did about four thousand years ago (in 2348 B.C., according to data in the Bible; in about 1500 B.C., according to other calculations), the earth will tilt, north will become south, east will become west, and everything will be over and done with, for knowers and skeptics alike!

But, you may think, the chances of the earth's colliding with a comet are infinitesimal: about one in 281 million, according to the calculations of astronomers.

An end of the world every ten thousand years

Geologists tell us that the earth is five to ten billion years old. From this we might conclude that the end of our earthly world must be very close, since it should already have happened long ago. Fortunately such 'mathematical' conclusions are not very exact. It is still true, however, that the earth is almost certain to be violently perturbed every five to ten thousand years, for although comets may not strike it, they can pass close enough to have a disastrous effect on it.

In his extraordinarily penetrating and well-documented book *Worlds in Collision*, Immanuel Velikovsky has reconstructed the genesis of the earth and its adventures with comets. He bases his account on traditions as well as the best scientific data. In his quest for truth he is sometimes in agreement on certain points with Professor Louis Jacot, who maintains that the speed of the earth's rotation has fluctuated drastically. In my judgment their erudite studies and recent discoveries by archaeologists, extended by interpretations of the Bible and apocryphal writings, provide all the elements needed for clearing up the mystery of human prehistory ten thousand years ago, and probably much farther back.

The north pole was in the south

About ten thousand years ago the north pole was in Baffin Land and the earth's axis was not tilted, so that the climate of each region remained the same all year round, without seasonal variation.

A comet or a wandering planet – Venus – passed so close that the earth was convulsed and set afire. Cities, forests, and even mountains burned and exploded while a rain of petroleum, soil, and incandescent meteorites fell from the sky. The ice floes of the north pole began drifting, setting off a formidable tidal wave that quenched the fires and finally destroyed what had been spared. Only a minute proportion of human, animal, and plant life escaped annihilation.

During these upheavals the earth was completely turned around, so that the north and south poles changed places. This situation lasted an undetermined time, perhaps only a few days.

Venus was caught in our solar system as though in a net and, like an artificial satellite, began revolving in the orbit it now occupies.

Toward the middle of the second millennium B.C. another cataclysm, much less devastating, brought the tidal wave, earthquakes, and meteorite showers of which the Bible speaks in Exodus and Joshua.*

* Velikovsky gives these dates: between 1500 B.C. and 1700 B.C. for the worldwide cataclysm, and fifty-two years later (at the time of the Hebrews' exodus) for the second upheaval. He also says that Mars collided with the earth in the eighth century B.C., causing a shift in the earth's axis. I agree with his account, except on a few points. There was not a direct col-

That, very briefly stated, is the history of the last five to ten thousand years, in which these well-known events occurred: a worldwide cataclysm, known as the Deluge, and a limited cataclysm in the time of the Hebrews.

But two points demand detailed explanation because of their fantastic nature: the inversion of the poles and the coming of Venus between Earth and Mercury.

As for the inversion of the poles by a 180° turn of the earth, ancient texts leave no doubt that it really happened. The Harris Papyrus, from Egypt, speaks of a cosmic cataclysm by fire and water and says that 'the south became the north and the earth turned over.' The Ipuwer Papyrus says almost the same thing: 'The world is turned backward as on a potter's wheel and the earth turns over.'

In *The Statesman*, Plato speaks of a reversal of the sun's course and the annihilation of mankind. Herodotus, the 'father of history,' reports Egyptian priests as saying that several times within known history the sun had risen where it now sets and vice versa. Papyruses found in the Pyramids state that 'the sun has ceased dwelling in the west and now shines again in the east.' The Polynesians, Chinese, Hindus, and Eskimos also witnessed these phenomena.

And finally, this accumulation of evidence, which had long intrigued archaeologists and astronomers, was greatly strengthened by the discovery of two maps of the sky painted on the ceiling of the tomb of Senmut, Queen Hatshepsut's architect.

One of them is normal, with the cardinal points correctly placed, but in the other, because of the position of the stars, east is to the left and west is to the right, which is highly significant, especially in the tomb of a man whose profession required him to be well acquainted with astronomy and the configuration of the earth.

---

lision (otherwise the earth would have been shattered to bits!) but a light glancing blow. The worldwide cataclysm may have occurred longer ago. In any case, the Egyptians and the Hebrews would not have been able to repopulate and rebuild their respective civilizations in fifty-two years.

Hatshepsut was a queen of the eighteenth dynasty, in the middle of the second millennium B.C.; her architect Senmut therefore lived during the period when, according to Velikovsky, the earthly cataclysm took place. The map in his tomb may have been meant to commemorate an extraordinary event that happened in his lifetime.

Furthermore, in certain volcanic regions geologists have found lava polarized in the opposite direction from that of the local magnetic field, and this is inexplicable without the assumption that the lava crystallized at a time when the poles were reversed.

Venus could not be seen

We are used to a cosmography in which the planets of our solar system go through their motions without the slightest irregularity. If some day our clocks should indicate noon when the sun had not yet risen, we would not believe our eyes. Yet (and astronomers agree on this) there have been days and nights thirty to forty hours long.

We know from the Bible that when Joshua made the sun stand still the day was miraculously prolonged. The water clock of Pharaoh Amenhotep III, which has been recovered, was designed for a day of twelve hours and eighteen minutes at the winter solstice, instead of the present ten hours and twenty-six minutes.

It is certain that a comet passing close to the earth would slow its rotation in proportion to its mass. This has happened in the past and it will happen again.

Venus seems to belong to our solar system in the same way as the other planets, but there is a difference: it appears that five or six thousand years ago Venus, now the brightest, most conspicuous planet in the sky, could not be seen from Earth. Where was it? Beyond Jupiter in the solar system, perhaps, or billions of miles away, in some remote galaxy.

In any case it is certain that at a relatively recent time, within sight of everyone, Venus passed close to the earth, wiping out most of mankind, and then settled into its present orbit. It was an event that the ancients could not forget!

It is acknowledged, of course, by the many astronomers to whom tradition and logic mean nothing. Having
no scientific proof of it, they prefer to deny it, purely and
simply. But it seems certain to anyone who accepts the
demands of logic.

Rational analysis of it can be divided into two phases:
first, proving that Venus was not visible, as a planet, five
thousand years ago; second, proving that its arrival was
the cause of the cataclysm known as the worldwide
Deluge.

The Tirvalour Tables

In the eighteenth century some Hindu astronomical
tables showing the great antiquity of science in India
were sent to France by Christian missionaries and Jean-
Baptiste-Joseph Gentil, a famous Orientalist. Among
them were the Tirvalour Tables, which prove that what
was known as the Age of Caliugam began on February
16, 3102 B.C., at twenty-seven minutes and thirty seconds
past two o'clock in the morning.

'The Indians,' wrote the royal astronomer Jean Slyvain
Bailly, in *Traité de l'Astronomie Indienne* (1787), 'say
that in the Age of Caliugam there was a conjunction of
all the planets. Their tables indicate that conjunction, and
ours show that it actually took place. ... At that time
they saw four planets successively emerge from the rays
of the sun: first Saturn, then Mars, then Jupiter and
Mercury; and these planets were seen gathered together
in a rather small space.'

Bailly was, of course, surprised to find no mention of
Venus in this observation. Unable to believe that there
had been a system of only four planets, he concluded that
Venus must have been behind the sun at the time of the
observation, or had simply been overlooked.

But neither of these explanations is valid. The Hindus,
like the Chaldeans, were highly skilled and meticulous astronomers, and they said specifically that there was a
conjunction of *all* the planets, not just some of them. They
noted it so precisely that we can determine its date to
within a second, in relation to our present calendar, after

more than five thousand years. That rigorous precision enables us to say with certainty that Venus was not overlooked in the observation or the report, especially since it is now the brightest and most visible of the planets.

The idea that it was behind the sun is also unacceptable, since it could not have stayed there long and would then have emerged as the other plants did: 'first Saturn, then Mars, then Jupiter and Mercury.' It would have been impossible for it to remain hidden during the whole time it took the four others to emerge.

Furthermore the Tirvalour Tables make no mention whatever of Venus, not even of its absence or reappearance, which would surely have been noted if it had occurred.

Since those precise, painstaking Hindu astronomers specifically said that they were describing a conjunction of *all* the planets, we may conclude that Venus was not part of the solar system five thousand years ago. And Hindu astronomical tables later than the Tirvalour Tables are based on a system of five planets, including Venus.

The Babylonian Tables

Babylonian astronomy deals with the four planets mentioned above, but here too Venus is absent. And ancient texts call Venus 'the great star that joined the great stars.' In their prayers, the Babylonians invoked Saturn, Jupiter, Mars, and Mercury, but never Venus. An ancient calendar found at Boghaz-Keui, in Asia Minor, mentions the stars and planets, but Venus is missing from the list.

There is only one logical explanation: Venus was not known to the Babylonians of five thousand years ago. Either it was not in our solar system, or else it was too far away from Earth to be seen by the ancients.

Mexican tradition says that 'the great serpent of fire of Quetzalcoatl attacked the sun and there was darkness for four days, then the great serpent was changed into a radiant star [Venus].'

In the Samoan Islands, the natives say that the p Venus once 'ran wild' and grew horns on its head.

In Greece the learned Democritus, particu

versed in astronomy, maintained that Venus was not a planet, but without giving his reasons. This is rather disturbing from a great initiate!

Saint Augustine reports, according to Varron, that 'Castor the Rhodian left a written account of an amazing transformation in Venus: it is said to have changed its colour, size, shape and motion. There has never been anything like this, before or since. It is said to have happened in the time of King Ogypes [let us recall the flood during his reign], as it is attested by Adratus, Cyzicenus and Dion, noble mathematicians of Naples.'

All these concordant accounts have keenly interested scientists, who can only make conjectures about the reasons for the phenomena. Many have thought, and Velikovsky agrees, that Venus was a comet, or was confused with a comet.

'But,' says the *Grande Encyclopédie*, 'could a comet have been confused with a planet? And even if such an error had been made, would it not soon have been revealed by the reappearance of Venus? What observer, what scientist or mathematician, would dare, without due consideration, to affirm such a great event, still unique after thirty-six centuries?'

Moreover, since the Chinese, the Greeks, the Hindus, and others spoke of 'bright hair, or 'a mane of fire' that trailed behind Venus, we are forced to agree that that planet simply did not exist in the sky of the ancients, that it appeared there in the manner of a comet, and that its arrival caused great upheavals.

And finally I will point out again that according to Incan tradition the first woman of the human race, Orejona, came from Venus in a spaceship 'brighter than the sun.'

Although the mystery of that planet remains nearly ⋯ith certainty that Venus came into ⋯housand years ago with the appear- ⋯produced disastrous effects on Earth. ⋯d that a mysterious satellite, natural ⋯n near Venus in the seventeenth and eighteenth centuries by eminent astronomers: Cassini, Short, Montagne, and others.

Thus the planet associated with Lucifer appears to have followed an irregular course and to have been responsible for the worldwide Deluge, thus giving rise to its reputation for bringing bad luck.

Is it so absurd that a planet of our solar system should have engaged in such eccentricities? Not at all; it is the opposite, in fact, that would be abnormal.

The atom, as astrophysicists and scientists in general like to say, is made in the image of the solar system – or vice versa, if you prefer. The sun corresponds to the atomic nucleus, the planets to electrons, and, as in the atom, it is an electric process, still imperfectly known, which determines the life, motion, and gravitation of the planets.

In the atom, electrons leap from one level to another; that is, they change orbits. In the solar system, planets should be able to behave in the same way, and from the same causes. (As Hermes Trismegistus said, 'What is above is like what is below.') In the atom, the phenomenon may cause concomitant reactions, as in the laser; in the solar system, it may cause what the ancients called an 'end of the world.'

In 1696 the English mathematician William Whiston stated that the comet of 1680, whose period is five hundred seventy-five and a half years, had caused the Biblical Deluge. I cannot guarantee the accuracy of his calculations, but if he was right the next end of the world can be expected in the year 2255!

Sumer and the Bible

I do not believe the thousands of people who claim to have seen flying saucers or Martians (I am speaking only of gullible or deceitful 'witnesses,' because I know there are honest and sincere investigators of unidentified flying objects), or the hundred of thousands of hallucination victims who claim to have seen ghosts; but I do believe the millions who, for four thousand years, from the equator to the poles and from the east to the west, have attested to the error of conventional science by insisting that a wandering planet set the earth ablaze and caused the worldwide Deluge, and that the planet was Venus.

Unfortunately the error of scientists who accept the system approved by 'conspiracies of the orthodox' is not the only one that has falsified the history of mankind! But then whom are we to trust, on what are we to base our certainty, if we can find no data that are not flawed or deliberately warped? We might as well believe in nothing! We might as well not believe in the Bible, or in Sumer as the cradle of the first civilization!

Yes, astronomers and archaeologists have dozens of proofs that Egyptian civilization preceded Sumerian by several thousand years. Hindu civilization is also much older than Sumerian. The Tirvalour Tables (more than five thousand years old) give evidence of a culture going back nearly seven thousand years.

The Sothis (Sirius) Calendar is more than sixty-two hundred years old; it proves that Egyptian civilization was earlier than Sumerian and enables us to place its beginning at seven or eight thousand years ago.

In the Calendar of Ptolemy we find the heliacal rising of Sirius at 4241 B.C. Since the rising of Sirius was vitally important because it announced the overflowing of the Nile, it has been concluded that this calendar was drawn up by Egyptian astronomers.

But official doctrine maintains that civilization began in Sumer about five thousand years ago, so the Sothis Calendar is rejected and, by subtle calculations designed to 'correct the error,' its age is reduced from sixty-two hundred years to less than twenty-eight hundred. And Sumer is saved!

It takes a certain courage, or foolhardiness, to play Don Quixote in the realm of illusory images! Especially since the conspirators of the System, turning the truth around as they did in the Glozel trial, will be sure to cast discredit, and opprobrium if possible, on any attempt at reconstruction.

But no matter! In the maze of millenia and machinations, I will try to come as close to the facts as possible and suggest those explanations that seem most logical to me.

On my hypothesis, extraterrestrials came to our planet several thousand years before the Deluge, though it is not possible to give even an approximate date for their arrival during the great darkness of primohistoric times which may have extended to the period of Neanderthal man.

Atomic war between Atlantis and Mu

According to the Bible, men who had been initiated into a new and superior civilization sank to the point where their 'thoughts and inclinations were always evil' (Genesis 6:5), which may suggest a parallel with our present age of base materialism and iniquity.

What happened then?

The destiny of civilizations is an eternal recommencement, an inexorable movement toward death and rebirth. For reasons no doubt similar to those which now lie behind the opposition between the eastern and western blocs, war broke out between Atlantis and Mu.

It happened at the early limit of our prehistoric times and it is now shrouded by the mists in which actual events are diluted into legends reported by traditions. Men have kept a memory of those events, but they have adapted it to their own times, their gods, their heroes, and their imagination.

The Mahabharata, the Drona Parva, and the Maha Vira tell of an atomic war that was fought on Earth, producing radiation sickness and mutations. The Ramayana, like Greek mythology, describes a struggle between the gods and demons or Titans. There are so many similarities, and the heroes resemble each other so closely, that the Greeks believe that Homer was translated in India. It is more likely that a universal truth, known to everyone in primohistoric times, inspired the *Iliad*, the *Odyssey*, and most traditions. The main element of that truth is the war of the Titans against the gods; that is, the worldwide cataclysm.

The atomic bombs of Mu devastated Atlantis and the

American continent, and at the same time the Atlantan response brought death and annihilation to Mu.

We have already identified two centres of destruction: California-Nevada in the west and the Gobi Desert in the east. But there were probably others, now far below the surface of the Atlantic and the Pacific.

That senseless war plunged the world into ruin: all civilization was wiped out, the human race degenerated intellectually and physically, and its reproduction was impaired. Survival must have been made still harder by the fact that millions of people suffered from birth defects.

In a mysterious conjunction, the cataclysm set off by men was followed by the natural cataclysm in which the whole solar system was imperilled by the wandering motion of Venus. (Plato describes the priests of Sais as saying that the scorching of the world by Phaethon was actually a planetary cataclysm.)

After the Deluge, the human race declined day by day, descending the evolutionary path it had ascended, gradually sinking into brutishness. In a last glimmer of lucidity, men erected the Puerta del Sol at Tiahuanaco and carved on it representations of technological devices whose function was no longer very clear to them, meant primarily as a message to future generations. In Egypt, initiates drew winged globes that would later appear on the doors of temples as mysterious, incomprehensible symbols.

I know that this reconstruction of primohistoric times will offend upholders of the conventional system and theologians attached to their traditions and revealed truth. Yet it is no more fantastic than accounts written by historians and prehistorians who disregard such essential data as stories of angels, ancient heroes, legendary monsters, and deluges and cataclysms that wiped out several earthly civilizations.

Commentators and theologians have not yet studied the Bible and apocryphal writings with full awareness of certain facts that cannot be ignored indefinitely: we are becoming increasingly bound up with the cosmos, the earth is not a closed universe, interplanetary exchanges will begin within a short time. In other words, there are outdated and sectarian people who want to go on thinking as earthlings when we are already citizens of the universe.

Since Pope John XXIII there has been a broad tendency toward intellectual freedom in Catholic circles, along with a certain tolerance. The Old Testament is already a subject of controversy and on November 2, 1964, at the Vatican Ecumenical Council, sixteen bishops asked that tradition be allowed to fill gaps in the Scriptures. For those revolutionaries, the books of the Bible were written by men in specific circumstances, according to the literary genre they had chosen. There is a distinct movement in favour of a new interpretation that will 'take into account the discoveries of modern science.' That is what I want to do in this book, with as much objectivity as possible.

The Bible and other sacred writings stress the fact that intervention by extraterrestrials is the main element in our genesis. I have tried to reconstruct primohistory on the basis of that fact, correlating my hypothesis of vanished civilization with the extraordinary events that took place in Biblical times.

Chapter 9

THE ASTRONAUTS OF HYPERBOREA

Have I convinced you that the 'angels who came down from the sky' could only have been extraterrestrials? Do you think my views on the cosmic wanderings of Venus can reasonably be set in opposition to the decrees handed down by conventional astronomers?

I venture to believe so, especially since I will support my theories with other accounts and their application to history will clear up some enigmas that have so far remained impenetrable.

Not everything is revealed, of course; far from it. I could not have said everything or attacked all the superstitions that imprison us. But through the interpretation I have given, the last ten thousand years take on a new aspect and a meaning that begins to satisfy our need for logic, rationality, and wonder.

Others will later correct, curtail, and add to what I have done, and gradually, with time and good will, an approximate truth will emerge from the darkness in which it has been plunged not only by forgetfulness but also by error and preconceived ideas.

I ask the reader to excuse me for the fact that in my exposition, for the sake of convenience, I will mingle the probable and the conjectural, though trying to stray as little as possible from the line of reason.

Venusians land in Armenia

Few people doubt that the history of the world runs in cycles. Within the framework of our solar system these cycles or eras can affect all the planets to some extent.

Six to twelve thousand years ago,* the inhabitants of one of them found themselves faced with such disastrous

---

* How are we to establish precise dates when time is a rubber standard that stretches and contracts? A year in the Tertiary may have been equal to a century in our own era. The time standard is a function of the earth's rotation, which constantly varies.

biological conditions that they decided to attempt an exodus in order to survive. They sent space explorers to carry out a reconnaissance mission on a more hospitable planet similar to theirs in size, atmosphere, and general conditions of life.

The evidence is all in favour of identifying those two planets as Venus, in danger as a result of the cosmic adventure I have already described, and Earth, in an ideal orbit and similar to Venus as far as its vital characteristics were concerned. (This is only a hypothesis. The important fact is the arrival of extraterrestrials. I believe they came from Venus, but my general view would not be altered if they came from some other planet.)

At that time Venus was not between Earth and Mercury, but perhaps between Mars and Jupiter; in any case it was far enough away from our globe to make the ancients unable to see it.

An exodus by the whole population of a planet presents enormous difficulties, no matter how high the degree of technological development may be. A reconnaissance expedition was essential. Explorers with specific instructions were sent in several spacecraft to Earth, where the Venusians knew they would find a suitable atmosphere and plant and animal life already well advanced along the path of evolution.

Another consideration guided their choice: only Mars and Earth were close to Venus in size, but Mars was appreciably smaller and its barrenness was an obstacle to human settlement.

Since Venus was larger than Earth (it later lost some of its matter in its fantastic rush toward the sun), its inhabitants were taller than earthly human beings.

All this was well known to Venusian scientists and weighed heavily in their selection of Earth as the refuge planet.

In our time, astronauts could find favourable conditions for colonization only on Mars (weaker gravity than ours) or Venus (gravity a little stronger). If we should have to leave our planet, Venus would theoretically be the best possibility.

It is probable that the Venusians came in at least five groups, each composed of several spacecraft, and landed in Hyperborea, Atlantis (U.S.A., Peru), Mu (Gobi Desert), Egypt, and Armenia, in the area marked by the flaming petroleum deposits of the Middle East. (I have given these places the names by which they are now known.)

Interplanetary travel presupposes attempts at contact by emissions of electromagnetic waves or light signals. Are we now receiving signals from other planets? Yes, if it is correct to attribute an intelligent intention to the recent emission from CTA-102. We are also sending signals but we began only recently, whereas in ancient times the earth emitted a constant signal: the fire of the petroleum deposits burning around the Caucasus, in Azerbaijan (Land of Fire), Persia, and Iraq. Chroniclers attest to this in their writings. In an immense semicircle, the petroleum deposits of the Near East served as markers for landing sites, and if extraterrestrials came to Earth in the past, where would they have landed if not in Armenia, in the area marked off by those fires? When our astronauts go to Mars or Venus, if they see fires by which they can guide their spacecraft they will surely come down near those accidental or intentional signals.

On most of the continents where they landed, except for the Near East, the astronauts (the angels, demigods, heroes, and flying men of tradition) left a memory of themselves as highly cultured and benevolent initiators. This was apparently not true of those who landed in Armenia, however; they must have been daredevils of the kind likely to be found in any group of pioneers and adventurers used to risking their lives, among whom desperados and criminals are not rare.

We must also assume that, having been seen to explore an unknown and perhaps hostile planet, the astronauts had to be builders, colonizers, and initiators as well as warriors. They did not behave unscrupulously, but those who were lucky enough to land in a part of our planet where the women were particularly beautiful did not resist their charms. Circassian and Armenian women have always been famous for their great beauty, the smoothness of their skin, the brightness of their eyes, the nobility of their bearing. Unions between alluring Armenian women and Venusian giants (about six and a half feet tall) resulted in the birth of children who were unusually tall, handsome, intelligent, and strong. On this hypothesis, then, the heroes and demigods of antiquity were the descendants of Venusians and Armenian women.

If the planets were inhabited, the size of the inhabitants of each of them was in proportion to its mass. Jupiterians were bigger than Saturnians and the other sizes were in this order: Neptunians, Uranians, Earthlings, Venusians, Martians, Mercurians. Five to ten thousand years ago Venus was a little larger than Earth; its inhabitants were therefore slightly taller than those of Earth, but their height must not have been much greater than six and a half feet. It is interesting to note that mythology is in agreement with scientific laws: the Titans, tall as mountans, were sons of Uranus the Sky (that is, of Jupiter, no doubt, since Jupiter is the largest of the planets), the Cyclops were sons of Saturn, and the Hecatoncheires, hundred-handed giants, were sons of Uranus.

Same blood, same race?

An important biological problem arises: how was it possible for men from another planet to have children by earthly women? Why were their sexual relations not sterile? The fact is that they were not, and there are a number of possible explanations for this.

The extraterrestrials of Hyperborea may have had scientific knowledge that enabled them to overcome what seems to us a major difficulty. If women had monstrous children with animals, as they are believed to have done, there is no reason to assume that it was impossible for them to procreate with men from another planet. Nor is there any absolute reason why plant, animal, and human life should not be almost identical on all inhabited planets.

For the Pawnee Indians of North America, the morning star (Venus) is, after the sun, the most important of the celestial powers. The Great Spirit gave it the gift of life, with orders to spread it over the earth. And as in Western traditions, Venus fought a great cosmic battle (against 'seven monstrous birds').

When the world was created, say the Pawnees of Nebraska, Tirawa, the Great Chief, assigned tasks to the gods. He said to Venus, the bright morning star, 'You will remain in the west and you will be called the mother of all things, for by you all living beings will be created. I will send you the clouds, the winds, lightning and thunder, and when you have received them you will place them near the Celestial Garden. There they will become human beings.'

American Indian traditions, which have remained unaltered, state clearly that all human beings were conceived by the planet Venus. If so, they are all of the same blood and can procreate among each other. Moreover, how are we to explain, if not by a common base of truth, that traditions all over the world give such a preponderant role to Venus and never to any other planet?

Man, particularly, may be a universal animal. In that case the human race on Earth is essentially the same as that on other planets of the solar system as the result of the successive migrations from planet to planet which I have explained within the framework of Louis Jacot's theories.

The headquarters in Hyperborea

The astronauts of the other groups necessarily had sexual relations with the women of the regions where they landed, and they too procreated superior human beings: *idolos* in Peru, fairies (superior women) in northern Europe, mythological heroes in other places.

General headquarters for all the exploration groups was in Hyperborea (Thule or North America), 'between the north and the west, where the angels had received ropes to measure the place reserved for the righteous and the chosen' (the *Book of Enoch*, Section 12). This was where Enoch, the Armenian astronaut, went to report on his missions.

The Hyperboreans taught fragments of their knowledge everywhere they went, but of course the primitive peoples of Earth could not, in a few generations, have made the great leap that would have brought them to the intellectual level of their initiators. Furthermore, those initiators were cut off from their homeland; they may not have been professional scientists and they did not have libraries, laboratories, and other necessary means of teaching everything they knew.

Imagine the fate of atomic scientists parachuted into the Brazilian wilderness in the twentieth century and deprived of contact with civilization: they would be as helpless in wild nature as Robinson Crusoe on his island. This was the case with the Venusians. It seems, according to the *Book of Enoch*, that they let themselves be partially absorbed: each group settled down on its own continent with, understandably, no great desire to go back to the endangered home planet.

Were the Hyperboreans more conscientious? Did they send a courier craft back to Venus? Were they able even to attempt a return journey? These questions will probably never be answered.

Be that as it may, the extraterrestrials stayed on Earth, whether by choice or from necessity, and created two main civilizations. One was in Atlantis, the vast continent that then lay in the Atlantic Ocean and extended into America. The other was in Mu, the Pacific continent that extended into the Gobi Desert and part of India. There were also smaller settlements in Egypt, Greece, and Armenia.

Within a few thousand years Hyperborea, Atlantis, and Mu reached their apogee; they had regained the scientific knowledge of their homeland and they again possessed the secret of nuclear energy.

Meanwhile Venus must have been going through the horrors of its decline while its inhabitants became decadent to the point of being unable to escape to another planet.

Chaos after the Deluge

We know from traditions that in all parts of the world thousands of men and women who took refuge in high mountains were able to survive the presumably atomic cataclysm and the Deluge that followed it, Egyptian manuscripts, however, say that the whole human race perished except for a very small number of survivors. These accounts must actually refer only to the plains of the Nile and the nearby desert, where the ancestors of the Hebrews paid a particularly heavy toll.

The genealogical lists that the Hebrews drew up in the Bible to give themselves ancestors are too long, and too obviously designed to prove something, to convince us. As for the incredible story of Noah in his Ark, it is contradicted by the Bible of the Egyptian Gnostics and is only a naïve mask for this important point: in reality the world was not completely destroyed, but it did undergo an essential deterioration and was repopulated at random.

From whom were the Hebrews descended? Could they have formed the rootstock of the human race at a time much earlier than the Biblical period? It is possible, because a mystery surrounds their origin.

'At first sight,' says the *Grand Dictionnaire due XIX*[6] *Siècle*, 'one might think that no other people had such complete information on its origins; but if we consider the mixture of theological elements and wondrous stories that we find in its history, we are inclined to conclude, on the contrary, that few ancient histories offer as much uncertainty and obscurity.'

The special intellectual qualities of the Hebrews gave them a certain superiority over other peoples, and for that reason one might think they were descended from the extraterrestrials, especially since the latter probably selected them to continue their mission.

This hypothesis is supported by Biblical history: 'clouds' (celestial vehicles) bring the initiators to the people of Israel to dictate the Law to them, to teach them, to lead them in the desert, to take them through the waters. . . .

Intervention by the Hyperboreans can be detected in most of the great events related by the Old Testament and we have already seen that a number of important Biblical characters were born of Hebrew mothers and fathers who were 'angels'; that is, men who came from the sky.

Hebrews versus Hyperboreans

The Hebrews did not consider that a child born of an 'angel' father was of the same blood as themselves. They never hid their hostility toward intrusion by extraterrestrials into their private lives. Also, no doubt, having lost through the centuries the sense of their mission and the original truth, they wanted to give their race the honour of having been the first initiators of mankind.

For that purpose they took over all the heroes of primohistory. Enoch, Noah, Moses, Melchizedek, and so on, thus became pure-blooded Hebrews, and the 'angels' were frozen into the image of guileless holiness preserved by tradition.

This concealed goals of appropriation, which motivated the expurgation of ancient texts, also explains why the Bible avoids speaking of the cosmos and the planets: anything in the real sky was automatically subject to great mistrust. Moreover, the Bible describes in detail what happened *before* the arrival of the 'angels,' but it is silent on the important matter of what happened *afterward*, between that supernatural landing and the Deluge. A strange omission. . . .

When the Christians wrote the Gospels in about A.D. 150, they may not have understood the secret meaning of the Hebrews' policy, but by a kind of extraordinary clairvoyance they took up the thread of the unknown past.

Jesus was born of Mary and a father unknown to earthly men (God). The initiatic tradition continued in secrecy, but the Jews refused to recognize that Messiah: his birth was a little too much like the births whose 'miraculous' nature had been so hard for them to conceal! From their viewpoint, he was not of their blood; he was not a Jew.

To sum up, the important fact of those protohistoric times, full of uncertainties and wonders, is that a vast chess game took place between the Hyperborean initiators

and the Hebrews to determine who would finally provide
the race of superior ancestors.

Since the Hebrews did not exist as a people until the
reign of Moses, credit for the first initiation cannot be
withheld from the Hyperboreans.

One difficulty in resurrecting this protohistory is to
reconcile the ruin of the civilizations of Atlantis and Mu
with the fact that, long before the Deluge, 'clouds' and
flying machines played a modest but effective part in
postdiluvian history.

Operation Noah

It is an irritating problem, but if at the time of the Deluge the Hyperboreans still had spacecraft they obviously
used them to save their elite. It was a 'survival operation,'
similar to those that are planned in most twentieth-century civilizations. (Since 1964 in Great Britain, for example, there have been practice sessions for an operation designed to save fifteen thousand privileged people in case of
nuclear war. The first ones were directed by Captain
Rushby, commander of the Royal Observer Corps, and
took place in the atomic shelter of Maidstone, Kent.)

We can consider at least three hypotheses:

1. By scientific methods known to our modern astronomers, the Hyperboreans had foreseen the cosmic cataclysm and taken measures to make sure they would be
able to save their knowledge and their elite by leaving
Earth. We may call this 'Operation Noah.'

2. They sent the craft of Operation Noah into space for
the hours or days during which there were violent upheavals: grazing of Earth by Venus, rains of stones, fire, earth,
etc. They may have prepared a temporary refuge on another planet; or perhaps on Lilith, our second satellite
once observed by the Cabalists; or on that problematical
anti-Earth which they situated behind the sun, directly opposite Earth. Either of the latter two may have been the
Eden to which Melchizedek was transported. (We are still
seeking a solution for that Eden, that original earthly paradise. It may actually have existed somewhere other than

on Earth, perhaps on Venus, as the result of a natural sentiment on the part of the Hyperboreans: no matter how much it may have deteriorated, their home planet must have held a strong nostalgic attraction for them after centuries of absence.)

3. They had shelters on Earth where they would be protected from the effects of the cosmic cataclysm and the Deluge.

This last hypothesis, the most plausible, brings to mind those centres of initiation whose existence is reported by tradition, or perhaps legend: the sealed city under the Egyptian Pyramids* where 'high personages of the West' came to take shelter; the underground Agartha of Tibet, beneath the mighty Himalayas, *also built in the shape of a pyramid.* According to Oriental traditions, the sages of all times and the 'Masters of the World' live in the Agartha.

There were probably also other refuges that were submerged with Atlantis and Mu, or crushed like Tiahuanaco (the underground city whose entrances were identified by the naturalist d'Orbigny in the nineteenth century).

In any case it is quite certain that the naïve and charming survival operation carried out by Noah with his Ark belongs to the realm of pure legend. It is not a lie, however; only a kind of fable.

The extraterrestrial Noah and the beautiful Armenian women were unfortunately not the Adam and Eve of later times, but only survivors among thousands of others.

Operation Noah was the swan song of the Hyperboreans: their continent was submerged; their initiates were decimated, scattered, and reduced to the role of witnesses; their civilization, already disrupted by an ab-

---

* A fascinating idea: the Pyramids may be markers, almost eternal since they cannot be buried under the sand, which were built to show men of future times that the secrets of 'the beginning, the middle and the end' are buried here.

When men decide to build a monument of twentieth-century science, they will have to indicate its existence and location with a marker capable of defying the millennia. Will they use a pyramid again? Or a radioactive deposit whose radiation will be detectable for thousands of years?

surd nuclear war, was now almost entirely destroyed, along with their laboratories, spacecraft, and other technological developments.

The little that remained after the Deluge was not enough to enable the former Masters of the World to keep their preponderant power. We can conjecture, however, that with their last usable spacecraft, operating from their underground retreats, they still tried to control a few major events.

Here we have a reconstruction of the past in which the implausibilities of traditional accounts are replaced by explanations that are rationally possible, if not probable.

Many points still remain obscure. With the uncertainties brought about by time, it is now hazardous to try to unravel the plot patiently and skilfully woven by powerful conspiracies, a plot whose threads, if we could follow them, would lead us to this primordial truth: the initiation of mankind was the work of 'angels who came from the sky'; that is, the astronauts of Hyperborea.

Chapter 10

THE JEALOUS GOD OF THE CHOSEN PEOPLE

Whether he is an integral part of the animal kingdom or was created spontaneously, man must have been made in several different prototypes that did not all develop in the same way.

Furthermore, in the course of its existence our planet has no doubt been subjected to radioactive bombardments, natural or set off by man, which increase mutations. (The 'atomic nations' *clandestinely* dump their radioactive waste in the oceans. Birth defects almost inevitably occur in the contaminated areas and radioactivity on land also raises the rate of mutations. Large numbers of defective babies are born, but of course that fact is kept secret.)

Some species disappeared in certain parts of the globe (the horse in America, for example) while others took on an anarchic, monstrous character.

A species exposed to radiation may have had a sudden, extraordinary development of its intellectual faculties. Is man the product of one of those fortunate mutations?

One fact favours this idea: the slow, hazardous procreation of mankind, which is contrary to what happened with other animals. One of the first results of exposure to radiation is a deterioration of procreation.

If there was a first man – Adam – or a first woman – Eve – who was produced accidentally by mutation and was therefore one of a kind, he or she could have reproduced only by having sexual relations with animals of the species from which he or she originated, or with animals of another species. (It is also possible that the first human being was hermaphroditic. This is almost a classical view.)

If there were several human prototypes, which is quite likely, they were all necessarily dissimilar. At any rate, monsters naturally came from either the original single specimen or the different prototypes. It is interesting to conjecture whether these monsters had any connection with those of mythology, and consequently with the heroes and demigods who played an enigmatic part in the protohistory of mankind.

Although copulation between animals of different species is physically possible, biologists maintain that it can never result in procreation. This theory is questioned by some people, however, especially since it has no scientific basis.

In 1965 Professor Henry Harris and Dr. J. P. Watkins, of Oxford University, succeeded in fusing cells from human beings and mice and obtaining hybrid cells. Other matings between different species and classes of animals have been successful. At the cellular level, hybridization between mammals and fish, and perhaps between birds and plants, is possible.

It is by no means beyond the realm of possibility that a woman may be able to have children by a male animal. The experience of Thérèse X. in Vichy, France, seems to prove this.

Thérèse, aged sixteen, lived with her father and a little monkey in a trailer parked in a vacant lot. One day she found herself pregnant. Suspecting the possibility of incest, the police made a discreet investigation. The girl's father, a very ignorant but deeply religious man, was soon exonerated, especially since he sincerely believed that by the workings of the Holy Ghost, exactly as in Bethlehem (and why not?), his humble trailer was going to be honored with a miraculous birth!

Thérèse finally gave birth normally, but to a monster that was part human and part monkey. It was not only alive, but perfectly viable. She then admitted having had sexual relations with the monkey. Their offspring was killed with an injection a few days after its birth. It was studied by Dr. T., of Vichy; his scientific report and the records of the judicial inquest are preserved in the city archives.

Animal hybridization thus seems to be an open question. Moreover, what is true for animals in general may not be true for man in particular, since he is specially privileged with regard to his emotional and intellectual qualities, and perhaps his reproductive faculties.

We may also speculate that the men who came from another planet and had children by earthly women may not have been conditioned exactly like us. And it is not impossible that they had scientific knowledge enabling them to bring about procreation between animals and humans, perhaps for experimental purposes.

If our modern astronauts some day land on a planet where there are major obstacles to normal human life, it is conceivable that they will try, by artificial insemination, to create a hybrid species on that planet, half native and half earthly.

In any case the science of the future will surely overcome what is now an insurmountable difficulty. The explanation of mytholological monsters may lie in the mysterious science of the Hyperborean astronauts.

Andes traditions say that the earthly human race descends from a tapir and a Venusian woman astronaut named Orejona. The Spanish biologist Garcia Beltran takes a favourable view of this claim.

Genesis according to the Book of Enoch

Copulation between women and animals occupies an important place in traditions, especially in Egypt and Greece.

In the grip of an irresistible erotic passion, the beautiful Pasiphae made love with a white bull and thereby became the mother of the Minotaur.

The Propoeitides prostituted themselves to all comers and did not hesitate to arouse the lust of animals. The same is also said to have been true of the Armenian and Lydian women who devoted a shameless form of worship to the goddess Anaitis (the Anahid of the Orientals).

Carved stones representing men with distinctly canine heads were found in the Magdalenian cave of Lussac-les-Châteaux, France.

. We should also, no doubt, pay special attention to a passage in the Book of Enoch in which the author, referring to a vision, describes strange scenes of procreation. In

Chapter 85, Section 17, Verses 2-4 he says, 'I saw a bull
come out of the earth, and the bull was white. Then came
a heifer and, with her, two calves, one black and the
other red.' The white bull (the colour of justice) represents Adam; the heifer is Eve; the black calf is Cain; the
red calf is Abel. In Chapter 85 Enoch describes the proliferation of bulls and heifers and says, 'I looked at these
things with wonder, and the bulls became aroused and
mounted the heifers. The heifers conceived and gave
birth to elephants, camels and asses.'

Next comes the story of a battle among elephants,
camels, and other animals, then the building of the Tower
of Babel, followed by great confusion on Earth, and
finally Noah and the Deluge.

This version of genesis, quite different from the Biblical
version, lends support to the contention of mythology
that there was a mysterious interaction between bulls and
human beings. Whatever meaning is given to the bulls
and heifers in the story (wheher they are regarded as
people or animals), Enoch says that the other animals
were engendered by them and that their mother was
either a heifer or (as is much more likely) a woman.

A North American Indian tradition reported by Father
Charlevoix says that when the whole human race had
been destroyed by a great cataclysm, God changed animals into people to repopulate the earth.

I give no credence to these stories, of course, but it is interesting to note that ancient peoples, rightly or wrongly,
did not consider procreation between animals of different
species to be impossible.

Oannes the fish-god

It is not known whether the Chaldeans were of the
same race as the Hebrews, and it seems unlikely; but their
traditions would lead one to believe that a strange being,
neither man nor beast, was their superior ancestor:
Oannes, the god and civilizer of the Babylonians.
(Oannes, Oan = Ogen, Okean, Okeanos = Oceanus. He
is the wise and initiated Janus of the Romans and also the
Prometheus of the Greeks.)

He is depicted as a monster, half human and half fish (he is also said to have been half frog), who came from the Erythraean Sea; that is, the Persian Gulf and the Red Sea. He had two heads – one of a man, the other of a fish –and legs that grew out of his tail, and he had the power of speech. Every morning he came out of the sea and went among men to teach them science, the arts, letters, and agriculture.

In Syriac the name Oannes means 'stranger,' which gives us little information on the origin of that initiated god.

Did Oannes's clothes give him the appearance of a fish, or was he, by some incredible miracle, the result of a monstrous hybridization?

On November 1, 1964, a female dog in Corthezon, France, gave birth to seven puppies, six of which strangely resembled fish: elongated muzzles, no ears, webbed paws, slender bodies tapered at the rear like that of a fish. Their skin even had the glistening appearance of scales. Were they the product of monstrous crossbreeding or a fantastic mutation? Inexplicable though it may be, their birth actually occurred.

Logic makes me inclined to see Oannes, assuming he really existed, as an extraterrestrial who came to Earth in a spacecraft that could be used as an underwater home after his arrival.

Be that as it may, it is clear that ancient peoples were not frightened by men with an abnormal physical make-up, as though monstrosity were nothing extraordinary, but a rather common phenomenon.

However far back they may go, those traditions and legends form the essential subtance of an understanding of man's unknown history, even if they seem contrary to the scientific laws of a universal evolution that is much more adventurous than is usually believed. For if the world has been destroyed several times, if deluges have drowned the human race, how could evolution have continued without profound alterations? And we find many such alterations in all forms of life.

Monsters, fantastic animals, and physically extraordinary men must have a logical, rational place in the advance of matter, intellect, and spirit toward the latest link in the chain: man.

Is it foolish to believe that at the time when the first men were created certain mutants endowed with intelligence, and perhaps also with perversion, engaged in an implacable struggle against *Homo sapiens* for supremacy on Earth?

The Fantastic Beast

Traditions of all countries report that giants or monstrous beasts, sometimes semihuman, sometimes entirely animal, demanded tributes of boys or young virgins, or decimated populations. We may wonder to what extent those monsters – the Minotaur, the Sphinx, the Volta, giants, satanic creatures – perpetuated the memory of an ancient scourge.

In the labyrinth of death, normal men finally won out over the Fantastic Beast; human evolution was then able to take place freely and the globe was populated at a natural rate.

Was the Fantastic Beast of the ancients a symbol, a formidable mutant, an actual beast, or a deadly pestilence?

Behind the veil of fable and legend hides a truth that we are afraid to identify.

Man is able to keep a memory intact for only about forty years; after a longer time than that, facts begin to be deformed and gradually enter into legend. The Napoleonic Wars would long since have become legendary if written records of them had not been kept.

The memory of the semihuman monsters has thus been transformed into wondrous tales and the problem is to discern the particle of initial truth they contain.

The formidable Beast of Gévaudan was not even an ordinary wolf, but a big cat or lynx! Roland's titanic battle against the Saracens at Roncesvalles was actually no more than a skirmish!

As a general rule, ancient events have been magnified with time, but in some cases their magnitude has been diminished. For example, the war between the Titans and Zeus, which is said to have shaken Olympus and made the gods tremble, was most likely a worldwide cataclysm that wiped out a large part of the human race.

Between these two extremes, how are we to interpret stories of ancient monsters such as the Cyclops, the Minotaur, the Titans, the Gorgons, satyrs, angels, ogres, Hydras, the Leviathan, and the Behemoth of mythologies and traditions?

Immanuel Velikovsky has proved that the Deluge occurred in about 1500 B.C. and that our whole planet was profoundly disrupted by a cataclysm that was probably caused by the near passage of a comet. Aristotle maintained that our solar system was regularly perturbed and restored to order in the course of the 'supreme year,' which included a great winter called *kataklusmos* (deluge, catastrophe) and a great summer called *ekpyrosis* (conflagration). This tallies with Velikovsky's thesis of a worldwide deluge and fire.

Were the mythological monsters that date from the last deluge engendered as the result of radiation produced by the passing of a comet?

Since the Bible makes no mention of that proliferation of extraordinary beasts, I believe we must place their appearance before the Deluge, at the undetermined time (a figure of nine thousand years ago has been advanced) when, according to my hypothesis, there were nuclear explosions in America and the Gobi Desert. Afterward, the few people who had escaped being killed in the disaster, suffering from radiation poisoning, may have procreated monsters and struggled against them for the right to survive. And if there was only a very small number of them, they may have had to have sexual relations with animals in order to perpetuate their race.

Or are monsters still more ancient? Do they date from primohistoric times, when man was created by exceptional mutations? It is hard to believe so, for the events would be so remote that no trace of them would be left in human memory.

If we do not fall into the error of conventional thinkers who regard the earth as the centre of the world, we can try to formulate a better explanation.

Giants

Why not go on considering that the earth was once a kind of zoo and botanical garden for extraterrestrial human beings? Everything is then coherent and logical: groups of men from another planet landed on our globe, bringing civilization, seeds of unknown plants, and specimens of animals that they hoped to adapt to the new environment.

They also found earthlings, of course, and tried either to colonize them or integrate themselves with them, but not without risk, not without paying tribute to blood, because the astronauts were not biologically identical to us. Their relations with earthly women produced children who were larger than normal by earthly standards and, with the magnification of time, were remembered as giants. All ancient peoples attested to the existence of these giants before the Deluge. (During excavations in 1964, skeletons of men between 9′ 2″ and 9′ 10″ tall were found in a cave at Alguetca, near Manglis, U.S.S,R.)

A tradition of the Cholula Indians, recorded in a manuscript now in the Vatican, says that 'before the great flood which took place 4008 years after the creation of the world, the land of Anahuac was inhabited by giants, and those who did not perish were changed into fish.'

In Egypt, the giants were said to have fought a war against men, then emigrated after taking on the forms of animals.

Jewish rabbis have tried to establish, on the basis of memories too remote to be precise, that the first man must have been several hundred feet tall. The Bible speaks at length about giants, particularly the last of them: Og, King of Bashan, who perished in his struggle against Moses. This semilegendary Og must have had descendants, since the Hebrews still had to fight long wars against them.

The ancient Thais maintained that the earliest men

were of colossal size, and the Scandinavians, referring to Hyperborean traditions, said that the first men of creation were as big as mountains.

However, allowing for imagination, time, and the magnifications that is common in legends, we may assume that those ancient giants were not much more than six and a half feet tall.

The giants of Hyperborea

One aspect of Greek mythology tends to support the idea of extraterrestrial men taller and more intelligent than earthly men: the giants were so powerful that even the gods could overcome them only with the aid of mortals. Allowing for exaggeration, this may refer to men who were much more civilized than earthlings and therefore appeared to be invulnerable.

In further support of this idea I will point out that the Scandinavians situated the land of giants in the direction of Thule, where it is thought that the first men from another planet must have landed, for according to Celtic and Scandinavian traditions Hyperborea was the homeland of the superior men who were destroyed with their continent when the atomic cataclysm occurred in Asia and America.

The Hyperborean giants may have descendants in Japan: the *sumotori* (sumo wrestlers), who are highly popular and held in such esteem that they rank immediately below the gods and the emperor. They are prodigiously strong; some of them weigh more than four hundred pounds and are well over seven feet tall.

'At first,' writes the historian Pierre Darcourt (*Le Monde et la Vie*, February, 1965), 'the *sumotori* were recruited from among the light-skinned Ainu giants. The Ainus are a white people, proto-Caucasians, who are said to have migrated across Siberia. Their god Kamu included the sun, the wind, the ocean and the bear. Those mountaineers of Hokkaido, hairy, massive and powerful drinkers of hot alcohol, were formidable wrestlers.'

The other, darker-skinned Japanese are said to have

come from the Polynesian Islands, Malaysia, and China. They conquered the giants by means of their superior knowledge and weapons.

'The victors,' continues Pierre Darcourt, 'rode off with the beautiful white women of their adversaries, and from their coupling were born the Asian giants who became the first bodyguards of the emperor.'

On this view, northern Japan could thus be regarded as the Far West of the globe, with its Hyperborean natives; or perhaps as a surviving portion of the ancient land of Mu, whose inhabitants were of the same extraterrestrial race as those of Hyperborea.

We are dealing here only with a clue, but it is one of many and it favours the hypothesis of superior ancestors who came from Venus or another planetary system.

From those extraterrestrial Hyperboreans may have come, first, the giants described by the Bible as 'the heroes of old' and 'men of renown,' and then, through deterioration, monstrous coupling (the lecherous 'sons of the gods' in Genesis) or radiation poisoning, the semi-human monsters of legend and the giants in animal form who are said to have migrated into Egypt.

Unless one purely and simply denies the existence of ancient giants and monsters – and in that case one would have to reject the Bible, apocryphal writings, and all traditions – I can see no rational alternative to this interpretation.

The giants of the Bible

According to the Bible, the giants were superior beings, since they engendered kings, heroes, and initiates.

In Genesis 6:4 we read: 'In those days, when the sons of the gods had intercourse with the daughters of men and got children by them, the Nephilim [or giants] were on earth. They were the heroes of old, men of renown.'

Here we have an explanation concerning the giants which we need only apply to the animal kingdom in order to have the key to the mystery.

In the first place, did not those 'sons of the gods' – who had come to Earth to steal the daughters of men or rape their wives – fornicate with certain animals? Such abnormal practices are still common today among the sexually obsessed, and they would have been all the more likely among men who must have been deprived of sex for a long time. The astronauts may very well have engendered monstrous children: half human and half horse, or half human and half cow. . . .

Furthermore they brought animals with them and released them on Earth, and before dying out or becoming adapted, these animals, as the result of perturbed natural crossbreeding or extraordinary couplings, must have passed through phases that necessarily involved physical monstrosity.

This may be the explanation of human giants, bull-men (the Minotaur), horse-men (centaurs), goat-men (satyrs), lion-men (sphinxes), Gorgons, mermaids, and so on.

Monsters against men

These monsters may have been mutants produced by exposure to radiation and their deformity has surely been exaggerated by legend. The Minotaur, for example, was most likely only a giant with a face that resembled a bull's.

They probably tried to play a part in society and found themselves opposed by normal people determined to preserve their prerogatives. Then came an almost fratricidal war that ravaged mankind for long years. The monsters had the advantage of strength and brutality, but their intelligence was limited. Their adversaries were less strong but more intelligent, and also more numerous.

The 'mythological beasts' took a heavy toll of human youth that was later recalled by blood sacrifices. But finally the 'heroes' (that is, 'giants' descended from extraterrestrial fathers and earthly mothers) overcame the tyranny of the monsters.

It may be that, to commemorate the great battle of ancient times, the victors erected the sixteen hundred enigmatic monsters of the Temple of Karnak the Pyramids, a colossal statue of the vanqui the Sphinx of Giza.

What a magnificent epic for ancient bards, and how easy it is to understand the enthusiastic changes they made in the facts! The victorious heroes were promoted to demigods, but truth remained in the midst of all the embellishments.

The jealous God's exhortation

The Bible contains some highly significant passages on this subject.

In Exodus 34:15 the Lord, who has called himself 'the Jealous God,' says to the Hebrews, 'Be careful not to make a covenant with the natives of the land.' Verse 24, same chapter: 'For after I have driven the nations before you and extended your frontiers. . . .'

The intention, of course, is to show the Lord's covenant with the tribes of Israel, but further on, in Leviticus 18:22-24, God gives a strange basis for making the Hebrews the Chosen People: 'You shall not lie with a man as with a woman: that is an abomination. You shall not have sexual intercourse with any beast to make yourself unclean with it, nor shall a woman submit herself to intercourse with a beast: that is a violation of nature. You shall not make yourselves unclean in any of these ways; for in these ways the heathen, whom I am driving out before you, made themselves unclean.'

This is clearly stated, and it is extremely important for human evolution: there was a time, after the Deluge, when it was a common practice for men and women to have sexual relations with animals. Did monstrous pro- creation result from it? The Bible seems silent on the subject, but Greek mythology tends to support the idea that such procreation took place.

Is this the mystery of the Chosen People?

The Chaldeans had a fish-initiator: Oannes; the Egyptians boasted of being descended from gods with the heads of jackals, vultures, ibises, cats, bulls, etc.; the Greeks did not hesitate to claim animal forefathers. Among the civilized peoples of antiquity, only the He- rews appear to have been free of any mixture with animals. And their God promised to give them earthly dominion for various reasons, one of which was that they had not 'made themselves unclean.'

Though I want to avoid drawing simplistic conclusions, it is still interesting to bring all these coincidences together.

Mythological monsters remain an unsolved problem but it is clear that the Hebrews presented themselves as the descendants of an unknown but pure race which we may assume to have been earthly.

Is this the mystery of the Chosen People?

The Hebrews always showed great reluctance to interbreed with extraterrestrials as well as races they regarded as impure. What obscure atavism, or what esoteric reason, made them consider themselves, like the Gypsies and the Norsemen, a 'people apart'?

In this respect, at least, their unknown history is worth exploring back to its remote and strange origins, which we can place in the time of Moses, whose revealed mission was to give the Hebrews a soul, a God, a homeland, and the social structure of a nation. Yet that prodigious patriarch, father of the Chosen People, was not a Hebrew, as I pointed out in Chapter 7, referring to the work of Sigmund Freud. The same idea is presented with extremely convincing arguments by many historians: Flavius Josephus, Yahuda, E. Mayer, O. Rank, J. H. Breasted, and others.

Ikhnaton, a monotheistic pharaoh

The mystery began in Egypt more than thirty-five hundred years ago, at the end of the eighteenth dynasty, when Pharaoh Amenophis IV proclaimed a religious reform and decreed that worship of Aten, the only god, was to be the sole official religion. Full of zeal for his new god, he changed his name from Amenophis ('Amen is satisfied') to Ikhnaton ('Glory of Aten') in the sixth year of his reign and abandoned Thebes for a new capital that he built in Middle Egypt: Ikhutaton, on the site of the modern Tell el-Amarna.

The pharaoh was also the high priest of the religion. He

conducted services in the Castle of the Obelisk and composed hymns that leave no doubt about the identity of the Creator: 'You, sole God, beside whom there are no others. . . .'

As in the religion that the Hebrews later embraced, it was forbidden to carve or draw images of Aten. He could, however, be represented in the form of a red solar disk whose rays ended in hands.

Other gods were banned, their statues were broken, their bas-reliefs were mutilated, and even the word 'god' was effaced when it was written in the plural.

The new religion rejected the idea of hell and forbade magic and sorcery. Its essential commandments can be found in the Bible: 'You shall have no other god to set against me. You shall not make a carved image for yourself nor the likeness of anything in the heavens above, or on the earth below, or in the waters under the earth.' (Deuteronomy 5: 7–8.) 'You shall not allow a witch to live.' (Exodus 22:18.) And the main commandment coincides with that of the Catholic Church: 'You shall honour one God and love Him perfectly.'

It is important to stress these close connections between the religion of Aten and the later religion of the Hebrews.

The Egyptians had been firmly attached to their ancestral beliefs for thousands of years. Although they sometimes pillaged the temples of Amen out of greed, they accepted the religion of Aten only under constraint and they quickly returned to their old gods when Ikhnaton died in about 1358 B.C.

Nefertiti and Moses

Moses is presumed to have lived at the pharaoh's court (he may have been a member of the royal family) and to have been converted to the religion of Aten.

Besides his one god, Ikhnaton also worshipped, in a different way, his beautiful wife Nefertiti, who is believed to have come from Syria. Did she bring with her the germ of a monotheistic religion? The writer and Egyptologist Jean-Louis Bernard believes so, but he notes in his book

L'Egypte et la Genèse du Surhomme that Ikhnaton's father, Pharaoh Amenophis III, had a certain inclination toward the god Aten, since he gave the name of 'Aten's Splendour' to the pleasure boat in which he took his wife Tiy for cruises on the lake.

'Nefertiti was not only radiant but captivating,' writes Bernard. 'She was refined, noble and intelligent, but also haughty and stubborn. There was something excessive, implacable and aberrant about her femininity.'

There are thus three main people involved in the worship of Aten: Nefertiti the advisor, Ikhnaton the unfortunate ruler, and Moses the man of action, who was to become the liberator and lawgiver of the Hebrews by bringing them a new and already formulated religion.

Did Moses dream of succeeding Ikhnaton, or was he his propagandist in spreading worship of the One God? In any case he must have soon realized that he could not carry out his mission among the more affluent Egyptians; like all reformers, he chose the poorest, most wretched, and oppressed people to receive his teachings.

The Hebrews, crushed and despised by the Egyptian nobility, offered him an ideal field of action and he took advantage of it: he immediately made himself their leader and took them away – without any opposition, it seems – toward a more hospitable land than the valley of the Nile.

An Egyptian religion and an Egyptian leader

According to the Bible, the exodus of the Hebrews took about a million people into the desert. This figure, however, is completely groundless. A million Hebrews could not have survived in the desert, or crossed the 'Red Sea' between tides. We have no basis for estimating their number. It may have been a few hundred, at most a few thousand.

Freud calculates that their exodus took place between 1358 and 1350 B.C., after Ikhnaton's death and about a century before the dates put forward by the Catholic Church.

Only after enormous difficulties with his barbaric horde

did Moses succeed in replacing the god Adonai with Yahweh. This probably happened in the fertile oasis of Meribat-Quades, and not on Mount Sinai.

The Hebrews thus had an Egyptian religion and an Egyptian initiator. And circumcision, the 'sign of the covenant' between Israel and God, was an Egyptian practice. There are ancient Egyptian bas-reliefs depicting the rite and archaeologists have often exhumed mummies showing obvious traces of the operation, in which the Egyptians took great pride.

Herodotus says of them. 'They practised circumcision and were the first to adopt it, for reasons of hygiene. They also abhorred pigs because Set, in the form of that animal, had wounded Horus. ... Out of pride, they considered themselves the highest and purest of all peoples, and the one closest to God.'

All this takes nothing away from the genius of the Hebrews, but it is clear that they owed their religious foundations and even their laws to the Egyptians, from whom they also borrowed superstitions and rules of hygiene.

Israel became a genuine people when the tribe from Egypt merged with desert tribes; the Mosaic religion took on its definitive form in about 550 B.C. when rabbis wrote the Bible. Since Moses had been dead for eight centuries – assassinated by the Hebrews, say several historians – when his words and deeds were put into writing, it is easy to imagine how approximate the accounts of them must be!

This analysis gives me a feeling of uneasiness and sacrilege because it tends to destroy a legend which was dear to me in my childhood and to which I am still attached by sincere affection, but history is not made of sentimental concessions and I must express what I believe to be a truth.

It is a conjectural truth, however; although it undoubtedly comes close to certain facts, it also contains great uncertainties. But I had to attack that fortress to continue my quest, just as I had to demolish – with much fewer qualms of conscience – the erroneous doctrines of prehistory.

Death of the Egyptian gods

Egypt, with its prodigious temples, its countless gods with the heads of cows, wolves, dogs, or bulls, and its heretical pharaohs, dropped the torch of civilization and it was taken up by the humble Hebrew shepherds.

Population had considerably diminished in the Mediterranean region, where it had once been very dense, and for a thousand years the desert had been steadily swallowing up arable land and ancient cities. Abydos, Thebes, and Memphis were now only shadows of their former splendour.

It is hard for us to form a picture of the world at that time but, if we are to believe sacred writings, the effects of the Deluge had been catastrophic for mankind. In that general decadence, when ancient civilizations were collapsing from a mysterious, lingering illness, only the Jewish people were aware of the mortal danger.

Whether he was Egyptian or Hebrew, a great initiate named Moses had the immense merit of setting out to save a race and prepare it for a lofty destiny. The Bible exoterically reports the event that gave birth to the Chosen People.

Was it done for the purpose of imposing on the world the tyranny of a privileged race? Some people have thought so, and that tragic error has darkened history without honour or benefit to anyone.

The mission and the Chosen People

After the Deluge had decimated mankind and perhaps damaged human reproduction, it became necessary to repopulate the world with a selected race stemming from the Hebrews and the extraterrestrials.

The latter had already assured themselves of descendants, first in Armenia and the Caucasus, but with the people of the desert they must have wanted to create a race of mutants or superior men capable of transmitting, without risk of adulteration, their scientific knowledge and subtlest secrets.

Unfortunately the Hebrews thwarted that intention by either misusing their advantageous situation or losing the esoteric meaning of their privilege and keeping only a crude idea of it.

According to indications in *Hosea*, the mission ended during the reign of Jeroboam, son of Johoash and King of Israel in the eighth century B.C.

In Hosea 1:2 the Lord says to Hosea, 'Go, take a wanton for your wife and get children of her wantonness; for like a wanton this land is unfaithful to the Lord.' And in 4:12-14, 'New wine and old steal my people's wits: they ask advice from a block of wood and take their orders from a fetish; for a spirit of wantonness has led them astray and in their lusts they are unfaithful to their God. Your men sacrifice on mountain-tops and burn offerings on the hills, under oak and poplar and the terebinth's pleasant shade. Therefore your daughters play the wanton and your sons' brides commit adultery. I will not punish your daughters for playing the wanton nor your sons' brides for their adultery, because your men resort to wanton women and sacrifice with temple-prostitutes.'

Such may be the explanation of the Chosen People, and also, no doubt, the wondrous secret of the Cabala from which, after the advent of Christianity, imperfectly initiated Hebrews drew knowledge of their genealogy with a feeling of frustration.

They may have believed they were only guinea pigs improved by crossbreeding, not a pure race, and so that they could lay claim to the glory of the first initiation they decided to make the past impenetrable. The Maasseh Merkabad of the Cabala then became a state secret that was transmitted only orally, and only to high-ranking initiated rabbis.

The extraterrestrials' plan sank into oblivion and the Jews sought to obliterate all trace of it by including in their race the foreign initiators and patriarchs of the time of Genesis and Exodus. From that great conspiracy came a darkness that enveloped the true history of mankind.

Chapter 11

APOCRYPHA AND FANTASTIC STORIES

There are certain apocrypha and ancient writings that bear on our subject. They contain details which may give us useful clues even if they are legendary.

Paradise is in the northwest

In *The Combat of Adam and Eve*, an apocryphal work translated from the Ethiopian, the author says that Adam's descendants were divided into two branches: the Cainites and the Sethites. The former, descendants of Cain, were devoted to Satan, the pleasures of the flesh, and immorality. They lived in a fertile land far away from Eden. The Sethites, descendants of Seth, had remained faithful to the Law and lived in the mountains near Eden, but they soon began mingling with the children of Cain, 'sullied themselves with their impurities and engendered with them children who were called *gariani*, that is, giants, for they were such strong and colossally large men that there were no others like them.'

This story tells us nothing about the geographical location of Eden, but some ancient works, such as Saint Ephraem's *Hymns to the True Paradise* and Cosmas Indicopleustes's *Christian Topography*, place it at the western edge of the world's highest mountain.

The ancients believed that the earth was flat; some said it was circular, others rectangular, surrounded by high arched walls that formed the celestial vault.

In Cosmas's cosmography, near the north pole there was a high mountain around which the sun, the moon and the stars revolved. Eclipses and phases of the moon occurred when the mountain came between the heavenly body and the earth.

According to tradition this high mountain, to which Enoch was sent on a mission, is the earthly paradise or Eden, and is near the north pole, 'between the north and the west,' which corresponds to the presumed location of

Thule and Hyperborea. (Even among the Chinese the north pole is the centre of knowledge. The Palace of Great Light in Peking was built under the sign of the northern stars and the Great Bear.)

It is also said that 'the Lord, compassionate and merciful, who governs all things in his infinite wisdom, wished Adam to live west of the Garden when he had been driven away from it, for the land in that direction is vast.'

Adam's treasure

The Combat of Adam and Eve next relates a strange story in which the Lord orders Adam to remain in a cave opening into the rock below the garden. Why a cave? Because Adam must bring his treasure there: precious objects from Eden, which the angels had given him before he sinned.

Many Oriental writings say that Adam was buried in a cave because he was not cursed by God, and he remained the holiest and most venerable of all the patriarchs.

When Noah had built the Ark, he brought Adam's body to it: 'Methuselah said to Noah, "My son, when you die, tell your firstborn, Shem, to take with him Melchizedek, son of Cainan and grandson of Arphaxad, for he is the priest of the Almighty God, and together they will take from the Ark the body of our father Adam, and they will carry it away and bury it under the earth, and Melchizedek must remain on that mountain before the body of our father Adam and celebrate the divine service there until eternity.'

Here is a new idea: of all the people who have ever been on earth, including prophets and messiahs, the most important of all is Adam. Melchizedek himself, a great priest of God and a great Master of Righteousness, is committed to divine service until the extreme limit of time.

Who was Adam? Have we not been mistaken about his true essence because we have given too much credence to Biblical creation?

The fact is that all of protohistory is only a summary of

semifabulous events assembled in a chronological order which has been believed to be correct, but may very well be false.

Who were they?

Adam, Enoch, Melchizedek, Moses – in short, most Biblical heroes until the time of Jesus – were described hundreds or thousands of years after their death. According to a number of historians, Adam is a myth and Enoch was a son of Cain, or Methuselah's father, or (and this is my view) a mysterious mediator between the Hyperboreans and the astronauts of Armenia. Melchizedek is hidden in almost impenetrable mystery and Moses was probably a high Egyptian dignitary, either a pharaoh or a priest.

To understand the irritating uncertainty of ancient data, it is enough to try to identify some great historical characters.

Who was Jesus? The son of God, say Christians, but most of the world's peoples deny his real existence.

Who were the first kings of France in the fifth century *after* Christ? We know only vague details about them, and the Merovingians, who have left us hundreds of of thousands of sarcophagi, are all but unknown to us. Was Charlemagne, the powerful Emperor of the West, clean-shaven or bearded? No one knows.

Who was Joan of Arc? I have so much affection for the Maid of Orleans that I would hate to see her image tarnished, but the truth is that her story is very strange! She was probably about to say pagan prayers to the fairy trees of Bourlemont when she heard her 'voices.' She miraculously recognized King Charles VII at Chinon, but as her comrade-in-arms she chose a sorcerer who sacrificed children to the devil: Gilles de Rais, executed at Nantes in 1440 as a heretic, a practitioner of black magic, and a murderer.

Was Joan a witch? Perhaps; she may have been an adorable, benevolent witch who 'drove the English out of France' with the magic sword unearthed at Sainte-

Catherine-de-Fierbois in incredible circumstances. And she accomplished her marvellous mission while carrying an effective relic that had been brought to her from the Abbey of Charroux, in Vienne, by order of Charles VII: the Bellator, the largest known piece of the True Cross.

But what is the True Cross worth if Jesus is fictitious? And what is the worth of Joan's ordeal at the stake in Rouen when we know that five years later her own brother Jean du Lys (as is recorded in the archives of Loiret) came to Orleans with the news that she was still alive? So much alive, say historians, that she reappeared in the flesh and was recognized by her family and La Hire, the commander of her army.

I again ask the question: who were Adam, Enoch, Moses, Melchizedek, Jesus?

On reflection it appears that the story of Adam being driven out of paradise can quite well be interpreted as the story of someone who came to Earth from elsewhere, after being banished for some sort of misconduct, or for reasons unknown to us.

Was Adam a Robinson Crusoe of space, an isolated astronaut, an adventurer from the sky? Or was he the leader of the Hyperborean exploration group?

If we give credence to *The Combat of Adam and Eve*, this last hypothesis explains to some extent the exceptional honours that were given to Adam's body, during and after the Deluge, by Noah and Melchizedek. On this view, the treasure in Adam's cave, given to him by the angels, may have been composed of objects that had no great intrinsic value but were from another planet.

It is obvious that additions were later inserted in the text, notably the passage where we read that 'Adam and Seth hid in the treasure cave the gold, incense and myrrh that the Magi were to give to the Saviour in Bethlehem.' (Christian commentators have, naturally, situated that cave under Golgotha!)

I have mentioned this fraud, and all the different versions and interpretations that I have presented in no particular order, to stress once again the extreme uncertainty of documents relating to our genesis.

A letter from Jesus

Are we to believe in the authenticity of the letter that Jesus is said to have written in reply to a message from Abgar, King of Edessa, in Armenia?

Eusebius, Bishop of Caesarea, is the author of the famous and valuable *Historia Ecclesiastica* in which he gives an orderly and accurate account of the establishment and progress of the Church between the years 267 and 340. The letter from Jesus appears in Chapter 13 of his book, and also in works by Nicephorus, Procopius, and others.

Abgar, says Eusebius, suffered terribly from gout, and when he heard praise of Jesus for his miracles he decided to invite him to his court and ask him to cure him.

Edessa, now Urfa, in Turkey, was a city in northwestern Mesopotamia, between the Tigris and the Euphrates, rather far from Judea, where Jesus was journeying with his apostles. So he did not accept Abgar's invitation, but instead sent him this talismanic letter:

You are fortunate, Abgar, to have believed in me without having seen me, for it is written of me that those who have seen me will not believe, in order that those who have not seen me will believe and be saved. You have asked me to come to you, but I must do what I have been sent to do, and afterward return to Him who sent me. When I have done so I will send one of my disciples, who will cure you and give life to you and yours.

And Abgar is said to have been cured of his ills.

'It was added,' writes Procopius, 'that Edessa could never be taken by the barbarians.' But this second miracle failed to occur, even though the inhabitants displayed Christ's letter at the gates of the city in lieu of any other kind of fortification.

The original of this letter, writes the eleventh-century Byzantine historian Cedrenus, was venerated at Constantinople in the reign of Emperor Michael the Paphlagonian, in about 1035.

An Arab manuscript preserved in the Leiden library gives another version of Christ's letter. The general meaning is the same, but there are considerable differences in style and details:

Letter from Our Lord Jesus Christ to Abgar, King of Edessa, which he sent, saying:

'I Jesus Christ, son of the living and eternal God, to Abgar, king in the city of Edessa. Peace be with you. I say to you that you are fortunate, and blessed is your city of Edessa, because you have believed in me without having seen me.

'You and your people will be forever happy. Peace and charity will multiply in your city and a sincere faith in me will shine there, and wisdom will be in its public places.

'I Jesus Christ, King of Heaven, have come to earth to save Adam and Eve and their race.'

And he sent him seven aphorisms in Greek:

I submit voluntarily to the sufferings and passion of the cross.

I am not merely a man, but a perfect God and a perfect man.

I have been taken away to the seraphim.

I am eternal and there is no other God than I.

I have become the Saviour of Men.

Because of my love of man.

I live in all times, always and eternally.

'The Lord,' continues the scribe of the Leiden manuscript, 'sent this letter, saying, "I have ordered that you be cured of your maladies, sufferings and infirmities, and that your sins be remitted. And wherever you place this letter, the power of enemy armies will be unable to defeat you or overthrow you, and your city will be forever blessed because of you."

'These are the seven aphorisms that Our Lord Jesus Christ sent to Abgar, King of Edessa, concerning his divinity and his humanity, and how he is a perfect God and a perfect man. Praise be to him forever.'

The spelling of the king's name is already altered in the manuscript and it seems likely that two or three more retranscriptions would not have left much of the original text. (In this connection it is worth noting that the Bible is known to us through twelve hundred to eighteen hundred copies, the original being, of course, lost or sequestered.)

The letter from Jesus to Abgar was not found until the fourth century. The Church considers it apocryphal and Saint Jerome did not believe in its authenticity. Yet it is the only more or less historical document capable of attesting to Jesus's existence.

The word *Khristos* appears in the Egerton Papyrus, which dates from the time of Jesus, but without any personal indication, and *Khristos* ('the Anointed One') could apply to any consecrated individual.

Several traditions state that the messenger Abgar sent to Jesus was the painter Ananias. Unable to persuade Jesus to come to Edessa, Ananias wanted at least to bring back a portrait of him. He tried to paint one while he was speaking in the midst of his disciples, but could not do so, because of Jesus's movements or the radiance of his face. When he was told of the painter's intention, Jesus asked for some water, washed his face, dried himself with a piece of cloth, and gave it to Ananias. And according to Cedrenus and John of Damascus, who report the legend, Christ's image was imprinted on the cloth.

In a speech, Constantine Porphyrogenitus, ruler of the Eastern Roman Empire, said that the power of that miraculous image forced the Persians to lift the siege of Edessa, yet Emperor Romanus Lecapenus acquired it in exchange for great advantages granted to the Moslems, who had become masters of the city.

The portrait was brought to Constantinople on August 16, 944, and the Christians there paid great homage to it.

The treasure of the temple

Although they were written only a short time before the Christian era, the Dead Sea Scrolls offer no better guarantee of authenticity. Not that I suspect the scribes who wrote them of having deliberately tried to lead us into error, but we must bear in mind that two thousand years ago Oriental peoples did not consider historical truth with the idea of scientific rigour that we attach to it today – theoretically, at least!

For example, we do not know exactly how much credence to give to the treasure described by documents discovered in March, 1952, in Cave III at Qumran. In that cave, amid fragments of jars, were three sheets of copper about twelve inches wide and thirty-one inches long, rolled up and firmly stuck together by oxidation. Professor H. W. Baker of Manchester University undertook the laborious task of separating them without damaging them; he succeeded and the text appeared.

It was the first time a message engraved on metal had been found in the Holy Land and for this reason it was thought to be exceptionally important. It may well have been, because its contents were divulged only by this short fragment:

> In the cistern at the bottom of the wall, on the east side, is a cavity hollowed out of the rock. It contains six hundred bars of silver. Nearby, at the south corner of the portico, before the tomb of Sadoq and under the pillar of the exedra: a cedar-wood chest of incense and a cassia-wood chest of incense. In the pit near here, close to the tomb, in a cavern that opens to the north, is a copy of this scroll, with precise explanations, measurements and instructions.

The treasure referred to was probably from the Temple in Jerusalem that was pillaged by Titus's Romans in A.D. 70. For this reason, and perhaps for others that were not to be known, it was decreed that the text of the copper scrolls was either a hoax or the ritual of a sect, and therefore that no importance should be attached to the literal meaning of the words.

It became known a little later, but with few exact details, that the copper scrolls revealed the location of sixty treasures of gold and silver: a total of two hundred tons of precious metal, representing a fortune of a hundred million dollars.

Where was the lie: in the presumably Essenian text, or in the translation of it? The mystery still remains.

Chapter 12

THE OTHER WORLD OF THE GRAIL

In the course of its slow resurrection after the horrors of the Deluge, the human race, bewildered and living under chaotic conditions, oscillated among various social systems. The world's population, formerly several tens of millions, had fallen to an unknown but certainly much smaller figure, and we may conjecture that it took three or four generations to bring it back up to an adequate level.

There were few survivors in the area around the centre of destruction in Atlantis, which was especially hard hit by the cataclysm. Some animals species were entirely wiped out. Prisoners of their continental isolation, the Amerindians – the former Atlantans – developed without contact with the rest of the world.

On the other side of the earth, the Land of Mu had been largely submerged, but the region of what is now the Gobi Desert (which according to traditions was once a sea dotted with islands) had been raised, and a new, virgin continent had risen from the ocean: Australia.

In the north, the Celts and Norsemen had been less disastrously affected than other peoples, but their civilization was not highly advanced and their development was hindered by two factors: they did not live on a fracture line of the earth's crust, favourable to evolution, and they were beginning another stagnant golden age on their overly rich lands. But precisely because of their stagnation, which meant that they had no ambition of achieving a great destiny, they had preserved the true traditions of Hyperborea as nearly intact as possible.

It was in the West and the Near East that the human spirit was to be manifested with particular brilliance and first credit for this must go to the Greeks, champions of rationalism, and the Hebrews, inheritors of Egyptian magic. Between those two tendencies the ancient world chose a compromise that was no doubt the best solution.

It is important to note that the Greeks, Hindus, Celts,

Incas, and Mayas believed that the whole cosmos was involved in their genesis and they therefore cultivated a spirit of universal evolution. But the Hebrews, and later the Western Christians, narrowed the universe down to the Near East, repudiating the sun, Venus, Jupiter, and Mars. This was their great error, their sin of omission.

Projecting far into the future, the Hebrews remained faithful to their policy through all sorts of perils and they had great influence until the first few centuries before Christ.

The Greeks developed a particularly brilliant civilization, yet, like the Egyptians, they were unable to impose their numerous and picturesque gods. Moses's monotheism was truer and more profound and it impregnated other peoples in depth, but since Jehovah refused himself to non-Jews it was Jesus who gave himself to the West, unless it was the West that gave itself to Jesus.

What great mystery presided over the advent of Christianity?

In a century and a half, from the year 1 to the year 150, by a conspiracy of initiates (which has been called a conspiracy of the Sons of the Universal Secret), the Christians reformed a society that had been plunged into chaos, apparently because the Jews had failed in their mission.

Since Israel remained the only keeper of the secret, the path to the superior ancestors was cut off. The Latins, Celts, and Scandinavians, however, still had some of the original truth, a little glimmer, almost indiscernible but tenacious, which was to brighten the flame of Christianity in the Middle Ages. While the Jews were turning inward in the Near East, Christian vitality was seeking a continuum in the mysterious and still unknown West.

The mission of the Hyperboreans

That thrust outward from the little European universe had already been foreseen and attempted by initiates through the channel of secret societies in the Hebraic and Greek eras, but only the Christians gave it a meaning and an ideal. This was the mission of the orders of chivalry, whose emblem, as their name implies, was the horse.

On the American plains where it ran wild ten thousand years ago, the horse had acquired a high symbolic value because it was the totem of the Atlantans in the form of Poseidon, the horse-god of the sea. After the worldwide cataclysm the symbol seemed to vanish with Atlantan knowledge, but the initiates of the Secret Centres had not forgotten it and they brought it back with the orders of chivalry.

It is significant that now, as ten thousand years ago, the horse is especially honoured in areas where groups of extraterrestrials landed: America, the Gobi Desert, and Armenian-Caucasian region. (The best horses of western Asia come from Armenia, the best of eastern Asia from Mongolia.)

The most famous order of chivalry, and also the most esoteric, was that of the Knights of the Round Table and the quest for the Grail. It gives us the wondrous key to a vanished world which should have led to the discovery of America long before Columbus. (America was visited by Europeans and Asians much earlier than 1492; by the 'discovery' of America I mean extensive exploration of it by non-American peoples.)

The quest for the Grail has been endlessly debated, analysed, and distorted. It can be definitively understood only in the light of the primohistoric past. Religious communities had an interest in falsifying and monopolizing it in order to control it better, but its mysterious atavistic appeal was so strong that its deep meaning, imprinted in the subconscious, always persisted in spite of additions and alterations. Initiates working in the shadows continued to direct the quest, whose goal was to safeguard and elevate descendants of the superior ancestors.

The legendary Grail

In medieval belief, the Grail was both the chalice that Christ had used at the Last Supper and the emerald cup in which Joseph of Arimathea had received some of Christ's blood at the Crucifixion. Different authors have given it other meanings, depending on their beliefs: an Oriental literary myth transposed in the West, the Philosopher's

Stone, the archetype of supranormal knowledge, a symbol of universal chivalry, God's grace or virtue, the living, immortal, divine presence, the magic cauldron of the Celts and King Arthur, and so on.

The Grail entered Arthurian literature in Wales in the eleventh century and made its first appearance in France in about 1135, in *Perceval*, by Chrétien de Troyes. In the early thirteenth century the German writer Wolfram von Eschenback included the Grail in his works *Parzival*, *Titurel*, and *Willehalm*. He borrowed the theme from the French poet Guyot, who claimed to have received it from an Arab necromancer of Toledo.

A more secret tradition relates the myth to an Arab epic and to an idea of peaceful domination over the East and the West by means of orders of chivalry.

In Wolfram von Eschenback's work the Templars are the heroes of the marvellous quest, at least according to the hermit Trevizent in *Parzival*: 'Valiant knights dwell at Montsalvage, where the Grail is kept. These are the Templars; they ride far away in quest of adventures. ... They live from a Stone whose essence is all purity and whose name is *Lapsit Exillis*.'

In *L'Islam et le Graal*, by Pierre Ponsoye, we read with regard to the cup of chivalry that 'here, the symbolism of initiatic drinks is as follows: wine = spirit; water = absolute knowledge; milk = revealed laws; honey = wisdom; whereas the theme of the Grail, complex in itself as well as by its origins, which probably go back to the primordial tradition, directly concerns the symbolism of the Spiritual Centres, and that is why its true Islamic counterpart is the Black Stone of the Kaaba.'

The general meaning of the Grail is based on a magic function similar to that of the couldron of the Celtic god Dagda: giving inexhaustible nourishment to all men on earth.

Its esoteric meaning is much subtler, because the nourishment of the Grail is both knowledge of hidden secrets (initiation) and an electric potential, a magnetism, probably similar to radiation by telluric currents.

As for the Grail itself, it is the womb in which mankind

was born and the quest for it is, in physical reality, a return to the source, to the native land of the great ancestors.

In Celtic mythology, which is closer to the primordial truths than any other, the 'Magic Cauldron,' or Holy Grail, has such marvellous powers that the gods try to steal it out of envy.

King Arthur succeeded in conquering it in a land that lay 'beyond the ocean' in the west where the Hyperboreans, represented by the Celts, had lived, according to my interpretation of the Corbridge Stone in England and the 'angels' whose heads had haloes of radiant light.

The Templars attributed to their standard some of the same magic powers attributed to the Grail: anyone who had seen it during the day was sure not to perish in combat! anyone who had seen it during the week might be wounded, but not fatally.

This correlation sheds light on the secret mission of the Knights of the Round Table and the Templars, who may be regarded as the keepers of the Guarded Secret and the elite with the mission of drawing strength, power, and knowledge from the land of the superior ancestors.

In popular legend, stories of the Knights of the Round Table were a series of valorous deeds by Lancelot, his son Galahad, Percival, Gawain, and others. They all had the ambition of going to the castle of the Fisherman King to seek the Grail, whose empty place at King Arthur's Round Table offended the eyes and hearts of his valiant knights. The castle of the Fisherman King was in an 'Other World' that was both real and unreal but had an 'open way' which could be found in the west, beyond the ocean.

The Other World of the Grail

Besides the Grail, the Knights of the Round Table were to bring back from their quest marvellous objects whose constantly increasing number finally overwhelmed the chroniclers who wrote about them.

In the most exoteric tradition, the land of the Other World was either underground or in the sides of steep cliffs overlooking rivers. One could reach it by way of

underground passages beneath haunted hills, after performing initiatic rites.

This popular version was composed by minstrels and
adapted to the naïve beliefs of the time. It contains almost
imperceptible traces of certain truths which appear more
clearly in ancient Celtic traditions.

In the Irish version, the Other World was beyond the
seas and the Islands of the Blest, farther than the thick
fogs that forbade access to it. Like Antillas, Brazil Island,
and San Brandan, it moved away from any unworthy
seeker who tried to approach it, and even disappeared
from his sight. Yet it existed, with its Adventurous Castle,
the temporary residence of the goddess-queen Riannon
and King Bran, who had reached the land of the Other
World after a perilous crossing of the great western sea.

Anyone who sat at the king's table and heard the singing of the queen's marvellous birds lost his sense of time,
which can be interpreted as meaning that when an initiated knight was admitted into the castle he entered another universe, with different dimensional rules.

In that land lived fairies, spirits endowed with strange
powers, beings that could think, move, appear, and disappear in ways incomprehensible to men of the normal
world, subject to three dimensions and such physical conditions as weight, opacity, and perceptions of sounds and
colours.

In that Celtic Elysium, which can be identified with the
enchanted land of Hyperborea described by Diodorus
Siculus, was the Island of Apples (Avalon), with its tree
bearing magic apples that warded off death. (This paradise where the fruit of the tree of knowledge could be
plucked without sin or punishment seems contrary to the
earthly paradise of the Bible, where knowledge was dangerous. Perhaps it was the antithesis of the Biblical paradise.)

As in the Tir nan Og (Land of Youth) of Irish traditions,
located on the American continent, centuries were minutes, flowers bloomed in all seasons, the rivers flowed with
mead, and the inhabitants had the gift of eternal youth.
Feasts and battles were the favourite pastimes of the

warriors, who drank divine beverages and took succulent dishes and enormous fruit from never-empty vases. Their female companions were women of marvellous beauty who also had the ability to see into the future. (Again we are reminded of Hyperborea, where according to tradition the women were exceptionally beautiful and intelligent.)

But in that land across the Atlantic there were wars in our visible world and it was not quite a paradise, or no longer a paradise, since misfortunes struck good King Bran in the form of enchantments. And one mission of knights on a quest was to break the enchantment that weighed down on the king.

This notion, and no doubt the memory of a remote and almost inaccessible Other World that had once been real, was deeply rooted and very old in the West, since Caesar wrote that the Gauls boasted of having all come from a common god, Dis Pater (Tentates), king of the Other World that was the origin of all souls. They left it when they were reincarnated, then returned to it after death, in a steady flow of spiritual capital that remained constant. The Druids also taught this in their initiatic chants.

Florida or Hyperborea

Descriptions and data relating to the land of the quest enable us to give an approximate location for it.

Geographically, we can situate it at the place where Enoch went when he wanted to contact the extra-terrestrials in the direction of Hyperborea, 'between the north and the west.'

But since Enoch's time the north pole has shifted westward. Making allowance for this, we are led to Florida, in North America, where the land sinks into the ocean almost without transition, as if it were pursuing its ancient continental substratum under the water.

Florida is the golden horn of the New World, and also a horn of plenty. It is like a living memory of the submerged continent, with its long coastline facing both the Atlantic and the Gulf of Mexico, and, as though by a strange kind of predestination, beneath its offshore waters lie sunken Spanish galleons laden with prodigious treasures of Incan and Aztec gold.

With its marshy Everglades, Florida is a blend of land and water and it is known as having the finest climate in the world, with an unending summer that is like an eternal youth of nature (the Tir nan Og of the Celts). As in Armenia, magnificent fruit grows here, from strains of trees improved by skilled growers in prehistoric times.

Greek tradition was thus stating a physical truth when it said that Hercules went beyond the sea to pluck the real and unreal golden apples of knowledge.

The average temperature of Florida is about seventy-three degrees and the difference between winter and summer is only about seven degrees; as a result, the 'golden apples' (oranges) and other kinds of fruit that grow there have an exquisite flavour.

This is the Garden of the Hesperides, the Other World of Gilgamesh, the Green Land of the Egyptians, the paradise of Amithaba, and, going back still farther, the Hyperborea of the Norsemen.

And Florida is a land of cavities made in limestone by underground streams. Veritable rivers flow through gigantic openings into the bowels of the earth, where they disappear into a prodigious realm of channels and caves that constitute a mysterious invisible world.

For the Welshmen and Irishmen of the land of King Arthur, Florida was the Other World described by the bold Celtic, Norse, and Basque sailors who discovered America long before Columbus and, of course, told of their travels with details added by their imagination.

America had become a semilegendary country at the western edge of the world, beyond the ocean in the direction of the Islands of the Blest and San Brandan, where in A.D. 570 an Irish bishop had landed, later to be confused by tradition with King Bran.

That Other World in America was reached after going through the incredible Newfoundland fog banks that were well suited to striking the imagination and giving rise to fantastic tales, and were like an initiation ordeal that had to be successfully surmounted. Once he had arrived, the traveller found a land with a balmy climate, marvellous golden apples, fragrant blossoms all year round, and even the underground kingdom that made such a strong impression on ancient discoverers.

So much for the physical, geographical Other World. We must still clear up the mystery of the duality, the reality and unreality, of King Bran's kingdom, where one lost the notion of time.

It is easy to understand the perplexity of our ancestors before that problem. It was insoluble then, and it can be solved today only by the hypothesis of parallel universes and the revelation of the history of our Superior Ancestors.

The call of America

It is possible that Hyperborea was farther north in primohistoric times and that Florida is only an image of the ancient reality, but if so the solution of the problem still remains essentially correct because it was in America that the land of the quest was located. Otherwise, how could we explain the single direction (westward) of all those currents that swept away initiates, heroes, knights, and discoverers?

And the paths of fortune-seekers and purveyors of dubious initiations still converge on America, particularly New York, as though an atavistic memory of a necessary voyage to the Other World still persisted despite the passing of millennia and deterioration of the primordial truth.

But discovery of the physical Other World was only the first stage of the quest and could bring little more than illusory material gain. The Knights of the Round Table never reached that world in a physical sense, but perhaps they had access to it through the mystery of 'underground passages' (that is, initiation) leading from our three-dimensional world to the world of parallel universes.

This hypothesis is supported by such indications as the supranatural duality of the Other World, which was real yet imperceptible, and the annihilation of time when one heard the singing of the marvellous birds. Furthermore, the Other World is said to have been reached by way of an 'open door'; that is, a kind of airlock through which the traveller could pass under certain conditions.

Some writers have interpreted the meaning of the quest for the Grail as entirely initiatic. In my opinion that is a mistake, especially since ancient texts say such things as 'The land of the Other World exists and does not exist' and 'It truly exists beyond the seas, to the west.' And in any case those islands, those fogs, that continent, those golden apples, and that land of felicity coincide too closely with the United States to be entirely a matter of chance. It is undeniable, however, that symbolism is mingled with reality in this subject, particularly since early historians of the Grail were generally unable to imagine superior ancestors, a vanished world, or even a western continent.

In his book *Der Engel vom Westlichen Fenster*, Gustav Meyrink expressed the view that the quest was the *Mysterium Conjunctionis* signifying the 'chemical marriage' of the initiate with the Lady of Philosophy or Queen of the Eearth from beyond the seas. He also saw it as the mystery of Transubstantiation, of the confusion between the plus and the minus; that is, the reintegration of Adam into the primordial or occult Eve, who was a hermaphroditic being.

This theory makes the United States the primeval land where the first man was born. If that were true, the quest would be a return to man's source, but on a scientific level it would be hard to support the idea that the United States was the cradle of the human race. For my part, I see it only as the cradle of a primohistoric civilization.

From a rational, scientific viewpoint, the journey or passage into the Other World cannot be made by a normally constituted physical man; he would probably have to undergo a kind of elevation and transmutation that would, for example, place him in an extremely subtle state which would facilitate endosmosis. There would then be transubstantiation and incorporation into the fringes of a universe with five or six dimensions, a theory which has been developed mathematically by Professor E. Falinski.

A theory of parallel universes

Here is a very concise summary of the theory presented by Falinski in his treatise *Parapsychologie Pengéométrique:*

At the time of creation there was not a choice of the best of all possible worlds (Leibnitz's theory), but a choice among all rationally possible worlds. There is thus an infinity of worlds in which anything is possible, even the legends of Tom Thumb, Santa Claus and the Blue Bird of Happiness. These are *parallel universes.*

The theoretical reality of parallel universes can be demonstrated mathematically by a series of equations drawn from Gauss's hypergeometry, Lobachevski's pangeometry, Riemann's non-Euclidian geometry and Cantor's calculus of transfinites. Briefly, the demonstration establishes that, contrary to Euclid's postulate, an infinite number of lines parallel to a straight line can be drawn through a point outside it. Hence the existence of universes that are parallel to ours but do not exactly coincide with it, since they are displaced from it in time and space; that is, events in them are earlier or later than those in our known universe.

These universes can penetrate each other because in their structure, as in that of the atom, there is much more empty space than matter.

There are no fields of force between different universes that prevent objects from passing from one into the other. Time travel and the 'miracle' of passing through matter are thus possible for anyone who succeeds in going from one universe to another. Fields of force operate only for inner elements, and in the interior of a given universe.

The fringe of non-coincidence between parallel universes is, so to speak, the 'airlock' through which an individual endowed with supranormal perception can pass to explore (see and hear) the past or the future.

On the occult level, passage through the 'mouth of the crack' can be viewed as conscious exploration in the astral body, a penetration of a parallel universe that would explain the mechanism of clairvoyance and precognition.

A traveller in the Other World of the Grail would thus have to establish a connection between the supranormal and a science which is still unknown, but which some day, no doubt, will be experimentally verified.

This theory does not dismay atomic physicists, for whom the behaviour of particles from the Other World of the cosmos is a profound mystery, along with the concepts of velocities greater than that of light, the hollow or curved universe, and space-time.

The Other World of the Grail is even more mysterious. As described by eleventh-century chroniclers, it suggests the survival of scientific knowledge that has deteriorated through the centuries but was at one time highly developed.

The process of integration may appear in a disguised form in the tests that had to be undergone by the Knights of the Round Table. (The process will be studied from a theoretical standpoint in Chapter 17.)

The tests

The quest for wondrous objects was subject to questions, tests, and perils; in return, the objects conferred happiness, awareness, invulnerability, and honour.

Their reported number increased as imaginative authors wrote different versions through the centuries, but the basic ones were always these:

> The Wondrous Cup
> The Stone of Sovereignty
> The Miraculous Basket
> The Drinking Horn
> The Sword
> The Lance
> The Inexhaustible Bowl
> The Cauldron of Abundance

Their fundamental number was thus eight, which was also the Templars' figure; and when the figure 8 is written horizontally it becomes the symbol of universal domination.

A symbolic value was unquestionably attached to each of them, but it seems that occultists have gone too far in speculating on their esoteric and alchemical significance. Yet the fact that the Templars continued the mission of the Knights of the Round Table leads us to think that occultism, and particularly alchemy, actually were involved in the mystery.

The two main objects, the Cup and the Stone (not to mention the Horn, the Sword, and the Lance of transcendent virility), can be related to the quest of alchemy, the Philosopher's Stone, the plus and minus signs, the occult Eve, and also, no doubt, the emeralds and the black stone that Lucifer is said to have brought from the planet Venus. It is a subject that could be discussed endlessly.

The ritual questions asked of candidates for the quest for the Grail were as follows:

1. Whom does it serve.
2. As what does the Grail serve?
3. Why does the lance bleed?

The first question meant 'In whose service is the Grail?' and the answer was 'It serves the wounded king.' The answer to the second question was 'It serves as divine nourishment.' The third question referred to the treacherous blow that wounded the King of the Other World and, by extension, to Christ's wound.

The tests were extremely numerous, but some of them occurred often enough to form a general rule:

– Spending the night in a chapel beside the body of a dead knight surrounded by candles; it was a terrifying night, with thunder, lightning, and the appearance of ghosts.

– The test of the turning bed, in which the candidate underwent a veritable bombardment of murderous arrows.

– The deadly game of the decapitated man, a kind of duel in which the loser was beheaded.

– Staying for several days, sometimes without eating, in the enchanted forest.

If the candidate successfully passed all his tests, he was given his name and was then entitled to his ancestors, his honour, and the soul reincarnated in him.

A whole system of initiatic meaning emerges from these tests. They have equivalents in the rites of all orders of chivalry, ancient and modern, and also in Freemasonry. Whether expressed clearly or in veiled terms, their function was to prepare an elite for a political mission which, from the eleventh century onward, was the conquest of the world by the peoples who were the direct descendants of the Hyperborean superior ancestors.

At the beginning of the Middle Ages the quest for the Grail was converted into a secret movement which still continues in an unexpected way.

A Christian aspect was deliberately added to it, and although it was a distortion of the original meaning it inspired the Arthurian legend. I believe, however, that it served to hide occult and political aims which were attached not to the Christian religion but to a universal religion corresponding to a plan of domination conceived by a vast conspiracy of knights whose spiritual empire extended from Jerusalem to faraway Thule.

In the thirteenth century a particularly well initiated emperor of the Holy Roman Empire, Frederick II of Hohenstaufen, illustrated this thesis, though it has escaped historians, most of whom are oblivious to the invisible history of mankind.

THE CASTLE OF THE MASTER
OF THE WORLD

Beginning in the time when men believed they had learned the limits of the earth, there were kings who dreamed of conquering it and ruling over all the invaded continents.

Until the last century, the generally accepted cosmology made the earth the centre of the universe, or even assumed it to be the whole universe, which meant that a man who had a desire to dominate the earth could hope to acquire the resounding title of Master of the World.

Some historians attribute both the desire and the title to such rulers as Charlemagne, Frederick II of Hohenstaufen, Charles V of Germany, and Napoleon. It would be easy to find other rulers and even private citizens who, out of megalomania, dreamed of earthly supremacy, but while it is wrong to bring the accusation against Charlemagne, Napoleon, and perhaps Charles V, there is reason to believe that Frederick II harboured that illusory ambition.

The most intelligent of all kings

In the heart of the Middle Ages, at the beginning of the thirteenth century, Frederick II was Emperor of Germany, King of the Romans, King of Sicily, and King of Jerusalem. He was a prestigious sovereign, an almost legendary figure whom his people sometimes confused with King Arthur.

The fact is, however, that the devoutly Christian sovereign of the Knights of the Round Table had little in common with Frederick, who was an implacable enemy of popes and religion and did not hesitate to say that Moses, Jesus, and Mohammed were imposters. In the thirteenth century, the time of Saint Louis and the Crusades, this credo was alarming to the Christian West, but there were sympathetic reactions to it among the common people, who were less devoted to the Roman Catholic religion than is usually thought.

Historians differ in their opinions of Frederick's character, but the facts are there: the great emperor spent most of his time struggling against the popes, driving them out of Italy, harrying them, undergoing anathemas and excommunications, and sometimes, when the danger became too great, coming back to the bosom of the Church, hardened unbeliever though he was.

The monk Salimbene called him the Antichrist; Dante promised him a place in the sixth circle of the Inferno, 'in the burning tombs where heresiarchs and their followers groan.'

German by birth but Latin by education, Frederick II was undoubtedly the most cultivated, intelligent, and independent sovereign in human history. He spoke Italian, Greek, Arabic, German, Latin, and French, and skillfully engaged in the practice of medicine, archaeological excavation, and undersea adventure. At his picturesque, learned court, the fisherman Colas Pesce (Colas the Fish) was a teacher of underwater science and brought his sovereign and friend the corals, shells, and treasures he found at the bottom of the sea.

But while a fisherman was the emperor's friend, occultists were his instructors and advisors.

He studied the Cabala, alchemy, and Merlin's prophecies

'This Caesar,' said Saba Malespina, 'who was the real sovereign of the world and whose glory has spread all over the universe, believing, no doubt, that he could become the equal of the gods by the practice of mathematics, began plumbing the depths of things and scrutinizing the mysteries of the heavens.' And it is here, I believe, that Frederick's personality is revealed; his mind was far superior to the general intellectual level of his time and he dreamed of becoming the Master of the World through science and magic.

He surrounded himself with seers, necromancers, alchemists, astrologers, and Cabalists who taught and initiated him.

He steeped himself in the legends of King Arhtur and the Knights of the Round Table, studied the Golden Number with Leonardo Fibonacci, the Pisan mathematician, corresponded with Juda Cohen, the Jewish scholar of Toledo, and consulted the most famous occultists of his time: Ezzelino da Romano, Guido Bonatti, Riprandino of Verona. He sent to Bagdad for the Saracen magician Paul, and to England for Michael Scot, an illusionist and a master of 'diabolical knowledge.'

His personal advisor was Theodore, a Greek scholar and expert in all the arts, who concocted strange drinks, love potions, magic sweets, and a 'violet sugar' whose wondrous powers equalled that of the elixir of youth.

Was Frederick under a spell? It is possible, but those who encouraged him in his aim of world domination were accomplished magicians and scholars of great worth.

Fond of fantastic legends, he was keenly interested in Merlin the Enchanter, King Arthur's companion and an inspired prophet whose fame in the countrysides of the West during the Middle Ages was so great that it strongly affected the fate of Europe.

His prophecies made it easier for Joan of Arc to accomplish her mission. The *Book of Merlin* said that 'the twelve signs of the zodiac will wage war against each other, and Virgo will then descend on the back of Sagittarius.' (It is interesting to note in passing that any publicly announced prophecy has a good chance of being fufilled because there will always be a visionary to take personal charge of it when the time comes: if a seer predicts a saviour for Europe in a given year, say 2000 or 2004, a certain number of Europeans will take the message to heart and the announced 'saviour' will inevitably appear.) The imagination of the French people saw the reference to Virgo as the announcement of a virgin who would save France, and Joan of Arc came to be known as 'la Pucelle' ('the Virgin').

It seems likely that in the thirteenth century Frederick II regarded himself as King Arthur's successor, in the light of this passage in the *Book of Merlin*: 'May God give him a successor like him; I can ask for none better.'

The Pactio Secreta

Naturally inclined toward the grandiose because of his Germanic heritage, the emperor recalled that at Acre in 1228, even though he had been excommunicated by the pope, he had presided over a Round Table meeting of the elite of world chivalry: Templars, Hospitalers, Teutonic Knights, Saracen Fatas, Turks, members of the Order of Assassins, and others, all united by the Pactio Secreta (Secret Pact) for the purpose of establishing the universal religion in a world ruled by the Grand Master of the assembled orders.

Here again we see the connection between chivalry and secret initiatic orders, as the writer René Briat points out:

> The Templars were considered to be the guardians and continuers of a primordially important 'mystery' that was not to be revealed to any outsider, even if he was the King of France.
>
> Was it the Grail, symbol of the knowledge that was the first step toward world domination?
>
> It does in fact seem that the main dream of the Order, the supreme goal of its activities, was the resurgence of the concept of the Empire; that is, the Islamic East and the Christian West, a kind of federation of autonomous states under the direction of two leaders, one spiritual, the Pope, the other political, the Imperator, both elected and independent of each other.
>
> Above the emperor and the pontiff was a supreme, mysterious authority.

Who was that supreme, mysterious Master? Was he an inhabitant of the earth? An extraterrestrial? There are probably few initiates who could give the answer to this enigma.

The treasurer of the seven plaques

The conspiracy of the chivalric orders and the Pactio Secreta have always aroused the curiosity of historians, but without ever being divulged. An accidental discovery, however, may have shed some light on the mystery.

In 1952 a woman living in the Seine-et-Marne district of France unearthed, on an estate at Rampillon, a small chest containing a net bag made with pearls, a seal in the shape of a scarab, and a red ivory box with many swastikas carved into it. Inside the box were a gold standard weight and some silver medals worn smooth as though from long use, some of them dating from the fifteenth century.

Near the treasure were two copper cases containing seven plaques, the largest of which had about the same area as a child's hand. They bore carved signs: Cabalistic, Templar, Masonic, Hebrew, Arabaic, Rosicrucian, and others hard to identify.

Anyone who sees them – with their unidentifiable material, their patina, their strange shapes of gears, octagons, and rectangles, and their mysterious carvings in which a full-blown rose sometimes appears like a reassuring smile – cannot help thinking of the Templars, the Rosicrucians, and a super-secret society in which Christians, Jews, and Moslems fraternized.

To anyone interested in the Grail chivalry, and the castle of the Master of the World at Castel del Monte, Italy, the relation between the symbols of these objects and those incorporated into the architecture of the Italian castle is obvious. Furthermore, an octagonal plaque bearing key signs coincides exactly with the plan of the castle.

The plaques are believed to have been tokens of membership in a hermetic order specifically devoted to alchemy.

Was Jacques Coeur, a maker of gold according to tradition, a member of that sect? It seems quite possible, especially when he is considered in association with those mysterious 'pilots' of King John II of Portugal who, by his secret order, withdrew to the Azores or the Madeira Islands, far away from indiscreet questioners, after having gone off to seek gold from the mines on Brazil Island ten years before the 'discovery' of America by Columbus.

As we will see later, the swastikas on the red box found

at Rampillon are related to the alarming modern resurgence of an order of chivalry.

Be that as it may, in 1240 Frederick II was affiliated with Pactio Secreta, the occult conspiracy of knights, and his castle at Castel del Monte, whose meaning had not been understood by anyone until recently, proves the reality of his dreams of domination.

Under the sign of infinity

Was Frederick II elected Imperator at Acre? He firmly believed so, but perhaps he was mistaken. In any case the sanctuary he was going to build in southern Italy – halfway between the Holy Land of the East and the Motherland of the West, and also halfway between Jerusalem, Avalon, and Santiago de Compostela – was to be a castle of Templar alchemists, governed by the Golden Number of the compass rose: the figure 8, which, when written horizontally, is the symbol of infinity and universal domination.

Frederick felt that everything was settled in this respect and also, on the exoteric level, with regard to the Teutonic Knights, the Hospitalers, the Templars, the Saracens, and the Jews. As for the Catholics, who were naturally hostile to his plan, he knew how he was going to deal with them: the pope would be overthrown.

The octagonal castle

The castle at Castel del Monte, in the Apulia region of Italy, was considered a 'unique wonder' in the Middle Ages. Its four basic measurements are borrowed from the Temple of Solomon (sixty, thirty, twenty, and twelve cubits). It is composed of two concentric octagons with inner divisions built on lines running from the geometric centre to the vertex of each angle, thus forming eight trapezoidal rooms. At each veretex is an octagonal tower rising from the surrounding wall, which is nearly nine feet thick.

The only entrance gate, facing southeast in the direction of Jerusalem, leads into the octagonal central courtyard known as 'the Master's Chamber.' This courtyard was once a vast covered room where, at each solstice, the leaders of the eight great world orders of chivalry were to gather around the Imperator.

It is an uninhabitable castle, with no utilitarian rooms such as kitchens, woodsheds, pantries, bedrooms, boudoirs, or storerooms.

The second story is a duplicate of the first, and at the centre of the two octagons is a cistern for receiving rainwater from the sloping terraces that serve as the roof.

According to tradition there was once at Castel del Monte a temple with a marble statue of an ancient god whose head was surmounted by a bronze circle that bore these words: 'At sunrise on the first day of May, I shall have a golden head.' In 1073 a Saracen guessed the hidden meaning, dug into the ground at the spot where the shadow of the head lay at sunrise on the first day of May, and found a great treasure which was used to build the first castle.

It is therefore probable that Frederick II had construction begun over the ruins of the old castle on the sacral day of the summer soltice in 1240 (the year has also been given as 1233).

Above the entrance gate, between the coat of arms of the Teutonic Knights and the lions of the House of Swabia, is a carved marble head surrounded by rays of light. It is either a symbol of the Unknown Master or a reminder of the god's head that located the treasure.

Michael Scot the gold-maker

In the thirteenth century, when chivalry and the myth of the Grail flourished, the octagonal castle corresponded to a triple mysticism that made it the athanor (alchemist's furnace) in which the fate of Europe and the other known continents was to be forged.

The emperor had a spiritual master: the monk Michael Scot. It is not now known whether Scot was Irish, Italian, of French, but it is certain that in his time he was widely regarded as a matchless magician. For years, first at the German court and then in Italy, he controlled Frederick by means of his knowledge and magic.

His contemporaries said, no doubt falsely, that he

sometimes gathered his friends around an empty table and then, when he made a certain sign, dishes of food appeared magically and placed themselves in front of the guests, as though brought by spirits. Scot would point to the dishes and say, 'This one comes from the table of the King of England, that one from the table of the King of France.'

He wrote many scholarly books, some of which were specially requested by Frederick. He was above all an expert on the transmutation of metals. One of his existing works as a transcription of an alchemical collection titled *De Sole et Luna* (Vol. 5 of the *Theatrum Chimicum*) in which he reveals the procedures for transmutation in cryptic language.

He announced to Frederick, long in advance, that he would die in a place 'consecrated to the flower.'

He also predicted the exact circumstances of his own death. It happened as if a curse from heaven had punished him in an exemplary way: he was praying in the Holme-Coltrane church (or in Melrose Abbey), in Scotland, when a section of wall fell on him and killed him.

His magic power was so great, says *The Lay of the Last Minstrel*, that by chanting incantations in Salamanca he could ring the bells of the Cathedral of Notre-Dame in Paris.

Dante wrote of him, 'He truly knew the workings of magic ruses.'

His sorcery books, and the books of spells by means of which he said he could invoke the infernal powers, were buried with him.

Such was the destiny of that prodigious magician who cannot be dissociated from his master and pupil in diabolical lore, Emperor Frederick II.

An enigmatic inscription

In order to reign on both the temporal and esoteric levels, Frederick needed to succeed in carrying out the alchemist's dream of making gold. As soon as his octagonal castle had been built, under the direction of the French architect Philippe Chinard, he shut himself up in it for

long days and nights with his scholars, astrologers, sorcer-
ars, and alchemists. To what god or demon were their
vehement invocations addressed? Did their archives give
them the secret of transmuting base metal into gold?

No one will ever know, except perhaps for a cryptographer sufficiently initiated to interpret the mysterious abbreviations on a bas-relief in the castle. It represents a woman humbly appearing before a ruler accompanied by several armed men. Below it is this enigmatic
inscription:

$$D^s \ I D C^a \ B^{10} \ C L P S H A^2$$

Here is hidden the mystery of Frederick II and his
magic castle.

In 1250, having experienced great political setbacks, he
was unwilling to withdraw to the castle that no longer
represented anything but a testimony to his thwarted
ambitions. He resigned himself to living in the Fiorentino
castle near Lucera. After again elaborating great dreams
of domination, he died there, in that place 'consecrated
to the flower,' as predicted by his magician.

Castel del Monte, now abandoned under the torrid sky
of Apulia, contains a small museum. A few tourists ad-
mire its severe Templar architecture and it is said that
certain more learned and subtle visitors make the trip
there as a pilgrimage. . . .

The Golden Sun and the Black Sun

Frederick's plan, which answered to the deep aspirations of the initiatic centres of his time, was pursued by
the Templars. Worried Christendom reacted brutally
against them in 1307, when Pope Clement V, in association with King Philip IV of France, ruined their order,
though it was able to keep itself alive clandestinely.

The mission of the Templars *was not to be interrupted
for any reason.* A few centuries later, under the sign of tolerance and universal religion (philosophy), Freemasonry
was born. The Pactio Secreta, renovated and purified, inspired the vast social and political movement which, after

Catholicism, has remodelled the face of the civilized world from 1798 to the present.

In esotericism, this plan has a symbolic name: the Golden Sun.

Other chivalric orders, notably the Teutonic Knights, have also been working in secret since the Middle Ages, but with a disquieting mentality and in the service of a truth that has steadily deteriorated. This is the Black Sun, born perhaps at Castel del Monte from the dream of Frederick II.

Monstrously distorted, it continues its activities among Germanic ethnic groups whose traditionalists are convinced that their race has the mission of saving white civilization.

Chapter 14

THE THULE GROUP

Mysterious Hyperborea

The Thule Group is a powerful and mysterious secret society that pursues its activities on continents inhabited by white people. Its name, which evokes the real or legendary Thule – that is, Hyporborea, considered as the birthplace of the white race – is also related to the quest for the Grail and, in a direct line, to chivalry. The activists of the group are exclusively whites who claim to be champions and defenders of their race.

Greek and Latin historians, such as Herodotus, Diodorus Siculus, Pliny, and Virgil, spoke of the Hyperborean continent as a great island of ice in the Arctic, inhabited by transparent people.

Tradition soon came to regard those Hyperboreans as the archetype of the white race. After first being transparent, it was said, they became opaque when they were mixed with Western white peoples, but they still kept a spiritual subtlety superior to that of others.

Their capital, Thule, was often said by medieval navigators to be in Norway. or even the Shetland Islands. Seen only in that light, Hyperborea would belong entirely to the realm of legend, but there are better reasons for believing in its real existence as a continent or an island.

In the first place, the geological upheavals that occurred in the primohistoric era give us the certainty that the distribution of land masses above the surface of the oceans has been altered several times.

If we are to believe the maps of Piri Reis,* which are

---

* The maps of Piri Reis, a sixteenth-century Ottoman admiral, were discovered in 1957 in the Topkapi museum at Istanbul. They are said to have been drawn from very old Greek and Portuguese documents which in turn reproduced maps drawn before the last ice age, about eleven thousand years ago.

unfortunately sequestered in America for unknown reasons, in that period Greenland (where archaeological excavations and finds have recently been made near the modern town named Thule by the Americans) was not covered with ice and consisted mainly of three large islands. It is probable that two continental plateaus rose above the ocean: one of them (Atlantis) to the south, in the area of the Azores, and the other in the Arctic, between Greenland and southern Norway.

On this assumption, Hyperborea was located either around Iceland, a zone of earthquakes and volcanoes, favourable to the development of civilizations, or in what is now the United States, the Green Land of mythology.

The Celts, Vikings, and Germans kept a memory of it as a veritable Eden, similar to the land of the Other World of the quest for the Grail.

More than all others, the Germans still cling to Hyperborea. Their pagan worship and occult political aspirations are based on it. The myth is so deep-rooted in them that their literature and folk music are impregnated with it, particularly in *Parzival*, *Willehalm*, *Titurel*, and *Faust*.

Goethe's *Ballad of the King of Thule* has an esoteric meaning that escapes the uninitiated but is clearly understood by traditionalists. Here is the story told by the poem:

The king's beloved had bequeathed him a golden cup to help him keep her memory alive. Her love was preserved in it and each time he drank from it his eyes filled with tears. When he felt that the end of his life was approaching he divided all his property among his heirs, except for the cup. He summoned all the noblemen of his court to his table, then stood up in silence, drank from the golden cup, and hurled it through the window into the sea below. From that time on he was never seen to drink again.

The cup of the King of Thule is the Grail, a magic treasure that evokes the vanished Motherland. Like King Arthur, he gathers around him the knights who are to go off in search of the womb-cup. He bequeaths everything except that cup, which is about to enter into the occult.

Once he has thrown it into the sea, the die is cast. The
Grail has disappeared. It is in the western ocean, on the
submerged land of Hyperborea. The Knights of the Round
Table must now set off on their quest for it, to be followed
by all of later knighthood and finally the Thule Group.

The esoteric Grail is thus the womb of superior mankind, by analogy with 'cracks' in the earth's crust; that is,
the primary source of the telluric and cosmic radiation
that gives virility and power over the unconscious minds
of ordinary people.

As we will see later, the Grail, Thule, and certain
myths belong to the same cycle, disguising a transcendent
primeval truth in symbolism. What is commonly called
'mythology,' the term being interpreted to mean 'imaginary stories,' is actually a retranscription of real events
masked by local colour.

Paradise is in the west

If it were otherwise, how could we explain all the
relations, under the sign of the planet Venus, that connect extraterrestrials and Prometheus the Atlantan, on
the one hand, and, on the other, the Other World of the
quest, the Grail, the Andes legends, the Gate of the Sun
at Tiahuanaco (see *One Hundred Thousand Years of
Man's Unknown History*), the Garden of Hesperides,
and the United States of America?

The keys to that enigma are hidden in the symbols of
tradition, history, and Greek mythology: Hercules,
Antaeus, Atlas, the Garden of the Hesperides, the Grail,
the Other World, and the modern Thule Group.

With disturbing unanimity (except for the Bible), traditions place the true paradise and the kingdom of happiness in the motherland of Hyperborea: the Green Land
of Celtic, Scandinavian, and Egyptian mythology, the
Hindu paradise of Amitabha, the great Buddha of the
western sky, the Hesperides of the Greeks, the land of
the Other World of the Babylonians and Polynesians.

In Babylonian mythology the land of the Great Ancestors who were 'made immortal by the Deluge,' according

to tradition, is at the western extremity of the earth, beyond the vast ocean that had to be crossed at the risk of death.

The hero Gilgamesh goes to the dwelling of the goddess Siduri Sabitu, who 'lives at the extremities of the sea, where stands the tree that bears the most beautiful fruit in the world,' to ask for the secret of immortality.

Gilgamesh, whose name means 'he who discovered the source, or 'he who has seen everything,' receives this strange answer: 'O Gilgamesh, there has never been a passage, and no one has crossed the sea since the most remote times. The passage is difficult, the way is arduous, and deep are the waters of death that block access to it. Where, then, Gilgamesh, will you cross the sea?'

By means of a certain magic, however, after sailing on the ocean for a month and a half Gilgamesh reaches the paradise of Utanapishtim, 'he who found life.'

One is struck by the similarities between this odyssey and that of the Greek hero Hercules: the garden of marvellous fruit, the voyage to America, the 'airlock' or passage through which the traveller must go to reach his destination. . . .

In *La Pensée cosmologique chez anciens Mexicains*, Jacques Soutelle writes that the Omeyocan of the Mexicans, the place where the gods and unborn children lived, 'is identical to the Paradise of the West, Tamoanchan, the land of the old gods and past generations, of ripe corn, mist and mystery, the region where the ancient peoples came out of a hole that opened in the earth.'

The Paradise of the West, past generations, the land of mist, and a hole in the earth – like the adventure of Gilgamesh, 'he who found the source,' beyond the mists of Newfoundland, this account evokes Florida, once inhabited by the ancient Mexicans, the home of ancient men, sons of Gaea the Earth.

And Celtic traditions, particularly those of Ireland, give such precise details that we are justified in wondering if the main centre of culture in primohistoric America was

Tiahuanaco (an assumption strengthened by the carvings on the Puerta del Sol) or if it was a Thule located in what is now Virginia or Nevada.

Celtic mythology gives curious details about the race of divine men who had knowledge not possessed by the Celts and came from a land across the Atlantic to fight the giants of Ireland. Since in other mythologies – Andes, Egyptian, Hebraic, etc. – the 'divine men' who come from the sky also bring an unknown civilization and struggle against giants, as in the Irish tradition, it is likely that these stories all have a common base and share a certain authenticity.

Here is the account of those divine men given by Roth and Guirand in their *Mythologie générale*: 'Finally, from the Islands of the West, where they had studied magic, came [to Ireland, about two thousand years before our era] the members of the Tuatha De Danann. They brought their talismans: Nuada's sword, Lug's spear, Dagde's cauldron and the Stone of Destiny, which cried out when the lawful king of Ireland sat on it.'

After the numerous wars described in *The Book of Invasions* the divine men, too few in number and perhaps diminished by the mysterious malady that consumed Prometheus, decided to return to the Land of the Beyond (across the ocean), demanding as compensation only that worship and sacrifices be observed in their memory.

Abandoning the island of Erin (Ireland), they went back to their homeland, named Mag Meld (Plain of Joy) or Tir nan Og (Land of Youth). There, centuries were minutes, no one grew old, and the meadows were covered with everlasting flowers.

Roth and Guirand write a little farther on, 'In British mythology, Avalon [the Island of Apples], where dead kings and heroes rest, corresponds to that Celtic Eden,' which recalls the Enchanted Land of the Hyperboreans.

Is it necessary to point out that these stories support the view that the United States was the cradle of mankind, with Florida corresponding exactly to the Celtic Mag Meld, the land of Hyperborea, and the Garden of the Hesperides?

The Garden of the Hesperides

In Greek mythology, to reach the Land of the Golden Apples one had to overcome the initiatic barriers symbolized by struggle with Antaeus, the demigod and giant who, when he was tired, gained new strength by touching his mother the earth with his foot.

It is interesting to know the genealogy of that magic wrestler whom the gods posted on the path of the Quest to stop the good hero Hercules.

Antaeus was the son of Gaea the Earth and Poseidon, the Greek god of the sea and sailing, and the supreme god of the Atlantans, whose capital was named Poseidonis.

Why did Hercules wrestle with Antaeus? Because he wanted to go and bring back the golden apples which the Hesperides, daughters of Atlas and Hesperos, kept in a garden at the western limit of the world, beyond the ocean. Like Hercules, Antaeus may not have been a real individual, but a symbol. His mission was to test the traveller to the Other World, as in the quest for the Grail.

Some symbolists and partisans of astrology will find it strange that I should seek a literal explanation of mythology where it seems that one can discern a clear correlation with the signs of the zodiac. I readily grant that there are sometimes correlations and even strong influences, but no matter how adventurous an attempt at historical reconstruction may be, its details cannot be based precisely on planetary fluctuations!

In the astrological view, chivalry, the Middle Ages, the Hundred Years' War, the rediscovery of America, the French Revolution, Napoleon, the American Civil War, the advent of Communism, and our present social conflicts are only earthly projections of the mechanism of the heavenly bodies. If so, to reconstruct history and foretell the future, one has only to study astrology. This has been done by various writers, but their complicated, tedious explanations, incomprehensible to anyone who knows little about astrology, have never been convincing.

Moreover it is reasonable and logical to believe that very ancient events can be transmitted through the centuries and preserved by initiates only if they are expressed literally, without changing 'one jot or tittle.' Even with that rigour, they are sometimes so radically deformed that they become unintelligible. Imagine a story systematically put into astrological symbolism: with ten contemporary authors writing in that way, there would be ten different versions and the ten authors would never reach agreement on them, since each would have his own method, key, system – and preconceptions!

To return to Hercules, he naturally emerged victorious from the test because he was an initiated hero. He continued on his way, killed the eagle that was devouring the liver of Prometheus the Atlantan (we still remain within our subject), and finally reached the Garden of the Hesperides. Mythology says that Nereus, son of Gaea and husband of the ocean nymph Doris (again the myth of the ocean), told Hercules how to go to the land of the Hesperides. He plucked the golden apples and took them away, but finally the wise Athena put them back where they had been, which is a strange conclusion for such an arduous expedition!

Were those golden apples actually oranges? That is what naïve commentators have claimed, but it is obvious that Hercules would never have gone so far away to get a kind of fruit that grows naturally in Greece and most neighbouring countries. No, they were apples, golden and therefore infinitely valuable, closely related to the apple that Eve plucked in Eden from the tree of the knowledge of good and evil.

The apple, which Cézanne believed he had synthesized in his painting, has a very elaborate exoteric meaning in Western tradition. It symbolizes the womb, love, woman, and knowledge, under the sign of eroticism (and not love, for love is only a static creation, whereas eroticism is enchancement and subtlety in creation). Cut in half, it curiously shows the female organs: at the centre is the vulva, concealing the ovaries, or black seeds; the lower part, rounded in the shape of the buttocks, has the mysterious and intriguing appearance of the female anus.

It is not by chance that Catholic peoples have identified

the apple (not named in the Bible; one would think of the fig instead!) as the forbidden fruit of the tree of sin, which Eve, tormented in her flesh and her imagination, gave to Adam, who was much less intelligent than she. It is thus not really to Adam that we owe the marvellous disobedience which generated birth, death, and consequently evolution. Eve is much more entitled than Adam to be regarded as the first intelligence of thinking mankind.

It was also an apple that Paris gave to Venus when she was newly born of the 'white foam' exuded into the vast, wet womb of the sea by Uranus's mutilated sex.

And the golden apples of the Hesperides explain the occult trajectory leading to intellectual knowledge from the plus and the minus; that is, by way of eroticism, which is the movement and intelligence of the universe.

I do not think that Cézanne, a wonderful painter-geometer but absolutely ignorant so far as love, women, and esotericism were concerned, was able to plumb the deep meaning of the apple. Through his bourgeois prudishness and multiple complexes, he painted his female bathers while watching a group of soldiers taking a dip in a stream. What would Renoir have thought of that?

In his Hesperides mission, Hercules was aided by the giant Atlas, and that brings us to another correlation. According to some traditions Atlas was the son of Oceanus, and according to others the son, like Prometheus the Atlantan, of the Titan Iapetus and the ocean nymph with the pretty feet. (Orejona, the Eve of Andes tradition, also had pretty feet.)

Prometheus had three brothers, one of whom was Atlas the Atlantan, who guarded the Garden of the Hesperides at the western limit of the world. After the revolt of the Titans, which 'shook the earth and the sky,' Prometheus, full of rancour against those who had exterminated his race, favoured men to the detriment of the gods.

In secret language we find here the Greek story of the submersion of Atlantis and the transmission of Atlantan knowledge to the people of our continent by Prometheus, initiator of the Egyptians and 'father of the human race after the Deluge.' This means that Prometheus can be

clearly identified with the Venusian Quetzalcoatl of the
Mayas and the Lucifer, friend of man, of Catholic mythology.

It is important to note that Prometheus is linked to the
planet Venus by his mother and his brother Atlas, and
that Lucifer bears the name of the planet (*lucis*, 'light,'
and *ferre*, 'to carry') that is the brightest in the sky.

Cukulcan, the civilizing Mexican hero, is also identical
with Prometheus, Lucifer, and especially Quetzalcoatl,
whose disappearance he imitated by going off one day
toward 'the direction in which the sun rises.'

Atlas was condemned to 'remain standing before the
Hesperides at the limits of the earth.' This brings us back
to the Atlantic Ocean, and we will be kept there by
Hesperos, son of Atlas and father of the Hesperides (who
were both the marvellous garden and its guardians).

Always Venus

Hesperos's genealogy leaves no doubt about the meaning intended by the ancients: he was the son of the planet
Venus and of Atlas the Atlantan, and brother of Phos-
phoros (another name for Lucifer, who himself represents
the planet Venus of the morning). Could the ancients
have expressed themselves more clearly?

For the Greeks, Hesperos was sometimes even 'the
most magnificent of the heavenly bodies that shine in the
heavenly vault.'

Correlations among Andes traditions, Greek mythology
and the meaning given to Tiahuanaco are too numerous,
precise, and explicit to be attributed to chance.

The planet Venus, the intervention of extraterrestrials,
the land of the Other World and America (Tiahuanaco
and Virginia) unquestionably play a preponderant part in
the primohistoric story that these 'myths' try to convey
to us.

In the land of the Other World, which heroes and
knights sought to reach from the dawn of mankind onward, were the golden apples of knowledge, and they
logically, inevitably lead us to the planet Venus and the
superior ancestors of Tiahuanaco-Virginia (the Green

Land). There, in the Green Land, was the earthly terminus of the pilgrimage to the source, and the Grail from which knights could draw authentic spiritual and physical strength.

Along with its mystical representation (the cup), the Middle Ages also sought the Other World that Columbus rediscovered without suspecting its real identity, since it finally became known as the New World, which was only relatively accurate. Columbus was not an initiate, but his monstrous lust for gold, which was the real motivation of his adventure, made him sense a glimmer of the truth. Furthermore he was well informed about America and knew that although he might not find the traditional 'golden apples' there, he could count on finding actual gold, which the Portuguese had been secretly bringing from Brazil Island since about 1480. It is possible that Templars or other initiates had encouraged and helped him for the purpose of checking the accuracy of their information.

The Grail, however, was strongly effective and has continued until our time to justify its reputation as a cup of abundance. The United States is the world's richest nation and the cup of abundance is now symbolized by the magic sign of the dollar.

But no matter how good a wine may be, it always has its dregs. Although the modern knights of the quest have remained faithful to the Grail, they have given it a more exoteric and less spiritual character, and from the cup as a principal they have passed directly to Thule, a centre of radiation.

The deteriorated secret

To understand the denaturation that the myth of Hyperborea has undergone in the twentieth century with the Thule Group, we must establish the fundamental meaning of the quest.

For the noble intentions, spiritual exaltation, and grandiose political and moral concerns of the ancient knights, modern adventurers have substituted a satanic dream of domination based on force, hatred, the spirit of

racial superiority, and the concept of a 'chosen people.'
The Hebrews once had that detestable ambition and
Joshua was to some extent a precursor of Attila, Gen-
ghis Khan, and Hitler.

After their defeat in 1918 a few Germans, initiated into
an infernal occultism and intoxicated with racist pre-
tesions, reorganized an Aryan society that became all
the more secret because it was outside the law in all parts
of the world. Their goal was to create a superior race;
that is, a privileged people who would subjugate and rule
the rest of the world.

In his successful book *The Myth of the Twentieth Century*, published in 1930, the talented writer Alfred Rosenberg stated the laws and philosophy of the Aryan champions. 'To rule the world,' he said, 'it is enough to have
pure blood.'

This new charter of the Aryan world was to be illustrated by rivers of blood, countless massacres, and
mountains of corpses.

Actually, however, Rosenberg had not invented anything. Identical ideas had been professed earlier by George
Grant, Gobineau, Houston Chamberlain, and, later, the
German Ludwig Wilset, in *Origin and Prehistory of the
Aryans.* And the French historian A. Pictet, in a work
titled *Migrations primitives des Aryas,* had announced
the advent of the master race: 'In an era before any historical record, lost in the mists of time, a race destined by
Providence to dominate the entire world grew little by
little in its primeval cradle, privileged above all others by
beauty of blood and gifts of intelligence.'

God, once again, had been involved in this adventure,
but the Thule Group kept him out of its dogma, no doubt
because three thousand years after Joshua it was becoming hard to make even fanatics believe that the Lord had
given preference to one race and authorized bloody
slaughter and genocide.

According to Duchinski the word 'Aryan' means
'noble,' 'illustrious,' and, by extension, 'owner.' The
homeland of the Aryans has been said to be the plateau of
Iran, but traditionally it was the region of the north pole;

that is, the land of the Hyperboreans. In Rosenberg's theory, the Hyperboreans, by a kind of psychic magic, had preserved the essential nature and transcendental character of the great ancestors.

The Thule Group was founded in 1910 by Professor Felix Niedner. Beginning in 1919, some outstanding adepts – Baron Ungern von Sterberg, Karl Haushofer, a disciple of Gurdjieff, the writer Dietrich Eckart – gave it a new impetus and an emblem: the swastika, symbol of evolution, the rotation of the stars around the pole, and the creation of fire among the Hindus. (The swastika is actually a universal sign found among all peoples. It is carved on a stone lamp in the Madeleine cave, the tablets of Glozal, the stones of Moulin Piat, and the prehistoric ramparts of Mississippi, and it appears in the inscription on the Newton Stone in Scotland.)

In his book *L'Europe païenne du vingtième siècle*, the historian Pierre Mariel writes that Dietrich Eckart was Adolf Hitler's initiator and brought him into the Thule Group in 1922.

Hitler was in great financial difficulties and may even have been a homeless vagrant, but he was consumed with ambition, rancour, and sincere, frenzied idealism. He was also somewhat clairvoyant; he served as a medium for the conspiracy, which became increasingly enveloped in the mists of a dubious occultism.

At the same time, similar movements were developing on the European continent. In London, Paris, Berlin, and Rome there were clandestine publications containing an odd mixture of anarchism, spiritualism, 'traditional research,' and eroticism.

In about 1920 the *Revue Baltique* appeared in France. It examined the problem of the direct descendants of the Hyperborean ancestors: the Lithuanians, whose writing has so many points in common with Sanskrit.

The magazine *Les Polaires* (Paris, 1921) had the ambition of resuscitating the old myth of Hyperborea, but this kind of writing flourished above all in Germany, with Niedner's *Altnordische Dichtung und Prosa*, Dietrich Eckhart's *Auf gut Deutsch*, and *Die Hanussen Zeitung*, published by the magician Eric Jan Van Hanussen, the man who is said to have replaced Hitler as the medium of the Thule Group, and who later became his semiofficial astrologer.

Hanussen

In the phenomenon of Aryanism we see the duality of the quest for the Grail: first, the Golden Sun and the knightly quest for knowledge; second, the Black Sun and the Thule Group's quest for political domination.

In copying certain ancient rites of the Hebrews, the Hitlerians no doubt wanted to create a confusion, but the fact is that Hitlerism is a psychopathic disorder which combines hysteria and outright insanity. Hanussen's entrance into the Thule Group gives frightening confirmation of this.

Herschel Steinschneider, born on June 2, 1889, in Vienna, was twenty-seven when, after having impregnated the niece of the rabbi of Lemberg, he decided he had better move elsewhere to avoid reprisals. In Zhitomir, Russia, he found a job in Signor Beltachini's little travelling circus. Under the pseudonym of Steno, he was a handyman at first, then was promoted to clown, sword swallower, and fortune-teller.

After World War I, in 1918, he was back in Vienna with a new identity. He was no longer Steno the fortune-teller or the young Jew Herschel Steinschneider, but a blond Aryan with sharp features and a mysterious, dominating gaze, and he bore an impressive name that suggested a Viking origin: he was Eric Jan Van Hanussen, a Danish nobleman.

A hundred mistresses in three months

He became a soothsayer in Austrian high society, making use of blackmail, corruption, and his extraordinary physical charm. The wives of the most eminent men in Vienna became his mistresses and betrayed their husbands' secrets to him, enabling him to make a veritable fortune by blackmail.

He is said to have had more than a hundred mistresses

in three months. Traces of some of them were found in a card catalogue:

Lilian, the 6th and 26th.
Maria, the 12th.
Marlene, the 20th.
Eva, the 7th, 14th and 21st.
Josepha, the 3rd and 23rd.

This list can be interpreted to mean that Maria and Marlene were of only slight interest to him, that Eva was rich, that Lilian and Josepha were satisfied to see him twice a month. . . .

In 1919 his fame was so great that he starred at the Apollo Theatre in Vienna, giving an exhibition of telepathy, clairvoyance, and hypnotism. In 1923 he was in a circus as a rival of Sigmund Breithart, the Austrian champion weightlifter. Then, after some extraordinary adventures, he settled in Berlin, where he directed the Palace of Occultism on the Lietzenburgerstrasse, and according to German newspapers he became 'the greatest clairvoyant of all time.'

He meets Hitler

One day in the house of the Nazi writer Hans Heinz Ewers, the apologist of Horst Wessel, a poet killed by the Communists, Hanussen was introduced to Hitler. The future master of the Reich immediately realized how he could make use of that intelligent, ambitious, and unscrupulous soothsayer. As for Hanussen, he was sure he could outwit that nervous, irritable and passionate little man who concocted grandiose plans and preached aggressive theories.

It was at this time, according to Pierre Mariel, that Hanussen joined the Thule Group. He also became Hitler's occult advisor and the prophet of the party and most Germans. Money flowed into his pockets and he had a spectacular sex life.

He published two magazines: *Dile Hanussen Zeitung*, which had a circulation of a hundred and fifty thousand

and sold for twenty marks, and *Die Andere Welt,* more specifically devoted to occultism. He carried on an intense propaganda campaign for the Hitlerian party, subsidized by the Thule Group, Count Helldorf, leader of the S. A., and even Prince August Wilhelm, whom he introduced to Hitler.

He had a luxurious apartment, a stable of race horses, a red Cadillac, and a white yacht, the *Ursel IV,* which flew his personal flag on the lake of Potsdam, and aboard which he liked to invite beautiful women for intimate gatherings that were a Prussian version of *la dolce vita.*

He tries to overthrow Hitler

Things began to go wrong in 1933, when the Nazi newspaper *Angriff* (Attack) published an incendiary article that contained these statements: 'Hanussen, that seer who belongs to the Party, is a charlatan and a swindler who has been in trouble with the police of Leitmeritz [which was true]. Furthermore, he is Jewish and his real name is Herschel Steinschneider.'

Hanussen succeeded in temporarily warding off the danger, but Goebbels was still determined to eliminate him because he suspected the amazing truth: the soothsayer was a spy.

He was certainly no model of virtue, but in spite of his sins, errors, and vices either he had remained faithful to his religion or, belatedly, he had realized the mysterious aims of the Thule Group.

The police began looking into the Jewish adventurer's past. In 1931, at the Prague Zionist Convention, he was said to have declared, 'I am a descendant of the miraculous rabbis of Prossnitz.' He had been married three times, always to Jewish women; one of the ceremonies had taken place on January 1, 1928, at the Ramburg synagogue in Czechoslovakia.

Frightened, Hanussen quickly went to a Protestant minister and officially converted to Christianity. The minister who baptized him was also the one who later conducted his funeral.

It was an important matter, so important that Hitler is

reported to have said, 'It's a dirty business; I would rather have lost three battles than to have it happen.'

The truth had not yet leaked out, however, at least not to the public. But Hanussen wanted to flee and carry out his secret mission: he, the famous astrologer, would denounce the evil of the Nazis' plans and prophesy that Hitler would soon die. The superstitious German people, he believed, would then withdraw their confidence in Hitler and the fate of the world would be changed.

First he attempted an impressive feat: on February 2, 1933, in the drawing room of the House of Occultism, before the writer Ewers, Prince August Wilhelm, son of the Kaiser, Count Helldorf, the actress Maria Portales, and the film star Siegfried Arno, he announced that the Reichstag was going to be set afire by the Communists. Four days later his prediction came true and his fame reached new heights.

On March 24, four hours before he planned to flee from the La Scala Theatre where he was giving a performance, Hanussen was arrested by the S. A. On March 29 his body was found at Treptow, in the Potsdam forest. He had been tied up with wire and shot four times. The Thule Group had 'liquidated' the man who wanted to overthrow Hitler.

The truth of this strange affair became known through the revelations of the Communist journalist Bruno Frei in *Berlin Am Morgen* and the later statements of John S. Goldsmith, an agent of the British Intelligence Service, and Pierre D., a former agent of the French Deuxième Bureau.

The Ordensbürger

Beginning in 1934, the Thule Group became a powerful secret society whose name was not to be known to the public or even candidates for admission. The latter, before their initiation, were given to understand that the organization was the secret Teutonic Order.

This secret order had, of course, no connection with the real Teutonic Order, which still exists in Portugal and the Netherlands. Under the name of the Knights of Poseidon (still the ideas of knighthood and the western ocean of

Atlantis), it has devoted itself to underseas adventure, as I described in *One Hundred Thousand Years of Man's Unknown History*, and is surely in communication with the Thule Group. It has been said that the Knights of Poseidon represent the temporal power of the German secret army, while the Thule Group is its spiritual power. This may be true.

The rites of the knights who had gone off in quest of the Grail were resuscitated in castles on the banks of the Rhine or in consecrated places. There, the elite of the young Nazis prepared themselves for heroic destinies, diving into rivers from high rocks, engaging in strenuous sports and dangerous warlike jousts. But it soon became obvious that this resurgence of chivalry was too romantic and outdated. It was replaced by the Ordensbürger, secret schools for training the new knights of the Grail, future members of the Thule Group.

There were three aspects of the education given in the Ordensbürger: military, similar to modern military and police academies; political; and occult, similar to the doctrines of Gurdjieff. (George Ivanovich Gurdjieff [1868-1949], born in the Caucasus, was both an adventurer and an enlightened occultist. Whether he was a miracle-worker, a secret agent, or simply a charlatan, he propagated in Europe and America strange, murky, and fascinating doctrines that troubled many weak minds. Perhaps he had a certain genius, but if so he was never able to express it in his books, which are unreadable, inane, and incomprehensible. He did, however, influence certain spiritualistic sects.)

In a Rhineland forest, amid tall firs, stands the white, impressive Vogelsang castle which was the Ordensbürg No. 1 of the Thule Group, with the main bureau of what would now be called psychological warfare.

The other Ordensbürger were located at Sonthofen in Bavaria, Krössinsee in Pomerania, and near the small town of Thule, in Westphalia, in the Werwelsburg Castle.

According to the historian Ray Petifrère, in *La Mystique de la croix gammé*, physical training involved two particularly savage tests:

1. The Tierkampf, in which the candidate had to fight barehanded for twelve minutes against mastiffs trained as attack dogs. The test could not be stopped unless the fighter's life was really in danger.

2. The Panzer test. The men lay in narrow individual trenches while tanks passed over them. Each of them was armed with a Panzerfaust, a kind of rudimentary bazooka. As soon as the tanks had passed, the men had to fire their rockets at almost point-blank range and theoretically destroy the tanks. Fatal accidents were common, but anyone unwilling to run the risk was dismissed from the Thule Group.

On the military level, members of the group were assigned to elite regiments and paramilitary organizations, but always in the upper echelons.

In our time, infiltration is particularly effective in paramilitary or sporting organizations; among deep-sea divers for example, where the practice of physical training is closely associated with technical knowledge that would have an unsuspected importance in case of war. The Knights of Poesidon, whose leaders are first-class divers, is the main activist section of the Thule Group.

Exercises in spirituality and mental concentration, which were the rule before 1940 and probably still are, were mingled with courses in the history of the Aryan people. Professors taught that the cradle of the white race in very remote times was Hyperborea, with its capital at Thule. They also inculcated hatred of the Jews who, they said, had unjustly taken over the title of the Chosen people, a title which rightly belonged to the Aryans and their most highly developed representatives, the Germans.

Racial exclusion was applied to Negroes and Gypsies, of course, but in 1940, bowing to political necessity, Hitler decreed that his Japanese allies were 'honorary Aryans.'

In Germany, however, the principle of pure-blooded race was so strictly observed that the government instituted Lebensborn ('fountains of life'), clinics for sterilization and reproduction in which artificial selection was practised.

The blood rite

The blood rite was one invariable feature of Satan worship that was found in the initiation of members of the Sonderkommandos, special formations in which each candidate for membership is said to have been required to perform, among other practices, the abominable 'cat rite,' which is directly connected with Satanic magic by bloodshed and horror. The candidate had to cut out both eyes of a living cat so deftly that the poor animal did not die.

Pierre Mariel reports the details of the test in his study of pagan Germany. Giving Dom Alois Mager as his reference, he states that the Nazi ideal consisted in identifying 'the three lusts of original sin' with the highest values of human genius. Hitler, says Dom Alois Mager, was 'Satan's medium.'

It is certain that magic had great influence on the leaders of the Thule Group, some of whom – Hitler, Rudolf Hess, Karl Haushofer – were genuine mediums, subject to trances and prophetic visions.

Consumed with occultism and devoted to the most primitive doctrines as well as the subtlest traditions, Hitler intended to govern the fate of Europe on the basis of the astrological data furnished by the pseudo-initiates of Lhasa. The influence of those picturesque men was unquestionable but equivocal: they led the gullible Hitler along the path to disaster not by genuine magic, which they were incapable of performing, but by bad advice and betrayals.

Thule and the Agartha

The lamas traditionally defended their race and a plan of domination that was in direct rivalry with that of the Germans.

The Tibetans are of unknown origin and speak a unique language. Like the natives of the Andes, they live at an altitude of more than twelve thousand feet on high plateaus strewn with salt-water lakes.

A legend – but is it a legend? – says that under the Himalayas, in the vicinity of Shambalha and Chigatze, lies the vast underground kingdom of the Master of the World. This kingdom, this Oriental magic centre, is named the Agartha. It is the opposite pole of the Occidental magic centre of Hyperborea, of which Hitler dreamed of being the Imperator.

We can now understand the strange collusion that may have existed between, on the one hand, Hitler and the Thule Group, an expression of the Hyperborean myth and the white race; and, on the other Gurdjieff (or so it is presumed) and the Chigatze Group, an expression of the Agartha and the *unknown* race represented by the Tibetans.

World War II was, we may hope, the last attempt at domination based on the myth of Hyperborea and the Grail, a myth that has been degraded in its principle and its rites by subjection to an odious political project.

Has the Thule Group persisted in that insane project? We may doubt it, if we believe in the good faith of the leader of the Knights of Poseidon who stated in 1964, 'Hitler sent the elite of Hyperborean youth to die on the plains of Russia. Because of that, he was the greatest criminal of the century.'

Chapter 15

THE VISION OF EZEKIEL

Twenty-six centuries ago, 'on the fifth day of the fourth month in the thirtieth year,' the prophet Ezekiel, in captivity in Babylon on the bank of the river Kebar, at a place that appears to have been about a hundred miles southeast of the present city of Bagdad, had what he called a vision.

Was that vision given to him by God, as theologians believe? Was it fictitious? Or did it represent a real experience? No one would venture to affirm the reality of all the events related, but the fact remains that Ezekiel's description of the celestial vehicle he saw is amazing because of its precise, unusual details and its correlation with a phenomenon known in our time as 'flying saucers.' Some commentators maintain that the prophet witnessed the landing of an interstellar spacecraft and that he was taught by its occupants.

Ezekiel (whose name means 'God makes strong' in Hebrew) was the third and strangest of the great prophets. He lived in the sixth century B.C., and during his captivity in Babylon he received from God the gift of prophecy.

The forty-eight chapters of his book, which is placed in the Bible between Lamentations and Daniel, are a series of imprecations and stories that are sometimes so scabrous, even though they are based on a great moral concern, that for a time they were forbidden to young Hebrews and are still not recommended for young Christian girls.

There is, of course, a hidden meaning in Ezekiel's vision and its bizarre details; I even believe that it contains the golden key which can open the inviolate tabernacle of the Cabala. I will therefore devote great attention to trying to penetrate the mystery and analyse the deep meaning of images.

The celestial vehicle lands

Here is the fourth verse of the first chapter of Ezekiel: 'I saw a storm wind coming from the north, a vast cloud with flashes of fire and brilliant light about it; and within was a radiance like brass, glowing in the heart of the flames.'

In my interpretation, Ezekiel's celestial vehicle or 'cloud' was, as he himself acknowledges, a flying machine. It is important to note that clouds are numerous in Biblical history: they precede or transport the Lord, guide the Hebrews, take Noah away to save him from the Deluge, and convey Him who dictates the Law. Moses in particular often has dealings with the Lord and his cloud; and, each time he does, the people of Israel must remain at a distance: they may hear 'the glory of the Lord' (the sound of the motor), *but they must not see!*

Moreover, the cloud comes from the north, the direction of Hyperborea. I see this only as a clue, but it has its importance.

Verses 5-8: 'In the fire was the semblance of four living creatures in human form. Each had four faces and each four wings; their legs were straight, and their hooves were like the hooves of a calf, glittering like a disc of bronze. Under the wings on each of the four sides were human hands; all four creatures had faces and wings.'

(Compare this with John's 'vision' in Revelation 1:15: 'His feet gleamed like burnished brass refined in a furnace, and his voice was like the sound of rushng waters.' Was this a reminiscence of the celestial vehicle?)

Ezekiel then describes the 'creatures' who came out of the flying machine. His description here makes them seem to be something like animals with human faces, but they are actually cherubim, because he uses that name for them in Chapter 10. He uses it repeatedly, in fact, and also continues to call them creatures, without discrimination; and further on in his story he calls them men.

The Biblical cherubim were not immaterial beings similar to angels, as is commonly believed; they were physical beings that fulfilled more or less the same functions as the sphinx of the Egyptians, the *anka* of the Arabs, and the *simurg* of the Persians. They were half human and half animal. Their traditional mission among the Hebrews was to guard paradise, and among the Greeks it was to keep watch over the golden apples of the Garden of the Hesperides. If we identify the cherubim as astronauts, we thus see them as guardians of the land of the Hyperboreans.

It was traditionally believed that the majesty of God was manifested between two cherubim, which explains the carvings of them on the Ark of the Covenant and the walls of the Temple of Solomon.

Exodus and I Kings tell us that the cherubim had human heads and hands.

All this is interesting and corresponds plausibly to the idea that primitive people might form of astronauts wearing space suits like those carved on the Puerta del Sol at Tiahuanaco, and also like the flight suits of our modern jet pilots.

Cherubim and helicopters

I will discuss the four faces later, but for the moment I will point out that while Ezekiel attributes only two hands to each 'creature,' he gives each of them four wings, which may correspond to the rotors of a helicopter.

Chapter 1, Verse 9: 'Their wings touched one another. they did not turn as they moved; each creature went straight forward.'

I do not claim, of course, that this description is rigorously accurate, because it was no doubt deteriorated by time and repeated copying; I do understand from it, however, that the cherubim each had a kind of individual helicopter.

Verse 10: 'Their faces were like this: all four had the face of a man and the face of a lion on the right, on the left the face of an ox and the face of an eagle.'

Chapter 10, Verse 14: 'Each had four faces: the first was that of cherub, the second that of a man, the third that of a lion, and the fourth that of an eagle.'

Chapter 1, Verses 13-14: 'The appearance of the creatures was as if fire from burning coals or torches were darting to and fro among them; the fire was radiant, and out of the fire came lightning. And the living creatures went out and in like rays of light.'

François Couten, one of the best French UFO specialists, sees this as an image of four men moving through the
air by means of individual helicopters, without their
bodies turning at the same time as the rotors.

These men were wearing flight suits or space suits
whose surface had a metallic appearance and reflected the
light of flames escaping from jets. As for their resemblance
to a bull, an eagle, or a lion, it may have been caused by
the shape of a helmet, a mask, a microphone, and so on.

The flying wheels

Ezekiel goes on to describe a strange flying machine,
Chapter 1, Verses 15-18: 'As I looked at the living creatures, I saw wheels on the ground, one beside each of the
four. The wheels sparkled like topaz, and they were all
alike; in form and working they were like a wheel inside a
wheel, and when they moved in any of the four directions
they never swerved in their course. All four had hubs
and each hub had a projection which had the power of
sight, and the rims of the wheels were full of eyes all
round.'

My interpretation is that there were four wheels
superimposed on each other like a pile of tyres. The machine was enormous, which explains why its occupants
were able to come out of it with their individual
helicopters, and it had rows of portholes on its quadruple
hull.

Verses 19-20: 'When the living creatures moved, the
wheels moved beside them; when the creatures rose from
the ground, the wheels rose; they moved in whatever
direction the spirit would go; and the wheels rose together with them, for the spirit of the living creatures
was in the wheels.'

'Ezekiel's wheel,' writes François Couton, 'is an exact
description of the flying craft that have been observed or
photographed so often in recent years by witnesses in all
countries. Notice that the prophet never mentions the
wheels and the wings at the same time. which shows that
they are two different things.'

Verse 22: 'Above the heads of the living creatures was,

as it were, a vault glittering like a sheet of ice, awe-inspiring, stretched over their heads above them.'

Does this refer to transparent helmets like those of twentieth-century astronauts?

Verse 24: 'I heard, too, the noise of their wings; when they moved it was like the noise of a great torrent or of a cloud-burst, like the noise of a crowd or of an armed camp; when they halted their wings dropped.'

The similarity to a helicopter whose rotors make a great noise when they turn, then drop when the motor stops, is too striking to leave any doubt.

In Chapter 8 Ezekiel describes a second vision, but this time the big machine with portholes is not there.

Verse 2: 'I saw what looked like a man. He seemed to be all fire from the waist down and to shine and glitter like brass from the waist up.'

We recognize here either an isolated astronaut wearing a 'rocket belt' or a parachutist who speaks to the idolaters of Jerusalem in Chapter 9, Verses 1-2: 'A loud voice rang in my ears: "Here they come, those appointed to punish the city, each carrying his weapon of destruction." Then I saw six men [he no longer calls them cherubim or creatures, having become familiar with the vision] approaching from the road that leads to the upper northern gate, each carrying a battle-axe. . . .'

It was a punitive expedition, for, says Ezekiel, sinners thought that the Lord had forsaken the country (that the Hyperboreans had left?) and the astronauts went into the city and killed many people who worshipped the rising sun.

Here, perhaps, is a key to the mystery: it is not toward the rising sun that God should be worshipped, but toward the west, or toward the north where the 'image of his glory is found.

A time gap

That vision, those vehicles, and those cherubim may give rise to many comments, but in my opinion the idea of a flying machine and men wearing 'rocket belts' is the only reasonable interpretation.

If a modern shepherd were to witness such a fantastic

event, would he not describe it in essentially the same terms as the Hebrew prophet?

If we abandon the concept of divine intervention and dare to accept the hypothesis that Hyperborean astronauts came to Babylonia, we are still left with the problem of explaining what they were doing there.

Can we believe in the existence of flying saucers six centuries before Christ? Whether we consider that time or our own, the data remain the same and only pose the question of 'extraterrestrialism': is it plausible or not?

For Russian and American astronauts and their four hundred million fellow citizens, for the technicians, scientists, and workmen of Peenemünde (Germany), Baikonur (U.S.S.R.), and Cape Kennedy, the answer is categorical: space travel has been theoretically possible since time immemorial.

It seems incredible to me that Ezekiel should have been able to imagine, almost invent, the helicopter and the jet-propelled flying machine. Was it a vision, a premonition, divine inspiration? We might think so if the miracle of the celestial vehicle had been followed by prophecies or events of exceptional magnitude. But what does it lead to? Commonplace curses against those unwilling to believe in prophecies, the inevitable ruin of Jerusalem, Tyr, and Egypt, the truth of God's word, and so on. In short, the naïve and hackneyed arsenal of all Biblical prophecies. It is hard to understand why the story should 'fizzle out' that way after the miraculous appearance of astronauts who burst into the streets of Jerusalem with weapons in their hands.

Did Ezekiel see the flying machines in physical reality? It is unlikely.

I can conceive of only two explanations: either Ezekiel knew the story of extraterrestrials from oral tradition and it tormented him for months and years until he caused his vision, or else he did not live in the sixth century before Christ, but farther back in the past, in the time when the spacecraft of the Hyperboreans still streaked across the sky.

However, since the time gap is only a matter of a few

centuries, we cannot be too cautious, especially since Ezekiel's book, even assuming that he actually wrote it himself, has been considerably altered, perhaps to the point of making it say the opposite of the original version or of the truth.

For example, when we read in Ezekiel 10:4 that 'the temple was filled with the cloud, while the radiance of the glory of the Lord filled the court,' is it not possible to conjecture that this may originally have been a description of astronauts exploding a bomb in the temple? And perhaps the noise of the rotors was transmuted into a great rustle of wings: 'The sound of the wings of the cherubim could be heard as far as the outer court, as loud as if God Almighty were speaking.' (Ezekiel 10:5).

We have seen that the 'creatures' of the vision were later called 'cherubim,' and finally 'men.'

A glimmer from the Cabala

We also read that God ordered Ezekiel to eat a book, and then to make bread in this unappetizing way (4:12): 'You are to eat your bread baked like barley cakes, using human dung as fuel,' though later (4:15) the Lord changed the order to some extent: 'So he allowed me to use cow-dung instead of human dung to bake my bread.'

The churchmen assembled in Rome in 1964 assured us that the Bible was written under God's inspiration and is therefore necessarily free of error, but it is hard for me to accept such an absurd passage as the one above, even if it is given a symbolic meaning.

In my analysis, I can give credence only to sensible and *gratuitous* stories; that is, stories which can be neither a help nor a hindrance to the Hebrews and the Christians.

To sum up, only one event in Ezekiel seems certain, though we cannot say precisely when it happened: the landing of the celestial vehicle. This may mean that Ezekiel only gave his own version of the very old myth of angels coming down to the earth, as he had learned it from the Maasseh Merkabad of the Cabala or the *Book of Enoch*.

The secret of the Book of Enoch

It seems to me that we are here approaching the source of the mystery or the great myth. The Cabala (the Zohar) tells us that the *Book of Enoch* is older than any other document of antiquity.

'The Holy One, blessed be he,' we read in it, 'took Enoch from this world to serve him, according to what is written. For God took him. Then was delivered the volume that is called the *Book of Enoch*. At the time when God took him, he showed him all the mysteries on high; he showed him the tree of life, in the midst of paradise, with its leaves and branches [knowledge and its different disciplines?]. And we see all that in his book.'

In the Slavic text of the *Book of the Secrets of Enoch* is the first known description of the 'angels' who came down from the sky to seduce the daughters of men. The description of these 'angels' has an obvious correlation with that of Ezekiel's cherubim and with most visions of saints through the centuries.

It is important to note that in this Slavic text Enoch does not speak of angels or saints, but of *men*: 'Two men appeared to me, very tall, as I have never seen men on earth; their faces were like the sun, which shunned their eyes glowing like lighted lamps; fire came from their mouths, and their garments were a spray of foam, and their arms were like golden kings at the head of my bed.'

This recalls Ezekiel 1:13: 'The appearance of the creatures was as if fire from burning coals or torches were darting to and fro among them; the fire was radiant, and out of the fire came lightning.'

The astronauts' clothes are described as 'a spray of foam,' which may refer to magnetic space suits, and the 'golden wings' may be helicopter rotors.

In 1224 Francis of Assisi, who had then withdrawn to Mount Alverno in the Appenines, had a similar vision: he saw a seraph (luminous angel) coming down from heaven with six wings of fire, and between the wings was the figure of a crucified man.

In the episcopal palace of Assisi, Francis had already

seen 'a chariot of fire on which was a globe of light as re-
splendid as the sun.'

Saint Francis of Assisi surely had a hallucination (he
was subject to them), and the same may have been true of
Ezekiel, but the chariots of fire of Elijah, Moses, and
Enoch were probably physical realities, as were the men
equipped with mechanical wings.

The identity of the latter is clear in Chapter 16 of the
Book of Enoch, where Enoch, having come as a delegate
to the Lord (the leader of the astronauts?), hears judgment passed on the rebels of Armenia:

'Tell those celestial intelligences, "You have had the
sky as a dwelling, but the secrets from on high have not
been revealed to you; however, you have known a secret
of iniquity. And in the impulses of your hearts you have
imparted it to women, and you have thereby multiplied
evil on the face of the earth." Also tell them, "You will
never obtain grace, and you will never receive peace." '

Interpreted in a modern, rational manner, the meaning
of these texts becomes extremely clear and fills in the gap
in the Bible with regard to the punishment we know the
Deluge to have been: the astronauts had taught the secrets of iniquity to earthly women. It was thus by having
revealed and practiced magic that our ancestors jeopard-
ized the evolution of mankind and the earth.

Did the oral Cabala relate these primordial truths? Did
the Maasseh Merkabad transmit them through the story
that misled Avicenna, Lully, Paracelsus, and all Cabalists
and false initiates? That is what we will try to discover.

Chapter 16

THE CABALA

While traditionalists consider it probable that additions and distortions have been introduced into ancient writings for a political and religious purpose, they consider it equally probable that authentic manuscripts and true accounts of the genesis of the world have been preserved in at least three sanctuaries: the secret Vatican library to which even the pope does not have access; a secret place (said to be in Spain) known only to a few initiated rabbis; and in Morocco, where precious originals are the property of Moslem leaders who are fiercely opposed to making them public.

In 1887 Sultan Abdul Hamid sent the learned Ibn At Talamid to Spain with orders to examine and, if possible, bring back certain manuscripts left by the Arabs at the time of their departure in the fifteenth century. Other delegations later tried to carry out the mission, notably at Granada, Cordoba, and Seville. The manuscripts must have had an inestimable value to motivate such concern.

It is likely that other documents, equally valuable and unknown, are secretly kept in Indian and Tibetan monasteries, and we may wonder if they will ever be made public.

It therefore seems logical to assume that fragments of truth and authentic accounts can be known only through governmental archaeological excavations or apocryphal writings, especially those which, like the *Book of Enoch*, have partially escaped the censorship of sectarian conspirators.

The Cabala of the Jews, however, with all its enigmas, symbols, and occultism, is regarded as containing revelations of transcendent truths, the mystery of primohistoric peoples and their knowledge.

The Cabala (from the Hebrew *qabbalah*, 'received doctrine,' 'tradition') is said to have been taught to Adam, at God's command, by Raziel, the Angel of Mystery, when Adam was driven out of the earthly paradise.

Rationalists, of course, give no credence to what they consider to be a fable imagined by mystical minds. Cabalists, on the other hand, believe they can explain the secrets of the universe by means of this magic book and that its teachings, foreign to our earthly science, also explain the 'Mysterious Unknown': the secret power of the human self, premonitions, clairvoyance, levitation, and so on.

These teachings have their own symbols, signs, figures, mathematics – in short, a writing that would be translated by initiates if they had the key to the system. For centuries, generations of occultists have sought that dangerous key. Most of them have sunk into black magic and alchemy, and those who have claimed to have a solution to the problem have never proved it.

My ambition is not to open the Forbidden Door, especially since I do not believe that the written version of the Cabala has the extraordinary importance usually attributed to it, but to elucidate a few enigmas by applying certain Cabalistic data to my view of human primohistory.

The heavenly chariot

Primarily, the Cabala is divided into two extremely revealing branches:

1. The Maasseh Bereshit, or story of genesis, summarized in the Sefer Jerisah.

2. The Maasseh Merkabad, or story of the heavenly chariot, summarized in the Zohar.

(According to some historians the history of the heavenly chariot, or Zohar, was written and perhaps imagined in the thirteenth century by Moses de León. We must bear in mind that the original manuscripts of the Cabala, the Talmud, the Bible, etc., either no longer exist or never existed at all. In the best of cases, we have only second-hand or third-hand retranscriptions. This means that the original text has more or less disappeared.)

The two main branches of the Cabala bring us to the heart of the mystery, especially when we realize that the number-one initiator or scribe of that Cabala was an angel whose name phonetically resembles those of astronauts mentioned in the *Book of Enoch* – and, says tradition, he was an Angel of Mystery.

The story of the 'heavenly chariot' is said to be several thousand years older than that of the mysterious vehicle in Ezekiel's vision, but both stories probably concern the same vehicle: a spacecraft, in my view.

The Maasseh Merkabad has always been regarded as the holiest and most important branch of the Cabala. Rabbis maintained that it must be divulged only to one disciple at a time, with stringent precautions and restrictions. Two thousand years ago only the greatest Jewish initiates could speak of it, and only among themselves and in the utmost secrecy. Then the oral tradition was set down in writing and the 'story of the heavenly chariot' is now condensed in the Zohar.

The fact is, however, that the written story resembles the original only in its title, because everything concerning the mysterious vehicle, including its origin, its occupants, and their superior knowledge, was censored by the rabbis, so that the real Cabala, as in ancient times, is still known only to initiates and is discussed only orally.

I may be reproached for giving too literal a meaning to 'the story of the heavenly chariot,' but it must be noted that all sacred writings have literal meanings: the Bible, 'the book'; the Talmud, 'instruction'; the Torah, 'law'; the Zohar, 'light'; and so on. Furthermore my interpretation seems much more profound to me than the symbolic explanation.

The Zohar is the universal code of the Cabala and also of the Bible, which cannot be interpreted without it. We get an idea of the bewildering machination concocted by the ancient initiates when we know that to understand the Bible one must be enlightened by the Zohar, and to understand the Zohar one must be enlightened by compilations known as 'little keys,' the most famous and least comprehensible of which is the *Little Keys of Solomon*.

And that is not all. The Zohar can be explained only by using a set of initiatic keys: *Temurah* (permutation), *notarikon* (sign), and *gematria* (geometry). This breaks down into three operations:

1. Changing the value of words by replacing the first letter with the last (*temurah*).

2. Studying each letter separately, the whole word being considered as a sentence; taking the first and last letter of each word of a verse and forming a new one which reveals the mystic meaning (*notarikon*).

3. Seeking the meaning of each word by replacing its letters with the numbers corresponding to them, as determined by their position in the Hebrew alphabet (*gematria*).

Hence the essential rule of Talmudists and Cabalists that 'not one jot or tittle' of the original text must be changed; if a single word is omitted, altered, or replaced, the whole text becomes incomprehensible.

Three postulates govern the metaphysic of the Zohar:

1. Everything has a mystic name which forces its bearer to obey when it is spoken.

2. It is impossible to conceive of God, since he is not measurable, limited, localized, localizable, etc.

3. There is another universe with multiple dimensions, unknown to our visible universe and containing superior forces, where images of all pre-existing things are hidden behind the cosmic veil.

The principle of the mystic name (which is also found in the story of the Grail) indicates the supreme power of the Word in relation to magic knowledge belonging to a Mysterious Unknown.

Only the high priest of Israel – and here we think of Moses and Melchizedek – knew the true pronunciation of the Tetragrammaton, or sacred name, which was written with the four letters YHWH (Yahweh).

The principle of an unknown and inconceivable God sheds singular light on the Bible and gives us a key for elucidating its most important points.

It is obvious that according to this postulate *God cannot manifest himself to men, or be seen, or even give orders.* But in that case, who spoke to Moses, whom did the great patriarch meet 'face to face' on Mount Sinai?

My position is firm on this point: Moses met 'demi-gods,' those superior men whom I have identified as extraterrestrials and who were known by Enoch, Noah, and Abraham.

Face to face with God

Moses's encounters with the Lord are very strange and conceal a reality which is, of course, very different from the orthodox concept.

'The Lord said to Moses, "I am now coming to you in a thick cloud, so that I may speak to you in the hearing of the people, and their faith in you may never fail." Moses told the Lord what the people had said, and the Lord said to him, "Go to the people and hallow them today and tomorrow and make them wash their clothes." ' (Exodus 19:9-10.)

I interpret this to mean that the Lord, that is, the extraterrestrial initiator, intended to land his spacecraft in concealment; and the order to make the people wash their clothes suggests a kind of light radiation whose effects could be avoided in this way.

This hypothesis is strengthened by the rest of God's instructions to Moses: 'You must put barriers round the mountain and say, "Take care not to go up the mountain or even to touch the edge of it." Any man who touches the mountain must be put to death. No hand shall touch him; he shall be stoned or shot dead: neither beast nor man may live.' (Exodus 19:12-13.)

My intention is not to draw wild interpretations from the Lord's words, but to give them a reasonable explanation. The first thing which appears is that it was *mortally dangerous* to approach the top of Mount Sinai, exactly as if there were a risk of exposure to radiation. Moses escaped its effects by means of precautions or treatments that are not explained to us, but the visitors must have provided them only for him.

Not being immunized, the people had to remain outside the contaminated area. Any person or animal that entered it would become a carrier of radiation and would have to be killed. And an important precaution is specified: the

contaminated person or animal had to be killed from a
distance, untouched by anyone, by means of stones or
arrows.

However strongly one may be biased against this interpretation, it would be hard to substitute a more plausible
explanation for it, especially since the Lord expressly re-
peats his mysterious order later (Exodus 24:1-2):'Then
he said to Moses, "Come up to the Lord, you and Aaron,
Nadab and Abihu, and seventy of the elders of Israel.
While you are still at a distance, you are to bow down;
and then Moses shall approach the Lord by himself, but
not the others. The people may not go up with him at
all." '

Here we come to a surprising instance of the inconsis-
tency of the Bible. In the passage above, Moses is told to
go up alone and the people are told to stay behind. Then
the 'face-to-face' dialogue takes place, solely between
God and Moses. The people could not hear what was said,
as Moses states in Deuteronomy 5:5: 'I stood between
the Lord and you at that time to report the words of the
Lord; for you were afraid of the fire and did not go up the
mountain.' This contradicts the earlier passage: the people remained behind not because God had ordered them
to do so, but because they were afraid.

Earlier, after having solemnly declared in Deuteronomy
4:2, 'You must not add anything to my charge, nor take
anything away from it,' Moses gives what is obviously an
altered version of the scene on Mount Sinai, since he
implies that the Hebrews heard God's words directly
(4:10): 'You must never forget that day when you stood
before the Lord your God at Horeb, and the Lord said to
me, "Assemble the people before me; I will make them
hear my words and they shall learn to fear me all their
lives on earth, and they shall teach their sons to do so." '
Then (5:22): 'These Commandments the Lord spoke in
a great voice to your whole assembly on the mountain.'

It would be good to know what is the truth here and
what is not. Did the people hear or not? Did they stay
away from Mount Sinai because they were afraid or

because they had been ordered to do so? Did God speak to all of them or only to Moses?

In any case, God's insistence in Exodus that the people must not come near the peak of Mount Sinai is strikingly interesting.

The Lord's glory (the cloud, which I believe to have been a spacecraft) shone on Sinai like fire – or like a hull of polished metal.

My thesis of radiation obliges me to think that the astronauts themselves were strongly irradiated. There must have been a compelling reason for this; perhaps it will become clear to us in the near future, when we too have travelled to other planets.

After his conversation with the Lord, Moses's face was radiant, and each time he encountered him in the taber-nacle he put a veil over his face. This may have been a way of protecting himself by insulation.

At this point it is interesting to make a comparison with the story of the destruction of Sodom and Gomor-rah a few centuries earlier: when the 'angels' who had come to announce the divine punishment were about to be mistreated by the men of Sodom, they struck them blind (Genesis 19:11).

Just before the destruction took place, Lot was told not to look back, but his wife died because she disobeyed the order, and when Abraham looked down toward where Sodom and Gomorrah had been (Genesis 19:28), 'he saw thick smoke rising high from the earth like the smoke of a lime-kiln,' no doubt with the mushroom shape of the cloud that rose above Hiroshima and Bikini!

All this can be explained only in the light of the idea of extraterrestrials who knew the secret of atomic fission; and furthermore, if God is not conceivable, as the Cabala says, we must assume an intervention by human beings if we are to account for the destruction described.

The Master of Mystery

The Cabalistic doctrine of the powers of the inner self gives a first impression of crude empiricism, yet it also contains some surprising scientific data rather close to Falinski's theory of parallel universes.

In the Maasseh Bereshit, the first man is created simultaneously in two different places, or, more likely, in two parallel worlds. And the whole discussion of angels in the Cabala accustoms us to moving from our world to a world of subtler entities capable of working miracles.

If a Cabalist knows the magic of names and the Word, he can call on the forces of the invisible, and he himself can operate in a universe outside of ours. One who knows the secret, who possesses the key, is a Baal ha Sod: a Master of Mystery.

Certain passages in the Zohar, hermetic but relatively transparent, may lead to the initial source of knowledge. The first verse of the first chapter says that 'the Book of Mystery describes the balance of the Scales. . . . Her skin is of ether, she is clear and closed. . . . Her hair is like pure wool. . . . The world will last six thousand years.'

This is an explanation of the cycle of our time, with an obscure beginning and a clearly formulated end: barring atomic or other man-made catastrophes, the next end of the world will occur in about the year 3500.

Translation problems

The Cabala presents greater difficulties in translation than the Bible, the Talmud, the Popul Vuh, and the Vedas. These difficulties are, in fact, all but insurmountable. Even the main outlines of the Cabala are hard to discern in that skilfully contrived confusion, which was meant to be penetrated only by those entitled to do so.

For it was out of the question to say clearly that men had come to Earth from another planet; that Moses was not a Hebrew; that the religion he established was Egyptian, like the rite of circumcision. Until the first century of our era, the extraterrestrials took pains to secure descendants of their race so that there would be a kind of lineage of initiates. But although the Jews were their specifically designated heirs, they tried to obliterate all traces of their superior ancestors. Alterations and

additions were made in sacred and apocryphal writings, as
well as other ancient texts, to conceal those embarrassing
facts.

To preserve its integrity through the centuries, however, the marvellous oral truth had to be transmitted by
rabbis under the obligation never to change 'one jot or
tittle' of the traditional text.

Unfortunately it is hard to believe that the truth has remained intact down to our own time. How much of it is
now left? Did the custodians of the Great Secret fail in
their task?

In the Zohar, transition from spoken to written transmission created a situation that can be illustrated with
two examples. In the first chapter there are these interpretations of a single verse: first, the primeval kings died
for lack of food; second, the primeval kings died and their
crowns were not found.

And in that same chapter, here are two interpretations
of the fifteenth verse. Pauly gives its meaning as follows:
'Before all things, the King permitted the transformation
of the void into a transparent ether, an imponderable
fluid like the light of a phosphorescent body.' Paul Vul-
liaud's version: 'In the beginning, the will of the King
sculpted the sculptures in the light on high, the glittering
lamp, and there emanated in the midst of the Secret of
Secrets, from the Head of the Infinite, smoke in formless
matter fixed by a ring that was not white, or black, or red,
or green, or any colour.'

All you have to do is to decide which version is correct,
then unlock it with the keys of *temurah, notarikon*, and
gematria!

History is an enigmatic conflict among the past, the
future, and the present – and the interpretations given to
texts.

Marrying a nymph

Despite its deceptive but bewitching mystery, the
Cabala would have been of no more interest than any
apocryphal work if alchemists and sorcerers had not
claimed to find the core of their magic arts in it.

It abounds in angels and wondrous creatures: water sprites, nymphs, gnomes, 'guardians of treasures, surface mines and precious stones,' salamanders living in fire, sylphs, and so on.

A nymph becomes immortal if she succeeds in marrying a wise man; a gnome acquires the same privilege with a mortal woman. All great men are born of these unions, which God willed on the first day of creation.

Do you want to gain domination over salamanders? 'You have only to concentrate the fire of the world by concave mirrors in a glass globe, and this is the artifice religiously concealed by the ancients and discovered by the divine Theophrastus. Inside the globe is formed a solar powder which is very effective for carrying out your plan.'

How to attract sylphs, nymphs, or gnomes: 'You have only to close a glass full of air, surrounded by water, leave it exposed to the sun for a month, then separate the elements according to science. It is a marvellous magnet for attracting nymphs.'

All Cabalistic incantations favouring alchemists begin with the sacred word *Agla*, composed of the first letters of four Hebrew words: *Atah, Gabor, Leolam, Adonai* ('You are powerful and eternal, Lord').

Rationalists have always said – with many valid reasons, it must be admitted – that the Cabala is a mass of nonsense. This is partially true, since the original substance of the doctrine has been greatly diluted in extremely dubious formulations, but now and then a pure particle of that substance shines through.

In the face of these interpretations and mysteries, however, one must decide either to reject everything or to try to find a guiding thread in that diabolical labyrinth. Occultists have chosen the second course, and the Zohar has therefore become a basic text for alchemists, magicians, and sorcerers.

III

THE MYSTERIOUS UNKNOWN

Chapter 17

THE MAGIC BOOK OF SCOT THE WIZARD

Since the survival of the tradition depended on memory, initiates were required to have almost miraculous intellectual faculties. Levitation, the creative power of the Word, and even the resurrection of the dead were based on teachings transmitted after initiatic tests. To write the incantations and formulas was to *betray*.

Modern sciences, however, such as atomic physics and astronomy, can be expressed only with a vast range of letters, figures, and operations. Calculating in the infinitely small and the infinitely great became increasingly laborious until finally it approached practical impossibility, and that was what motivated the development of computers. These machines, electronic calculating robots, can now perform millions of operations in a few seconds, which shows the dizzying complexity around which our civilization is oriented.

According to Cabalists, knowledge could be acquired by much simpler psychic and intellectual processes, but rationalistic scientists deny the existence of that mystery.

Without drawing on the familiar arsenal of occultism – radiesthesia, clairvoyance, divination – in which we might find manifestations that escape all scientific explanation, it is better to take examples from among certain phenomena in which the Mysterious Unknown is convincingly substituted for the prodigious calculations of electronic machines.

Mysterious knowledge

In studying the migrations of swallows and wild geese, ornithologists and biologists, such as the German Gustav Kramer and the Englishman Matthews, have demonstrated that they constantly take their bearings in relation to the sun, the North Star, and the moon, and perhaps also by taking account of winds, climates, terrestrial magnetism, and universal gravitation. Since the sources of light that seem to be their main guides are always in motion, they must take their position continually.

Matthews has calculated the successive courses of a migrating bird and concluded that, considering its speed, human beings would need a computer to duplicate its navigational feat. The birds, however, do very well without computers. Calculations of drift, flight speed, and the motion of heavenly bodies are automatically registered, corrected, and synchronized by their small brains, almost instantaneously and with mathematical precision.

Animals have information, senses, or abilities which, as in the Cabala, substitute a mysterious knowledge for that of men. The Mysterious Unknown, even if it is only an experimental science that is still unknown, is therefore not a myth.

The poor monk Amon

The machine obeys man, but man does not yet know how to make use of the possibilities, even more prodigious than those of computers, that lie within his psychic subconscious.

A Near Eastern tradition illustrates this idea of our strange powers.

In a Tabennite monastery Brother Amon prayed, meditated, and tried to reach the summit of God's perfection by total renunciation of his coarse nature. But his deep humility made him painfully uncertain of the merit of his feelings, and if he had been asked to name the unworthiest man in all creation, he would sincerely have named himself.

Tormented by this sense of inferiority, Brother Amon went one morning to the abbot and dared to make a request of him: 'I am not worthy of singing in the chapel with my brothers: my voice is harsh and rough, and cannot be pleasing to the Lord. I beg you to make me the gatekeeper of the monastery, though even that will be too exalted a post for my humble abilities.'

The abbot was surprised to hear this from a monk who was liked and respected by all, but he granted his request.

A month later, Brother Amon asked for another position: 'I thought I was capable of opening and closing the gates, but I am a little deaf and sometimes I do not hear the bell. Please allow me to spade the garden and carry manure, and may God grant that I shall do my work properly.'

Again his request was granted, but he came back repeatedly, asking to be allowed to split firewood, or repair shoes, or do heavy manual labour. Finally he was sent into the Grandmont forest to gather faggots on the way at the proper times to pray and praise the Almighty.

Increasingly humble and aware of his inferiority, however, the good monk despaired of being loved by God and honouring him. 'I do not have a well-formed body, a pleasant voice or a confident bearing,' he said to the abbot. 'Anyone who sees me feels great pity for the servants of God, if he judges from my wretched appearance. When I give to a poor man, my alms do him little good, and when I take care of a sick man I do not always save his life. Please allow me to make a pilgrimage to the Holy City so that I may pray to the Holy Mother of God and ask her to plead my worthless cause to her beloved Son.'

Once again his request was granted. Taking nothing with him but a pilgrim's staff, he set off on the long road to Jerusalem.

Some time later he had to cross a great desert, but he was fortunate enough to meet two Augustinian monks who were willing to accept his company.

One evening they arrived exhausted at a mud hut and decided to spend the night in it. They had spent a long, hot, arduous day on the road. To refresh themselves they had half a gourd of water, but not the slightest morsel of food.

'No matter,' said one of the Augustinians, 'I will say the right prayer.'

He went to a corner of the hut and mumbled a few words. Suddenly, miraculously, a big loaf of bread appeared in his arms.

Brother Amon looked on in amazement, admiring the power of the mysterious prayer, and also the faith of the man who had said it. How greatly he must be loved by

God, to receive such an outstanding favour! It would
never have been granted to him, poor Brother Amon.
But God was just and gave to each according to his merit.

At the second stop in the desert the same scene was repeated: the other Augustinian knelt in a corner of the
hut and murmured a prayer, and a loaf of bread appeared
from nowhere.

Brother Amon praised God for the miracle, praised his
companions, praised the whole world, performed his act
of contrition and ate some of the good wheat bread. But
on the third evening he could not restrain his curiosity:
he humbly begged his companions to teach him the miraculous prayer, which was surely addressed to a powerful
saint if not to God himself.

'We dare not pray to God for such a favour,' said one
of the Augustinians. 'As for the saints, they could not
grant it. We pray to a holy monk who gathers wood in the
Grandmont forest. He is certainly a cherished son of the
Lord, for he works all miracles that are asked of him. His
name is Brother Amon.'

The Magic Book of Scot the Wizard

Man's inner power, known in remote antiquity, was expressed by the power of the Word, of prayer or incantation. To pray or invoke is to call for the intercession of a
superior entity; to draw the creative power of matter from
within oneself, without asking for external help, is to
command the Mysterious Unknown.

It seems that there has always been participation by a
superior principle which believers and occultists identify
with either God or the devil.

Praying to Brother Amon so that he will make a loaf of
bread appear is not a method acceptable to rationalists;
on the whole, they would be less hostile to direct creation
by personal miracle.

The view originally held by the Cabala was related to a
power that came from man's unknown self, with the obli-
gatory intercession of an entity.

In his unpublished personal notes the great Cabalist
Michel Carguèse (Charles Carrega) formulated the

principle of that science. It was probably known to the Rosicrucians (AMORC), who are known as the heirs of the 'unknown science' and rightly feel that the time has now come to divulge certain truths. They still constitute a centre of secrecy in the beneficent sense of the term.

Carguèse's notes bear the title *The Magic Book of Scot the Wizard.* They were inspired by the 'all-powerful book' of the famous monk Michael Scot, even though that part of his work is generally considered to have been destroyed. They explain the Mysterious Unknown, in the case of Brother Amon, in an almost scientific form that could be integrated into Professor Falinski's theory of parallel universes.

Operation in the created-uncreated universe

To arrive at the materialization of bread, the phenomenon must go back to the initial cell and bring it, by the workings of evolution, to the stage of the grain of wheat. Everything is done by the Word, which analogically plays the part of the control button in the functioning of an electronic robot. Millions of years go by in a fraction of a second, just as millions of combinations present themselves in a computer as *possible eventualities.*

In the created-uncreated universe (or antiuniverse) everything is foreseen but nothing is determined; that is, all worlds, solutions, and developments exist as 'possible eventualities' among which free will makes a choice.

In my cosmology the created-uncreated universe corresponds to the zero point where a contracting universe is about to become an expanding universe (see the first section of Chapter 5). It can be described as the present time whose existence is theoretically impossible.

From the grain of wheat, materialization goes on to the states of the wheat field, the harvest, the flour mill, and the baker's oven.

A universe of machines, time, and humanity is necessary for involutive, then evolutive development in an almost absolute instantaneity. Everything returns to the zero point of noncreation after the useful creation – bread – has occurred. The energy-matter is taken from Brother

Amon, who unconsciously participates in the phenomenon without knowing that he is the generator of energy, the propulsive manufacturer of feelings and thoughts expressed as an ebb and flow. The law of the conservation of matter, enunciated by Lavoisier – 'Nothing is lost, nothing is created, everything is transformed' – is maintained all through the transaction.

Exploration in a parallel world

In a more detailed analysis, the thought formulated by the Word sets off a pulsation of energy that passes into a parallel world. The potential of this Other World thus acquires an intolerable excess which causes the materialization of the bread with a necessity to expel it, as a foreign body, into our three-dimensional world, which draws it in as though presenting an empty pocket eager to be filled. (The principle of this materialization is demonstrated in atomic physics: when an energy of nineteen million kilojoules is developed in a particle accelerator, material particles are created.) There is thus a double transfer of energy-matter, from one world to another.

The transfers are instantaneous in physiological time: an eruption, an irruption, a creation, an expulsion. The energy transmitted by the Word is returned as bread-matter.

Through the workings of the Mysterious Unknown, man is a powerful generator; he could create a mountain, but at the risk of losing his physical and psychic equilibrium. The transaction is beneficent, however, when it results in the unconscious expulsion of psychic residues. It is in this way that man refines, liberates, and spiritualizes himself; his waste products pass into the Other World, which gives new, neutral energy in exchange.

The Beyond of demons and spiritualists

The Magic Book of Scot the Wizard explains the contamination of the Other World by this osmosis. With the psychic residues of the three-dimensional world, the Beyond procreates a race of monsters which occultists call demons, incubi, succubi, genies, sylphs, nymphs, gnomes, etc. They are doubles of beings that now live or once lived on earth. Spiritualism is the science of invoking those monsters and making them pass from the beyond into our world through the 'airlock' of zero point.

The mystery of the Cabala, according to Scot and Michel Carguèse, was the scientific secret known to the magicians who formulated the oral version of the Maasseh Merkabad. It consisted in bringing about a transaction between two parallel worlds by means of the Word. And Carguèse says specifically that the transaction was between the world and the antiworld.

Since the written version of the Cabala could not divulge this dangerous magic secret, it wrapped it in so many veils, and concealed it in so many labyrinths, that only a few initiates can still find the guiding thread.

But even initiates are able to bring about materializations and transactions between parallel worlds only by an empirical method, without knowing the scientific mechanism of the phenomenon.

The mystery of the phoenix

In white magic, the psychic loss calculated in energy is compensated by an inhalation from the Other World which restores the balance. But, says *The Magic Book of Scot the Wizard*, the conscious transaction is always unfavourable on the physical level, which explains why saints pay with their own bodies, and with their earthly happiness, for the good they do. Are they not generally emaciated, covered with wounds and sores, myopic, and often tubercular?

Anyone who has a good thought or emits good radiation must pay for the benefits he gives; no one who gives sublimity receives sublimity in exchange. If you give gold – by analogy – in return you will receive only raw materials, such as stone, wood, base metal, or waste products, with which you must make gold again by your work and incubation, to your physical detriment.

In this sense, he who gives exhausts himself. Even God, who is alone in giving constantly, must constantly die and be resuscitated, like the phoenix, by way of compensation.

This is the mystery of Prometheus, Lucifer, Quetzalcoatl, Hercules, and all the Mexican, Incan, and Hindu gods who voluntarily have themselves burned on a pyre. It is also the mystery of Jesus and Buddhist monks.

In most cosmologies God sacrifices himself to create the world: in the Rig Veda the Supreme Being destroyed himself to create; the god Bel of the Chaldeans cut off his own head; the universe of the ancient Germans was composed of the sacrificed body of the god Ymer; and so on.

In everyday life the dishonest rich man who owns, for example, too much land and too many houses, yet buys more land and houses to aggrandize himself, preventing the poor man from acquiring the little piece of land or the modest house that would have brought him contentment, will have the greatest possible happiness, health, and success. But the honest man, the good man, the saint, must pay and receive in return unhappiness, illness, and misfortune.

From this it follows that the concept of justice, in the exoteric sense of the term, is misinterpreted – unless justice is not of this world. But does the concept of justice exist at the mysterious zero point of contracting and expanding universes, the zero point of antitime, the antiuniverse, the antiworld? Such is the secret of the Cabala divulged by *The Magic Book of Scot the Wizard*.

Black Magic

The eighth chapter of the *Book of Enoch* says that the extraterrestrial angels taught men and women the art of enchantments and spells, but *not the true knowledge of the saints*. It was probably this black magic preserved in the Cabala, that was used by the Egyptians and the Hebrews when they vied with each other in demonstrating their powers before Pharaoh.

To work a miracle, a practitioner of black magic may take the necessary energy from his own psychic nature, but usually he is not willing to do this, as a saint is, and prefers to make others pay. For that purpose, without warning his victim of the danger, he invokes the Other World by means of a medium, usually a woman, whom he hypnotizes or puts to sleep in order to steal a particle of her grey matter. In other words, he is a vampire who, like Gilles de Rais, sometimes does not hesitate to sacrifice children to carry out the abominable rite.

By practicing human or animal sacrifice, the ancient Hebrew, Egyptian, Incan, and Mayan magicians, who were all priests,* gave us proof that they were aware of the psychic transfer in their magic operation.

How could they have had that knowledge, which is the fruit of a highly developed science, if it had not been taught to them by superior ancestors?

Once again we are brought back to a tradition bequeathed or taught by initiates.

Here is a theoretical and practical explanation of black magic:

By incantation, prayer or sacrifice, the magician condenses the psychic influx from the unconscious mind of the subject or victim in an accumulator: a totem, statue, figurine, or ritual object. This energy is transmitted to an entity – a spirit or demon – in a parallel world, by the sole magic of the Word.

(In traditional belief, the Other World is populated by wandering spirits who wait for 'external' energy that will enable them to take on real consistency.)

The entity performs the transmutation – that is, the 'miracle' – and the expulsion into our universe. The transaction is completed: the Other World keeps the refined psychic energy and sends an equal amount of psychic waste products in the form requested.

The miracle, which is always a material creation, even on the infinitesimal level, can take several forms:

* Although they were the heirs of a magnificent civilization, the Incas and Mayas practiced human sacrifice – with no spirit of cruelty, it must be added. So did the Celts, but either the sacrifice was voluntary (suicide) or the victims were prisoners of war.

Among the Hebrews, Abraham narrowly avoided sacrificing his son Isaac. The blood rite was held in high esteem, since even the initiate Moses observed it, in a rather repulsive way, if we are to believe Leviticus. But oversensitivity was not a failing of our ancestors of thirty-five hundred years ago!

1. Inanimate objects: a bouquet of flowers, gold, poison, etc.

2. Incarnation: a demon, the physical appearance of a person.

3. Hallucinations and visions: ghostly images appear; sounds – rumblings, thunder, words – are magically heard.

4. Possession: the magician or the subject receives a discharge and goes into a trance; he is 'possessed by a demon' and performs some sort of miraculous act.

If there is a medium it is always she who, having given the most psychic energy, is in the state of greatest depletion and therefore receives the discharge, as in the experiment of Mesmer's tub.*

In classical science this explanation is unorthodox and inadmissible; in pure experimental science, however, it has a certain credibility, since clairvoyance, premonitions, telepathy, hallucinations, visions, and levitation cannot be disproved.

Whatever their value may be, these phenomena apparently belong to an empiricism that is not without a factual basis. Rationalism tries to ignore them for the sole reason that it cannot explain them.

Walking on water

With faith, one can move mountains. Christ walked on water. Hopeless invalids are cured at Lourdes. Saint Joseph of Copertino, Saint Teresa of Avila, and Saint Bernard placed themselves in a state of levitation.

Can we deny this supranormal which escapes the temporary laws of experimental science?

For a theologian, the explanation is simple: it is a miracle, which amounts to saying that God, charged with

* 1778 the Austrian physician Friedrich Mesmer, founder of the theory of animal magnetism, caused hallucinations and convulsions – and also cures, it was said – by means of his miraculous 'tub.' It was a wooden vat containing iron filings, powdered glass, and carefully arranged bottles, all submerged in water. Iron bars descended into the system, which acted as an electric accumulator. The magnetism that was propagated through the iron bars was the direct cause of the mysterious manifestations.

a high potential, discharges some of his power for the benefit of earthly creatures.

This is exactly the theory presented by *The Magic Book of Scot the Wizard.*

Prayers, or the influx of thoughts and acts of faith emanating from a saint, for example, go to God, who transmutes that sum of energy into positive miracles. It is certain that a praying saint gives all his vitality, all his potential, all his 'faith' to the God he worships, to the point of being psychically emptied. It is then that the phenomenon of Mesmer's tub occurs: the return flow is, if not much greater, at least much more condensed in time, which enables the miracle to happen.

This return flow annihilates gravity (walking on water, levitation) or produces a supranormal power such as walking through fire without being burned, prophesying, perceiving the past or the future, bringing about miraculous cures.

Making a magic statuette

It is relatively easy to make a condenser of magnetism or, more concretely, a magic statuette whose effectiveness can be verified.

The object should preferably be made of animal matter. Magicians usually choose ivory or beeswax, but plant matter, such as resin or even wood, may also be used.

It is extremely important that the statuette have the form and appearance of a particularly well-loved being, one who has aroused affection, love, or admiration: Christ, Buddha, Lucifer, a god, a goddess, a dog.

Incantations are addressed to the statuette to charge it with psychic potential identical or similar to magnetism, but they must be expressed with fervour, in such a way as to create a current between the operator and the matter.

After a rather long charging period of several months or even years, sensitive people will feel the beneficial effects of the charge, especially when thy touch the statuette.

This is the principle of totems, divine statues, and all worshipped objects. The beneficial radiation is especially strong in sanctuaries that have been frequented by worshippers for centuries. It is often concentrated in ivory or wooden statues of Christ which believers have approached closely and rubbed against in unconscious magnetic contacts. The object should be either suspended or insulated by a pedestal made of a substance that has low conductivity, such as glass.

This is the fundamental principle of white magic, and also of black magic – everything depends on the intention – if the statuette represents an evil person, a demon, Satan, or a wicked god.

Antique dealers who buy and sell magic objects often have occasion to observe how their sole presence can have pernicious effect.

Our lives are much more strongly subjected to good and bad influences than is commonly believed. Some people emit beneficial or harmful radiation, according to their nature, and the same is true of certain houses, objects, and places. Each of us, in varying degrees, acts as a magic statuette or an accumulator. In the course of a gathering in an auditorium or a stadium, for example, we may acquire a potential increased tenfold by intense polarization. In cities, the crowd discharges energy by touching metal handrails in buses and subway trains, or simply by pressing against each other.

It is for this reason that initiates in India avoid physical contact with individuals who may communicate harmful psychic energy to them.

Magic courtesans

Women are usually more highly charged than men because they attract greater admiration, love, and desire.

Courtesans and ordinary women, conscious of their sexual power, concentrate passion and become charged even more when they avoid being touched. Physical contact is a veritable magic act which reaches its critical intensity at the beginning of the sex act.

Film and theatre actresses, who drew a powerful influx from the admiration of the public, are charged with extraordinary magnetism, which often explains the blossoming of their talent and self-assurance. They are sometimes so highly charged that it becomes necessary for them to seek relief, usually by making love, but also, in a more unconscious way, by walking barefoot in the streets or in the country, to allow their excess charge to drain off into the ground.

Scientifically this charge is called animal magnetism, but esoterically it is psychic energy, less subtle, perhaps, than that which is produced by faith, but of the same emotional nature.

When the psychic charge has no outlet, it becomes concentrated in the individual and creates phantasms; that is, it is converted into neuropathic self-bewitchment.

The Mysterious Unknown thus extends into the known, the connection being made by magic and magnetism. This enables us to foresee that some day the empirical science of the Cabala will also be connected with experimental science.

Chapter 18

SORCERERS AND MATHEMATICIANS

Magic and sorcery, like all sciences, have their initiates and their gullible believers.

I am tempted to say, with the rationalists, that reason and science have killed occultism. This is relatively true, but the Mysterious Unknown, which has not yet been explained, resists the assaults of the ignorant.

Furthermore, magic is a natural need of oppressed people, and the first of the sciences in hierarchical order.

Let me make it clear that I do not want to defend absurd superstitions and infernal practices as vain as they are ridiculous; my intention is to study a valid esotericism whose social implications are still not well known.

The erudite Alfred Maury maintained that magic was the first form taken by man's scientific instinct, borrowing from nature the power of her secrets. For initiates this definition, favourable though it may be, represents only the external explanation of a mystery that draws its essence from our genesis. Moreover, magic cannot be dissociated from the Bible, religion, and philisophy; it impregnates the Talmud, the Cabala, and all the bases of our traditional and literary knowledge.

Initiated women

The people who composed the primordial human race were only elements in a nearly wild horde when the extraterrestrial 'angels' landed. The *Book of Enoch* says that the first concern of those travellers from the sky was to 'bind themselves to one another by oaths'; that is, they went up on the 'Mountain of the Oath' in Armenia and concluded a *satanic* pact that could be broken only under penalty of the most terrible reprisals. There was thus the formation of a veritable magic circle, and ever since that event Samyaza, leader of the rebels, has been frequently evoked in magic conjurations.

Then each of the 'angels' chose a woman, ' and

approached her, and cohabited with her; and they taught the women sorcery, enchantments and the properties of roots and trees.' They also taught them the use of make-up, precious stones, and dyes.

So there was already magic at the dawn of the human race, with women initiated into a knowledge that had been previously unknown on Earth.

Even from the viewpoint of the purest rationalism, it would be arbitrary to refuse to give credence or interest to what constituted mankind's first knowledge; and it is not paradoxical to say that the first science was magic, whose two main branches are sorcery and classical experimental science.

In view of this, we can now see what the secret teaching of the Cabala was, and in it, moreover, we find the name of the *Book of Enoch* mentioned as the first source of all revelation.

The Talmud and the Bible give great importance to magic. It was the occult base of the Scandinavians and Celts, whose esoteric centre, governed exclusively by women, was on the island of Sein. In Brittany, at the heart of the Druidic region, this extraterrestrial magic achieved its exoteric fulfillment with Merlin the Enchanter. More esoterically, the dolmens carved with circles and spirals suggest a cosmic idea of expansion related to a much more rational science.

The feminine initiation of early times is probably involved in the myth of the earthly paradise, where Eve the Knower listened to the serpent and chose free will, which is a kind of intelligent revolt against the rigours of determinism.

The witches' sabbath of the poor

Magic and sorcery are also revolts against dictatorships, whether of religion or society.

The deeper meaning of the witches' sabbath is evoked in this passage of the *Encyclopédia*:

God gave wealth and abundance to some, condemning others to hunger and poverty. Therefore, to punish God for his injustice, the people deny him and worship his enemy the devil. . . .

Similarly, for the poor people who went to it, the witches' sabbath was a celebration coming after the harsh labour of the week; it was the wild revel that succeeded despair. But that appearance concealed a veritable conspiracy.

While woman offered herself to what was called Satan, denying God, who had given her nothing but poverty and privations, man glimpsed something other than a fleeting, brutal pleasure. At the witches' sabbath he had beside him people as poor as himself, dissatisfied, mad with despair and rage; and from those demonic celebrations came a number of the terrible revolts that began breaking out in the twelfth century. . . . With the fourteenth century came the black mass, which later brought on the peasant uprising of 1358.

It is interesting to note that this uprising occurred on the day of Corpus Christi: May 28, 1358.

The witches' sabbaths of that time clearly showed a political character which timorous historians have failed to stress.

The altar of the ceremony was dedicated to 'the great rebellious stag, the old outlaw unjustly driven out of heaven, the spirit that created the earth, the master who causes plants to germinate.'

The witches' sabbath was a revolt by oppressed people hungry for food and justice. In despair they turned to Satan, feeling that they need not fear from him any greater torment than they had already.

This revolt is now found in Satanic and Luciferian societies, and if we go back through the millennia we find it even among the Hebrews, for example when, tired of waiting for Moses to return from his conference with the Lord on Mount Sinai, they melted their earrings and made the golden calf (Exodus 32:1-5).

In the Cabala, two angels symbolize the rebellion of matter against spirit, but also the people against the arbitrary: the White Samael, angel of punishment, and the Black Samael, angel of catastrophe. The fatality of magic is here evoked by a curious and profound image: 'Error is the skin enveloping the flesh of truth.'

The Talmud openly refers to superior knowledge to reveal methods of sorcery and miraculous cures which are actually empiricism in the literal meaning of the word.

These illustrious precedents, and the fact that magic is much older than any of man's intellectual knowledge, make that primordial science worthy of being studied with the greatest attention. Empiricism has made some scientists blind to it. This is unjust and vain, because it seems unquestionable to me that after its spectacular and masterful independent development, experimental science will soon be inevitably brought back to its great ancestor: transcendent magic, the magic of the masters and not that of the 'astronaut angels.'

The Cabala, the Talmud, and the Bible have never penetrated the 'skin' of transcendent science and magic to touch its 'flesh.'

Satan calls the tune

There is a Mysterious Unknown that puzzles us and a Mysterious Unknown that serves us.

The dictator, the politician on the rostrum, and the priest before the altar practice a spellbinding magic whose power over crowds is well known to them.

The sorcerer, who was one called a 'mathematician,' had his magic circle which, modernized by rationalistic science, has become the concentric waves of radio and television.

Like Caligula, Nero, and other ancient Roman emperors, government leaders use incantations, the magic of the Word, hypnotic images, and various subterfuges to bewitch the citizens of their countries.

The television screen is the old magic mirror of sorcerers, showing events that are happening, or have happened, at the other end of the world. It is a fantastic magic, a black magic, with human sacrifices: a Japanese prime minister is assassinated and we see the knife gleaming in the assassin's hand; a President of the United States is murdered and his murderer is killed before our eyes.

We could make those images disappear with a simple gesture, but we do not make that gesture because after those murders we need the spectacle of other murders, mounds of corpses, riots in America, men struggling against storms, floods, fire. . . .

What magic! What diabolical magic it is to see known and unknown dead people resuscitated, laughing and joking, after they have been buried!

This is a time of sorcery. Man rules the earth, its animals, and the sky. He tames and channels storms, sets off lightning, rain, snow, and earthquakes. He brings eruptions out of the earth that are more terrible than those of Mount Pelée, Vesuvius, and Etna. Flying carpets have been transmuted into rockets, invisible curses into speeding bullets. Doors open magically before us without our even having to say, 'Open sesame.'

And everything is materialized from an idea. A powerful sorcerer thinks, and from his thoughts come prodigious machines, made of steel, tungsten, or zirconium, for making other machines. Everything is done by enchantment and, as in the past at a witches' sabbath, the adepts, the 'enlightened masses' of our century, quiver ecstatically and are transfigured when on the magic mirror they see modern demons, succubi, and incubi: stars of the theatre and films, and especially the 'idols' of the young.

All this, which is satanic magic in the strictest sense of the term, is made possible by a close collaboration, a spiritual communion that goes from the scientist to the garage mechanic or butcher's helper who has become an 'idol.'

The most surprising part of it is that the laboratory scientist and his counterpart in the magic circle, the 'idolworshipper,' stoutly maintain that they do not believe in magic, the devil, and demons.

Scientific activity is entirely directed toward black magic, with its flying carpets, hypnotism, curses, and transmutations. The world's greatest scientists work on guided missiles, supersonic bombers, atomic fission, and hydrogen bombs, but none of them directly uses his intellectual abilities to lighten the work of peasants, improve medical care in rural areas, or give industrial workers greater safety.

There are certain parallels that show an obvious correlation: like the 'mathematician' at a diabolical gathering, the scientist maintains a stiff, dignified attitude; like witches at a sabbath, modern 'idol-worshippers' pull up their skirts or dress like men, dance barefoot and utter incoherent cries and hysterical shrieks.

In our modern world, devoted to Satanism, black magic has taken on an acute, endemic form; its only new feature is that it now denies its nature. In the past, in the time of obscurantism, it was the opposite: there was no sorcery and everyone thought he was going to a witches' sabbath!

Barefeet and pulled-up skirts

'Let no one be found among you who makes his son or daughter pass through fire, no augur or soothsayer or diviner or sorcerer, no one who casts spells or traffics with ghosts and spirits, and no necromancer. Those who do these things are abominable to the Lord, and it is because of these abominable practices that the Lord your God is driving them out before you.' (Deuteronomy 18:10-12.)

Despite these commands, the Hebrews were unquestionably fervent devotees of magic. Moses had already given them the example in front of Pharaoh.

The Romans carried stupidity very far in their magic practices, if we are to believe Horace. 'Canidia and Sagonna,' he writes, 'went to cemeteries at night to cast their evil spells.' He then describes a scene worthy of a horror film: the witches bury a young child alive and make a potion with his liver and marrow; they gather bones and herbs, cut the throat of a black sheep and pour its blood into a trench that they have dug with their fingernails. Finally they make wax figurines of the person they want to kill and burn them with many incantations.

On the Esquiline hill in Rome, before Maecenas built a palace on it, there was a cemetery for the poor, a kind of common grave into which their bodies were thrown without ceremony. Witches went there after dark, barefoot, with their hair dishevelled, wearing black robes pulled up to show their genitals. From that cursed ground they took the herbs and bones they needed for their magic preparations.

Fifteen reasons for being burned alive

To become a sorcerer, one had to enter into a formal pact with the devil, in which each contracting party undertook a strict commitment. The sorcerer renounced his baptism, devoted himself to sacrilegious practices and gave his soul to the devil. The devil, by his signature, obligated himself to obey for a certain time and allow himself to be enclosed in a bottle, a box, a ring, the body of a pet animal, etc. And, of course, he had to grant the sorcerer's wishes and give him extraordinary powers such as knowing the past and the future, procuring sinful enjoyments, troubling the tranquillity of others, obtaining a desired woman, getting rid of rivals and enemies, becoming invisible, flying through the air, controlling beings from the Other World, and rousing the dead.

The fact is that none of this ever actually happened. There were no such pacts, for if one had only to call Satan to make him appear, and sign an agreement with one's blood to obtain wealth, love, and power, the poor devil would be frantically overworked and happiness would reign all over the world!

With the advent of Christianity the old magic of formulas and incantations was transformed and took on a new ritual.

The poor believed that Satan was in league with all the vanquished divinities of the past, who had now become demons, and that this coalition opposed the victorious God. Belief in sorcery and its most characteristic manifestation, the witches' sabbath, became so strong that even saints accepted it.

The oldest French legal code, the Salic Law, deals with unsubstantiated accusations of sorcery in its sixty-seventh paragraph: 'Whoever calls someone a sorcerer, or accuses him of having taken a cauldron to a place where sorcerers gather, and cannot prove it, must pay a fine of 2500 denarii.'

Here, from *De la Démonomanie*, by Bodin (1581), is a list of the crimes imputed to sorcerers and witches:

First, their primary profession is to deny God and all religion. Their second crime is that, after having renounced God, they curse, blaspheme and spite him. Their third is still more abominable: they pay homage to the devil, worship him and make sacrifices to him. Their fourth crime is still greater: a number of them have been convicted of, and have confessed to, dedicating their children to Satan, a wickedness condemned by God in his law when he says that he will wreak vengeance on those who dedicate their children to Moloch. The fifth goes even farther: witches are commonly convicted by their confessions of having sacrificed to the devil small children whom they have first baptized, raising them into the air and then thrusting a large pin into their head. The sixth crime goes farther still, for sorcerers are not content with sacrificing their own children to the devil and burning them as a form of sacrifice, but they also consecrate them to Satan as soon as they are in their mother's belly, to bring death to both mother and child. The seventh and most common is that they promise the devil to lure as many people into his service as they can. The eighth crime is to call on the devil and swear by his name as a sign of honour. The ninth is that they are incestuous, for Satan gives them to understand that there has never been a perfect sorcerer and enchanter who was not engendered by a father and his daughter or a mother and her son. The tenth is that they kill people and, worse still, little children, then boil them until their flesh and humors become drinkable. The eleventh crime is that they eat human flesh and even little children and avidly drink their blood. And when they cannot obtain children they unearth bodies from graves or go to gallows to take the flesh of those who have been hanged. The twelfth is to cause death by poison or spells, for it is a much greater offence to kill by poison than by open force, and it is a still greater offence to kill by a spell than by poison. The thirteenth crime is to make livestock die, which is a common thing. And for that reason a sorcerer of Augsburg, in the year 1569, was pulled to pieces with red-hot pincers, having taken the form of an animal's skin. The fourteenth is also common: making fruits die and causing famine and sterility in a whole region. The fifteenth is that witches copulate with the devil, often beside their husbands, and they all confess that wickedness. Here, then, are fifteen detestable crimes, the least of which makes the criminal deserve death by torture.

The Holy Spirit of Françoise Bos

Ritually, the witches' sabbath, or meeting of sorcerers and witches, was held on a Saturday night in a clearing in a forest. The participants invoked Satan with formulas recited by heart or read from a book, said God's name backward, drank aphrodisiac potions, and engaged in debauchery worthy of our modern *dolce vita*.

It is certain that such gatherings actually took place and that curses were pronounced by 'mathematicians' against noblemen or rich burghers guilty of oppressing people of humble rank.

Fanatical men and overheated women took part in the spectacle, mingling lust and rancour in a single outburst of feeling, but frenzied imaginations added greatly to the scene, so that many participants claimed they had seen the devil and fornicated with him.

In that time of obscurantism, the masses were extremely credulous, as is shown by the trial that resulted in the death of Françoise Bos, of Guille. France, a poor, hysterical, weak-minded woman who had the misfortune of being pretty enough to tempt a scoundrel. Here is her deposition, taken from the record of her trial on Monday, January 30, 1606, at which she was accused of having had intercourse with an incubus:

The said woman states that a few days before All Saints' Day of the year 1605, as she was lying beside her sleeping husband, something fell on her bed, causing her to awaken in fear; and again, while she was awake and her husband was still asleep, that same thing fell on her bed like a ball. The spirit had the voice of a man. When she asked, 'Who's there?' she was told very quietly that she should have no fear, that the visitor was a captain of the Holy Spirit, that he had been sent to possess her as if he were her husband, and that she must not be afraid to receive him into her bed. She was unwilling to permit this. The spirit leapt onto a chest, then onto the floor and came to her, saying, 'You are very cruel not to let me do as I wish.' He drew back the bedclothes, took one of her breasts, lifted it and said, 'You must now know that I love you, and I promise you that if you let me take you, you will be very happy, for I am the temple of God and have been sent to comfort poor women like you.' She told him that she did not do such things, and was content with her husband. The spirit replied. 'You are wrong; I am the captain of the Holy Spirit and I have come to comfort and possess you. I assure you that I possess all women, except those of priests.' He then got into the bed and said, 'I want to show you how boys undress girls,' and when he had done so, he seized her, and finally went away, without her knowing what he looked like or if he had operated. She believes, however, that he is a good and holy spirit who is accustomed to possessing women. She adds that on the first day of this year, while she was lying beside her husband at about midnight, with him asleep and herself awake, the same spirit came onto her bed and asked her to let him get into it so that he could possess her and make her happy, which she refused to do. He asked her if she wanted to gain an indulgence; she said that she did. 'It was done,' he said, but he told her that when she went to confession she must not speak of the matter to her confessor. And when she was later

asked if she had confessed to having intercourse with
that spirit, she replied that she did not know it was
an offence to have intercourse with the said spirit,
whom she believed to be good and holy; that he came
to see her every night, but that she had allowed him
to have his will of her only that one time; that when
she treated him harshly he leapt out of bed and she
did not know what had become of him; that he had
ceased coming back eight or nine days before she was
imprisoned, because she had sprinkled holy water on
her bed and made the sign of the cross.

This story recalls the equally incredible adventures of
pretty women who were visited by 'angels' in ancient
times. But seventeenth-century judges, unlike ancient
husbands, were more credulous with regard to the devil,
and less so with regard to the Holy Spirit.

There were, however, aggravating circumstances in the
case of François Bos: she had invited her female neighbours to come and make love with the spirit, so that they
could have 'similar intercourse, and she promised them
that he would make them happy and help them to find
husbands for their daughters.'

The poor simple-minded woman (but was she really
simple-minded?) was convicted of 'having had intercourse with the devil, having fornicated with him.' On
July 14, 1606, after having made a public apology in
front of the parish church, barefoot and in a chemise, she
was hanged and burned *as a witch*. For the most amazing
part of her trial was that the judges did not identify the
'captain of the Holy Spirit' as an unscrupulous libertine,
but as a demon.

And there were often women subject to hallucinations
who, when they were brought to trial, confessed to imaginary infamous acts and climbed the steps of the scaffold
with enthusiasm.

Imaginary sabbaths

In the eighteenth century a judge in Florence questioned a woman who was firmly convinced of her guilt.

She confessed that she cast spells on her neighbours, sucked the blood of little children, went to witches' sabbaths, and fornicated with the devil. For once, the judge was sensible and humane. He ordered her to go back to the witches' sabbath that same night and told her that she would be pardoned if she did so.

Two young men, informed of what the judge had in mind, spent the evening with the woman and made her eat and drink heavily. After the meal she took off her clothes, rubbed several kinds of diabolical ointments on her body, lay down on a bed, and fell asleep. The young men mistreated her a bit, burning her on the breasts and thighs, and cutting her hair.

When she awoke and returned to the judge, she told him that she had gone to the witches' sabbath, naked and riding on a broom, that the devil had beaten her with red-hot rods, and that the 'goat' had carried her on his back and burned off part of her hair with a flaming broom.

The chronicler Minucci, who reports the case, ends his account by saying, 'By means of this strategem, the clever magistrate acquired proof of a truth that had already seemed certain to him. It was well worth torturing the poor madwoman in that way.'

During the reign of Louis XIV the philosopher Pierre Gassendi obtained identical results in an Alpine valley with peasants who had been in a lethargic sleep. They told him they had gone to a witches' sabbath, which showed that they were mentally unbalanced and mistook their hallucinations for realities.

Taken in its own terms, sorcery is fictitious, but the unknown self plays a mysterious part in it, transporting into a parallel world a series of physical acts whose inanity is apparent only in our visible universe.

The cult of the earthworm

Charred rooster bones on the altar of a ruined abbey near Torbridge, south of London; a skull with a pike thrust into it in the cemetery of the village of Clophill (it had belonged to a young witch burned in 1770); heads of cows and horses arranged in a circle nearby – these discoveries made in England in 1964 showed the survival of witchcraft and pagan rites that are still popular among Celtic and Nordic peoples.

English witches gather on the consecrated dates of the summer and winter solstices in twenty-six groups of thirteen, forming the ritual number of three hundred and thirty-eight. The high priestess of the sect is a woman with an admirable body, harmonious breasts, and shapely legs who, at sabbaths, officiates naked except for a gold necklace around her neck and a silver star in her blond hair. On an altar in the middle of a magic circle she places a sword, a flint knife, a wand, salt, water, and a censer. She then invokes heaven and earth for the benefit of the United Kingdom, certain persons designated by name and 'all people of good will.'

English sorcerers claim to engage in white magic, in opposition to what they consider the black magic of established religions, according to an ancestral rite addressed to the constellation of Orion and the earthworm; that is, the most beautiful constellation and the humblest form of life.

In tradition, Orion (the name comes from the Greek word for urine) was born of the mingled urine of Jupiter, Neptune, and Mercury. The mythological hero is a giant – one of the first men on earth – who received from Neptune the ability to walk on water.

The constellation is composed of the biggest stars in the sky; Betelgeuse, Rigel, Bellatrix. Its quadrangular shape, with three stars aligned in the middle, distinguishes it from all others.

Orion is regarded as dominating the sky and governing winter. Astrologically, it has an exceptional value and an especially perceptible magic influence.

The earthworm, on the other hand, represents telluric forces, the sign of Gaea, and the merciful Lucifer, driven out of heaven for having loved the human race. This Lucifer-earthworm is not the devil, much less an evil entity; he is a symbol of the damned, the banished, the victims of God's oppression and spitefulness.

English sorcerers venerate the forces of nature and deny that they direct their activities in the direction of evil.

They are naked at their sabbaths so that they can better communicate with the forces they invoke, and receive beneficial emanations from Mother Earth. Their pagan sabbath is not inspired by Satan and it has kept nothing of medieval tradition except the principle of protection from 'the malignant power of God.'

Honi soit qui mal y pense .

According to the writer Roger Delorme, a pagan cult based on black magic and going back to prehistoric times was given new life in the fourteenth century with the creation of the famous Order of the Garter. This cult is said to have continued among the English aristocracy until the end of the nineteenth century.

At a ball in 1348, when King Edward II was dancing with a woman who may have been the Countess of Salisbury, her garter slipped off. He picked it up and said, *'Honi soit qui mal y pense'* ('Shame to him who thinks badly of it'). In saying this, according to Roger Delorme, the king means to show that he belonged to the cult of worshippers of Janus, the ancient Roman god with two faces and the feet of a goat, who was of Etruscan and Norse origin.

In support of this idea, Delorme points out that Edward III publicly proclaimed the creation of a double coven composed of the twenty-six greatest noblemen of the kingdom, with himself as the head of one group of thirteen and the Prince of Wales as the head of the other. The words *'Honi soit qui mal y pense'* were not addressed to those who were shocked by the sight of a garter, but to orthodox believers who spoke against the ancient religion.

In the Middle Ages the cult involved human sacrifices, and it is thought that the Royal Coven even wanted to offer the life of a king as a bloody tribute. Unable to sacrifice a king, they sometimes substituted a close relative or friend.

William II, killed under mysterious circumstances by Walter Tirel, one of his courtiers, is said to have been a victim of the cult. Delorme notes that William's body was abandoned for several hours in the forest; by the time it was carried to Winchester by woodsmen, the new king had already been elected. Walter Tirel was never punished in any way for the accident – or the crime.

The death of Thomas à Becket, Archbishop of Canterbury under Henry II, is also classified as a ritual murder. I must add, however, that historians vigorously reject Delorme's view.

Near Castledown on the Isle of Man, Dr. Gardner, who founded a marvellous museum of sorcery, personally direct a group of sorcerers who worship the horned god of our prehistoric ancestors.

The first initiatic temple of this god was in the Trois-Frères cave in the Ariège district of France.

After World War I, in England, the witches' sabbath was given an elaborate and highly intellectualized revival by Aleister Crowley and the Hermetic Order of the Golden Dawn.

The Scarlet Women of the Golden Dawn

In that period a psychosis of mystery, mysticism, and folly swept over the world, giving rise in art and literature to startling manifestations that usually had no real value. But occultism was 'on the move,' and under cover of inner research, spirituality, release of inhibitions, and a return to ancestral truths, sects began proliferating under the sign of Satan disguised as an archangel. And Satanism involves sex in multiple and equivocal aspects, whether it be prohibited or, on the contrary, regarded as a means and a mystery.

In about 1920 the English secret society known as the Hermetic Order of the Golden Dawn, heir to the erotic traditions and sexual magic of the Hindus, contaminated Great Britain and spread into France and Italy.

MacGregor Mathers and Aleister Crowley – especially the latter, who was called the foulest man in England – plumbed the depths of the Black Grail and alchemically distilled the dregs of the dregs to extract the Philosopher's Stone of erotic magicians. Crowley proudly gave himself the title of 666, which is the figure of the Beast of the

Apocalypse, or of Baphomet, the occult psuedo-symbol of the Templars.

His 'Scarlet Women,' the high priestesses of the sect, were supposed to go further in erotic vice and perversity than anything that could be imagined by a refined mind stimulated by alcohol and drugs. Their prototype was the woman described in the Bible, Revelation 17:4: 'The woman was clothed in purple and scarlet and bedizened with gold and jewels and pearls. In her hand she held a gold cup, full of obscenities and the foulness of her fornication.'

Crowley proclaimed that everything was rooted in sex, that man could accede to God only through erotic initiation, and that a righteous man should die during orgasm.

Such theories found favour with a certain occultist and intellectual elite. The Hermetic Order of the Golden Dawn had its hour of glory. Crowley became a kind of demonic Moses, the pioneer of a new religion. One of his mediums, Rosa, dictated the *Book of the Law* while in a trance. Like Aaron in the Bible, high Priests were enthroned after a kind of sacrifice in which human blood was supplied by menstruation. The Imperator put blood on the priest's right ear, right thumb, and right big toe (as Moses did to Aaron, Leviticus 8:23) and the sacrilege was consummated by coitus with a Scarlet Woman.

These women soon became legion, each aspiring to the supreme title after incredible initiations.

To become a Scarlet Woman, the formidable 'Balkis' seduced her father, brothers, and uncles, became a genuine prostitute, and sold her charms in bars frequented by sailors. Finally she was received one night in the 'Temple of God' at a special session, having come directly from plying her erotic trade, and was presented naked on a platform, 'so beautiful and radiant,' says my informant, who witnessed the scene, 'that God surely inhabited her at that moment.'

In France, Italy, Egypt, and Scandinavia, identical scenes took place, under the sign of sexual spirituality.

In *L'Europe païnne du vingtième siècle*, the historian Pierre Mariel tells how, at Cefalu, Sicily, Crowley founded a *templum* named Thelema in which 'The Great Beast [Crowley himself] explored the extreme limits of ceremonial magic. All vices and many faults can be attributed to him, but there is at least one virtue that cannot be denied him: absolute, intransigent sincerity. He was convinced of his mission and believed that he had been called upon to propagate an ancient doctrine that had been forgotten or "corrupted" by Christianity: "Magick." '

Other Satanic sects held secret meetings in all countries of Europe and America. Spiritual 'masters' – all from the East, of course, like Gurjieff and Meher Baba – deluded their naïve disciples.

It is interesting to note that after World War II the same psychosis reached epidemic proportions in the same countries. More 'masters' appeared and, as a climax, there was even a 'Master of the World': the illustrious Prince Cherenzii Lind, Maha Chohan, Supreme Regent of the Agartha.

These charlatans claim, of course, to be philosophers, spiritualists, or practitioners of white magic, and their number steadily increases with the fateful approach of the year 2000.

The sorcerer and the sex act

In 1964 an extraordinary man named Paul Gregor, who did not hesitate to present himself as a sorcerer, came to Paris. He was actually a caster of spells, but in the sense of white magic.

In his book *Journal d'un Sorcier, ou l'Envoûtement selon la Macumba,* he described his objectives, which were to be achieved in a school of magic called the Macumba Institute. He propounded a strange theory whose basis was a 'change in the rhythm of the sex act' in accordance with Indian Tantrism, the precepts of the psychologist Havelock Ellis, and the secret discipline of Brazilian sorcerers.

'The strange orgasm which then ensues,' he wrote, 'is a light spasm that shakes the heart and the sympathetic nerve for several minutes. It is slower and charged with a sweetness a hundred times greater than ever. You feel the essence of your being split into two currents, one directed toward your partner and the other toward the secret centre of life. The flow of time and the aging process are slowed and reversed like the act of love.'

The practice is accompanied by a kind of dissociation and an amorous enchantment favoured by the use of plant stimulants.

It is no longer a matter of Satan, demons, and human or nonhuman sacrifice; with Paul Gregor, sorcery returns to its original concept: a mysterious science directed toward elevation of the unknown self.

Chapter 19

THE SEVENTH SEAL OF THE APOCALYPSE

The prophecies of Revelation in the Bible have not come true. The end of the world, believed to be very near, has hung fire. Yet a persuasive parallel truth impregnates our era as if it belonged to the 'exceeded time,' the post-Apocalypse. Are we in Biblical antitime?

Our evolutionary continuum resembles a vast fermentation, generating around our planet an aura charged with all the malignant emanations that come from us. As in the magic process, does this form of invocation pass into the Other World of God, then return to us as psychic waste matter; that is, as cataclysms?

However gratuitous this hypothesis may be, it fits in remarkably well with the data of tradition: *there is a correlation between great cosmic cataclysms and the deterioration of mankind.* Human degradation precedes an upheaval and acts as a premonitory symptom of it.

More specifically we can say, for example, that if man were to set off an atomic war a mysterious correlation would cause the end of our world to occur soon afterward, like the return shock in operational magic. The phenomenon could surely be explained in terms of nuclear physics if scientists would take the trouble to do so.

In this era of antitime everything seems to happen as if sovereign orders were coming from the Mysterious Unknown, a kind of electric potential which, to our understanding, takes on the appearance of a conscious entity. An order to revive the cult of blood. An order to the Scarlet Woman to brandish the cup of fornication, and to priests to measure the altar and the worshippers with a cane (Revelation 17:4 and 11:1).

But certain occultists believe that the 'orders' come from an earthly centre where magicians, no doubt unaware of it, constitute the great Satanic headquarters.

The daily holocaust

Our social organization is a vast conspiracy for the purpose of unbalancing the mind of the ordinary honest man. The fantastic things that occur in everyday life result from a supposedly rational system, but no one with a sense of mystery can fail to see a symbol in it, if not a characteristic sign of what is known as the time of Apocalypse.

On certain dates known as holidays, car owners leave cities and towns, mobilized by a mysterious and powerful order, to pay their tribute to an obscure god who may be Moloch. In France, the annual holocaust claims thirty five thousand victims. Fifty thousand gallons of blood poured on the altar of Moloch.

Enormous transport planes (such as the American C-5A), which can cause seven hundred and fifty deaths at once, are built by great firms, and the sonic boom of jet planes, scientifically distilled by the armed forces, ruins historic monuments, old cities, old people's hearts, and everyone's nerves. Like the voice of the Lord, that of the devil thunders in the clouds, destroying insect and bird eggs, impairing fetuses in their mothers' wombs, and driving farm animals into fits of wild insanity.

The act of heroism

The human race is evolving toward a suicide formula which may mean that people feel obsolescent and constant to the end of the world.

In the past, ordinary men and even heroes feared death: a Leonidas, a Bayard, or a Surcouf would surely have refused to ride in a rocket or a racing car. But in our time there are thousands of volunteers for suicide missions: kamikaze in planes packed with explosives, frogmen diving for hopeless expeditions, paratroopers eager to land behind enemy lines.

Millions of apparently sane men enthusiastically engage in flying and undersea diving; women show their disgust with life by enclosing themselves in caves a hundred feet below the ground; timid middle-class citizens are not afraid to gamble with their lives by driving on highways at top speed.

Does all this result from an insensitivity to risk and the rhythm of life? Only a libido of danger, of existentialism in the literal sense of the term, can explain this senseless behaviour in which even the instinct of self-preservation has ceased to play a part.

The furor of death and antitime is expressed in all organizations and at all levels of social life. Architects destroy sound buildings to erect skyscrapers that collapse before they are finished. Children of ten pillage their schools and attack passers-by in the street; at sixteen they kill cab drivers; at eighteen they attack banks.

In the soccer match between Argentina and Peru at Lima in 1964, there were 0.328 deaths and fifteen hundred injuries for every goal scored. In Athens that same year, spectators set fire to a stadium because the players were not brutal enough.

In Paris, men and women three-quarters naked wallow in a pile of rags and crumpled paper and throw bleeding chickens, raw fish, and bowls of jam at each other. It is part of an experimental 'intellectual' movement that seeks new artistic concepts in random combinations of human and nonhuman matter.

In fashionable Paris society, this is called a 'happening.' When the mass of chicken, fish, jam, and human flesh reaches its maximum 'potential,' a spark of genius bursts forth; a man may then, for example, plunge his head into a bucket of paint, shake his hair above a blank canvas and thus paint a picture that will be highly appreciated not only by the dimwits of fashionable society, but by a number of art critics as well.

Five of these brilliant demonstrations of human genius were given in 1964 at the American Artists' Centre on the Boulevard Raspail in Paris. There were, however, a few people who accused the participants of insanity and indicted the United States by pointing out that fights between women wrestlers using mud and fish had been presented in New York.

Despite the great and unfailing friendship that unites the French and American peoples – or perhaps because of that friendship – there were varying reactions in the

French press, some going so far as to demand that cultural relations be temporaily broken off.

Should the United States be destroyed?

In 1962 the French weekly *La Presse* received from one of its correspondents an incendiary article which, if it had been published, might have embittered Franco-American relations. Violently biased though it was, the article described a 'happening' and then showed how it illustrated defects that are undermining France and her great friend across the Atlantic. Here is a condensed version of the conclusion:

In the very near future life will become inhuman if not impossible for the French, whose old houses in cities, towns and villages, considered too dilapidated, will be demolished and replaced with cage-buildings made of reinforced concrete. This massive, inevitable reconstruction will destroy the soul and skeleton of old France, and at the same time it will cut the umbilical cord that connects the French with their ancestors.

The tragedy is complicated by the fact that instead of giving people 'human' houses which might become impregnated with a new atmosphere and a new past, 'sterilized' houses (the infernal houses of Le Corbusier) that will last only a few decades are now being built and will be built at an increasing rate in the future. The design and materials of these houses are hostile to coexistence and communion between the body and the soul.

A building made of cinder blocks or cement will never be a home. This is unimportant to foreigners passing through France and the materialists of the far left, but it is something that vitally affects the survival of the French nation. And what are we to say of our monstrous housing projects?

The situation is serious, very serious; millions of people will be cut off from their roots and doomed to live haphazardly, not knowing where they are going because they no longer know where they come from.

The French will dissociate themselves from their

*creative genius, their history, their customs and their
identity. They will lose their name, as young nations have
lost theirs. And it is the fault of the Americans.*

*For it is they who, because of their 'foundling com-
plex,' want to cut the umbilical cord of all living nations,
so that everyone will be without a father, a mother and a
house. So that everyone will be like them, people who
leave an illusory heritage: cement houses that crumble
in fifty years; furniture, clothes and knick-knacks that
disintegrate in one generation. 'Foundling people': that
is what the Americanized human race will be.*

*That is why the United States must be destroyed before
the great contamination deteriorates all mankind. The
world can then return to truly human social structures.*

This article was obviously too hard on our American
friends, but it reflected a basic, implacable and painful
truth.

Destroy the United States? Certainly not! But one
may wonder on a purely esoteric level whether the superior mission of the Russians or the Chinese may not be
precisely to save the world by an atomic attack on the
nation that, more than any other, has erected the principle of the heroic act into a system.

Will Atlantis be devastated a second time?

Only one lifetime

The article also stated all the grievances, genuine or exaggerated, that Europeans sometimes formulate against
America: juvenile delinquency, violent films featuring
gangsters or Western outlaws, spoiled children, racism,
gangsterism in the record and jukebox industries, deterioration of amateur sport, substitution of robots for intelligent workers, irresponsible automation, and so on.

Despite the extremism of the article, which seems to
reflect a political concern, it would have been better if it
had been published, for the guidance of both the Americans and the French.

It is unfortunately probable that because of scientific
progress (and the Americans may be more guilty than

anyone else in this respect, since they are in the vanguard of scientific research) the world is heading toward a trap in which it will die of asphyxiation, but all civilized nations bear responsibility for that destiny.

City dwellers are fatally contaminated, but country people are also losing their elementary common sense. In the past, a man planted trees for future generations; now he plants only for his lifetime, with no certainty that his humble efforts will not be destroyed by an urbanization project, a highway or, worst of all, an airport.

More and more, farmers are ceasing to grow potatoes, turnips, and Jerusalem artichokes and turning to industrial farming and more profitable crops. In twenty years only large-scale farming will be viable and the small farmer, like the small craftsman and the small shopkeeper, will be devoured by the new age. No more bushes around fields, but electric fences; no more walnut, chestnut, or medlar trees; in short, no more of anything picturesque, rare, or intimate.

Are these signs of the Apocalypse?

The desert is spreading

Because of overpopulation, there is a shortage of arable land, just as there will soon be a shortage of water. As far as water is concerned, the reason is clear: domestic and industrial needs are enormous and steadily increasing. But what about land?

Land is constantly being *mineralized*; that is, it tends to become desert sand or sterile clay.

Soil needs to undergo a three-phase process:

1. Millions of earthworms, working more effectively than ploughs, stir up millions of tons of arable land, including the crust and the mineral and organic elements.

2. Cows graze; this is the second phase of fermentation.

3. Excrement serves as fertilizer; this is the third phase of fermentation.

The cycle is completed and the earth lives.

But since the nineteenth century there has been a break in the fundamental cycle: the soil is being devitalized by overuse of chemical fertilizers composed essentially of minerals such as nitrogen, phosphorus, and potassium. It is dying for lack of organic elements, and even in the world's richest regions, in the United States, the Soviet Union, and France, harvests are gradually diminishing.

All over the world the desert is spreading, devouring good, nourishing soil like a cancer. The Israelis have tenaciously reconquered the Negev Desert, but Egypt, Algeria, and Morocco lose twenty-five thousand acres every year.

The earth needs rest and sleep, and perhaps in the Invisible someone is thinking that continents which have been above water too long must soon be plunged beneath the oceans again.

The same factors that deteriorate plant life also deteriorate human life. We have gone too far in sterilization and pasteurization. We sterilize our butter, milk, cheese, fruit, water, wine; in short, the basic elements of our diet. We even sterilize our own bodies by overuse of antibiotics.

As though to mock our pretensions to the infinitely great, the infinitely small takes vengeance with cancer, heart disease, disseminated sclerosis, and premature senility, whose viral nature is beginning to be discerned. Coal crumbles in mines, rotted by its own form of cancer, like the stone of cathedrals.

Chemical fertilizers, antibiotics, cancer – are they the Beasts of the Apocalypse?

The danger is grave; an error by our scientists may bring about man's irremediable downfall, as almost happened in the case of the sulfonamides.

And radioactive fallout strongly accentuates the imbalance against which man is waging a hopeless struggle.

According to the estimates of Dr. Linus Pauling, winner of a Nobel Prize in chemistry, Professor J. P. Vigier, and a number of Japanese physicists, each explosion of a superbomb has caused fifteen thousand abnormal births in the world. There are now more than half a million children with birth defects, and they in turn may engender children irreversibly different from other members of our species.

This is only a drop in the bucket if we consider the

projected figures published by the United Nations: the world's population was 2.9 billion in 1960, and it is expected to reach 7.4 billion by the year 2000. But will the human race live to see that year 2000 which impresses it so much?

Invisible soldiers in the Vanves fortress

Military technology is moving in a rather unexpected direction: toward invisibility.

Vision is the result of a complex process; each atom vibrates and emits faint radiation that is amplified within the billions of molecules that compose objects. These vibrations, which cover a wide range, varying in amplitude and period, are visible, audible, or thermal, or belong to classes of waves that escape our sensory perception.

Some scientists have considered it possible to transform vibrations perceptible to the human eye into vibrations within the invisible range. This would mean that colour would first disappear, then details, and finally general shape. In other words, objects would keep their opacity but their details would become invisible. The clock on the mantelpiece, for example, would lose its case, hands, and figures; you would no longer be able to tell time from it and you would probably see something like a fog in the vague shape of a clock, whose opacity would prevent you from seeing the wall behind it. This would not really be invisibility, but it would be a long step forward on the road to it.

At the Vanves fortress in Paris, technicians are secretly trying to achieve that result by enveloping objects in a magnetic field, thus disturbing visual appearance, if not normal atomic agitation.

In the same line of investigation, experiments are also being carried out with coloured coverings of foam made of natural or synthetic resins. They are said to have been already tested on tanks, airplanes, antiaircraft guns, and soldiers' clothing.

The prospect of a war between invisible combatants is so likely, and is taken so seriously, that since 1950 the great powers have had infrared cannons sensitive not only to the visible shape of objects but also to their thermal radiation.

But before thinking of destroying each other, people should think of protecting themselves against a common enemy: pollution of water, the air, and the earth. Air polution above large cities has become so dense that it has doubled the number of foggy days in one century.

Dr. Robert White of Cleveland, Ohio, believes that in the near future it will be possible to connect human brains to electronic robots and achieve 'transfers' equivalent to placing a scientist's brain in an athlete's body.

Such miracles will certainly be accomplished some day, which would seem to indicate that the end of the world may be close to our time.

But, says the sage, who is always right, you can speculate, invent, tyrannize, and prepare autumn and winter, but no matter what you do, you will not stop springtime! The Seventh Seal of the Apocalypse will never be opened.

Chapter 20

THE MYSTERIOUS UNKNOWN

The Mysterious Unknown is the strange phenomenon or fact that brings our reasoning to a dead halt.

Sometimes the unknown is the result only of imperfect scientific investigation. What is the cause of tides? Why are anticyclones always formed in the Azores? Why does the ocean turn around the south pole? Why is sulphur generally not produced by volcanoes, or petroleum by the oceans, but both by a bacterium?

Sometimes the unknown, while still remaining within the area of experimental physics or chemistry, also seems to overlap into a certain occultism. How can a living creature produce the minerals that enter into the composition of its body even when they are lacking in its environment? Hens deprived of limestone can, for a certain time, lay eggs with shells; spinach and cabbages grown in distilled water contain their normal proportion of iron and copper.

An experiment that is rather easy to perform is baffling to scientists. Put an ordinary bean and a little wad of moist cotton inside a clean glass tube. Close both ends of the tube by melting the glass, so that the bean and the cotton are in an airtight space. Place the tube on one side of a pharmacist's scales and balance it with a counterweight. Let us say that it weighs seven grams. Put the scales under a glass dome to avoid dust, and in a dark place if you see fit, to isolate the whole system from sunlight, whose photons have weight and might conceivably provide a partial explanation. After several days the bean will have germinated, absorbing the moisture in the cotton, and the tube will weigh about a tenth of a gram more than the seven grams noted at the beginning of the experiment.

What is the explanation of this phenomenon? So far the question remains unanswered.

Sometimes, finally, the mystery is directly linked to occultism – clairvoyance, alchemy, premonition, magic, sorcery – and takes on the true meaning of the Mysterious

Unknown. It can be explained only by intuition or inner sensation and, pending further study, rationalists refuse to believe it or grant it any importance.

To be fair, we must say that the Mysterious Unknown is discredited primarily by the incredible naïveté or aggressive dishonesty of most practitioners of the occult arts.

The error of occultists

The labyrinth in which occultists are forced to work by the nature of their doctrine is crowded with charlatans and swindlers. There have always been such examples as the healer who sold 'salts of gold' that allegedly cured cancer and actually made a fortune for him; the 'biologist' with his serum for curing leukemia; the 'great Italian professor' who collected fluid from the stars; the 'Gypsy clairvoyant' who has 'inherited the knowledge of the Egyptians'; the sanctimonious hypocrite who, because of a vow he claims to have taken, is willing to treat certain diseases free – and ends up charging an exorbitant price.

Newspapers carry advertisements in which charlatans use the Mysterious Unknown to attract customers: the 'fascinating gaze' of a hypnotist can solve your problems simply and easily; you can succeed by means of a ring 'made in accordance with the talismanic art'; you can infallibly attract love to yourself with a magic mirror; a 'wave bracelet' will cure your rheumatism.

The charlatan does not hesitate to bring ridicule to the occult by giving himself a title like 'Master,' 'Professor,' or 'Magus.' His business address is usually a post office box (it is safer) or an 'International Laboratory' or an 'Institute' (that sounds impressive).

But in addition to those crafty, unscrupulous charlatans there is a whole world of sincere occultists who are perfectly honest and firmly convinced of their powers, their mission or their truth.

Brother Bruegghe would have staked his life on the reality of the 'Celtic city' that he explored in his astral body, a hundred feet underground.

In Poitou, France, an honest bricklayer detected by means of his pendulum 'the world's greatest treasure' in a pyramid two miles high, buried directly below his house. 'I swear to you on my honour that this is the pure truth,' he wrote to me.

The treasure of the Templars

With equal confidence, certain radiesthesists say that the wondrous treasure of the Templars is in a castle at Arigny, in the Rhône district of France. Actually, there is no serious evidence for this, but the legend has already become well established, and what is more lasting than a legend? Someone might answer, 'Two legends,' and he would be right, because a second location, besides Arigny, is now attributed to the treasure of the Templars: Gisors.

The story goes back to 1942, when Roger Lhomoy, caretaker of the castle at Gisors and also a radiesthesist, detected a fabulous treasure under a knoll in the park. With a faith that could have moved the Himalayas, he dug a pit and a tunnel. Finally, in 1946, he said, he came to an underground church in which he saw thirty monumental chests which he presumed to be filled with ingots, coins, and precious stones. He could have opened them and taken the treasure for himself, but for some mysteriout reason he took nothing at all and remained as poor as ever.

But he talked about his discovery, and as the years went by his story of the treasure in the underground church began to acquire believers. Such a fortune could only have belonged to Croesus, Solomon, or the Templars. The Templars were finally chosen, and their second treasure was born. It will probably live forever. The legend was strengthened until it nearly became a part of history. It was accepted by a noted writer and then by a government minister, who had excavations made. Nothing was found, of course, and for good reason, but the treasure of the Templars had migrated from Arigny to Gisors.

It might be objected that Gisors was never a fief of the Templars and that it would have been stupid for them to take the gold they wanted to protect from the greed of their enemy the king and bury it in a town under his domination. But this did not faze believers in the story.

They could not accept the idea that Roger Lhomoy's pendulum might have been mistaken. It was easier for them to reject history, and that was what they did. But such fantasies do great harm to occultism and make scientists' mistrust of it comprehensible to some extent.

In Paris there is a Treasure-Seekers' Club. Its membership includes twenty-nine experts who, with electronic detectors and serious documentation, try to take stock of the mysterious hiding places that are scattered over the world, in the bowels of the earth, and the depths of the oceans. The secret archives of the club contain documents which take away from Gisors and Arigny the privilege of concealing the treasure of the Templars.

According to these archives, the treasure was taken to a manor in Charentes, then hidden again, in the fifteenth century, in the castle of Berbezières, where graffiti on the walls give its location.

A third legend? Perhap, but the odyssey of the Templars' treasure does not stop there.

The cryptographer of the Treasure-Seekers' Club, the erudite archaeologist J. de Grazia, who has devoted his life to the study of Templar esotericism, maintains that the real hiding place of the treasure is in a manor in the Seine-et-Marne district, where he has noted all the key signs of the Templars and the secret of their architecture.

A fourth legend? Who will ever know, since the charm of this kind of Mysterious Unknown is precisely that it escapes empirical verification.

Sethon the Gold-Maker

Like Christopher Columbus, occultists have a singular lust for gold, and it inevitably draws them toward the magic art of making gold at will: alchemy.

Have alchemists really been able to transmute lead into gold? Tradition says so, but the secret of the 'powder of projection' must have died with the last alchemists of the Middle Ages. (This powder, which has the power to transmute any metal into gold, is the Philosopher's Stone of materialistic alchemists.)

But there was one alchemist who, though not well

known, may have been the only one who ever gave proof of his ability. His name was Sethon, he was Scottish, and he lived in the late sixteenth and early seventeenth centuries. He was better known under the pseudonym of Cosmopolitan.

In 1602 he met Professor Wolfgang Drenheim in Fribourg, Switzerland. Drenheim was a declared adversary of all occultism, but he had to accept the evidence of his own senses: he saw Sethon transmute base metal into gold.

In a work titled *De Minerali Medicina*, Drenheim told of the experiment he had witnessed with Jacob Zwinger, a goldsmith from Basel:

We went to the house of a gold miner with several slabs of lead which Zwinger had brought from home, a crucible which we had borrowed from a goldsmith, and some ordinary sulphur which we had bought on the way. Sethon touched nothing. He told us to make a fire, place the lead and sulphur in the crucible, put on the lid and stir the mass with rods. Meanwhile he spoke to us.

After a quarter of an hour he said to us, 'Drop this little piece of paper into the molten lead, but make sure it falls exactly in the middle and try to let nothing fall into the fire.' Wrapped in the paper was a rather heavy powder, of a colour that appeared to be lemon yellow. It took good eyes to distinguish it.

Although we were as incredulous as Doubting Thomas, we did everything he said. When the mass had been heated for another quarter of an hour and stirred continuously with iron rods, the goldsmith was told to extinguish the fire under the crucible by pouring water on it. We found pure gold which, in the goldsmith's opinion, was of even higher quality than the fine gold of Hungary and Arabia. It weighed as much as the lead whose place it had taken. We were stupefied with amazement; we scarcely dared to believe our eyes.

Jacob Zwinger confirmed the facts in a Latin letter, *Epistola ad Doctorem Schobinger*, which was included in a book by Emmanuel Koning, of Basel. This letter states that before his departure from Switzerland, Sethon repeated his domonstration of transmutation in the house of the goldsmith André Bletz. Later, in Strasbourg, under the name of Hirschborgen, he transmuted again, this time in the house of the goldsmith Gustenhover, to whom he gave some perfectly operative powder of projection.

Although Sethon shunned publicity, the matter came to the attention of Emperor Rudolf II, who summoned Gustenhover to his castle in Prague. When he was ordered to reveal the secret of transmutation, poor Gustenhover insisted that he had only used the powder given to him by Sethon, but he was not believed and he ended his life in prison.

Despite his prudence, Sethon was lured to the court of Christian II, Elector of Saxony, where he was tortured to make him divulge the fabulous secret. 'He was pierced with sharp iron spikes,' writes Louis Figuier in *L'Alchimie et les Alchimistes*, 'he was burned with molten lead ... he was beaten with rods.'

Sethon held firm, however, and in 1603 his Polish colleague Michael Sendivag enabled him to escape by means of a ruse, perhaps in the hope that Sethon would initiate him into the supreme knowledge. But Sethon was now in very bad physical condition; he died shortly afterward, leaving his saviour only a few particles of powder of projection.

The marvellous secret was no doubt revealed in the only work that Sethon is known to have written, the *Book of Twelve Chapters*, but Sendivag mutilated the text to the point of making it incomprehensible.

Was Sethon a skilful illusionist? Did he actually succeed in performing the miraculous transmutation? Everyone is free to think what he wishes.

The Mystery of the Rosicrucians

Although it is easy to be ironic about occultists of bygone times, it seems that some of them, high-ranking initiates, had knowledge which experimental science took a long time to discover.

A few centuries ago, reports the traditionalist historian Charles Carrega, unknown masters asked candidates for initiation to explain this statement: 'The Pure Water of Truth leads to understand of the superior mystery of the Rose.'

Without venturing to propose an explanation of our own, we can still study the three elements of the problem: Pure Water, Truth, Rose.

The exoteric meaning of the rose is no secret, but on the esoteric level we can only marvel at the choice made by the masters, for the rose, with particular excellence, exists in at least four dimensions – length, width, thickness, time – to which must be added four subdimensions – form, colour, matter, odour – which are not so harmoniously combined anywhere else. (The mystery of the rose is unveiled in my book *One Hundred Thousand Years of Man's Unknown History*, Chapter XII.) The rose is thus an exceptional creation, almost in the absolute, and it has always been regarded as supreme in beauty, fragrance, and elegance.

It is also a symbol of death, for when it reveals its intimate secret, when it opens its petals and shows its heart, it is at the end of its life, not having, like most other flowers, the power to be reborn in a seed.

This same message of death is found in the other two elements.

Truth is also a message of death in the world of men, and anyone who proclaims it is sure to stir up a fateful danger. As the proverb says, he who tells the truth should have his horse saddled, ready to gallop away.

Pure water also signifies death. Alchemists vainly sought it for the accomplishment of the Great Work and, not finding it, replaced it with dew. To be consummated, the Great Work required regeneration by pure water (corrosive water).

Baptism is also a regeneration, a death followed by birth (on the spiritual level), and baptismal water is strictly defined as *natural water* (not pure water). It is, say theologians, any water from a spring, a well, the sea, a river, a lake, a pond, a cistern, or rain; *Non refert, frigida sit an calida, potabilis vel non potabilis, benedicta vel profana.*

Pure Water: Death

Baptismal water is thus not *pure water*; there can be no doubt of this because such water would mean physical death. Anyone who drank it or washed with it would be sure to die. It is more harmful than the most dangerous acids, and its solvent power is so great that it disintegrates nearly all substances. There is no pure water in France except at the Pasteur Institute, and since it dissolves glass, a special plastic had to be invented for making containers in which to keep it.

This power of death was known to initiates several centuries before scientists were able to obtain chemically virgin water.

May we conclude, then, that the meaning of the initiatic sentence is that the Pure Water (death) of Truth (death) leads to understanding of the superior mystery of the Rose (death), all this expressed on the level of the human world, of course, and not in the absolute?

One might find a strange meaning in the Age of Aquarius, the Water Bearer: water = golden age, the age of god-men = death.

In zodiacal symbolism, Aquarius is between Capricorn and Pisces. It is the eleventh and next-to-last sign, perhaps the last one of the physical universe before the psychic sign of Pisces.

If the Age of Aquarius is actually the age of god-men, we may fear a near end of the human adventure on earth, because it is hard to imagine man on earth striving toward a goal he has already reached. Moreover, the rapid increase in the population of most countries raises the possibility that millions or even billions of people will be killed in the next world war. In that case, the Age of Aquarius would indeed be the age of death.

For traditionalists, the self-destruction of mankind in

the Pure Water of Aquarius would be a baptism, a regeneration, leading to the advent of a new cycle, perhaps that of Truth, to be followed by the age of the Rose.

The magic hour

The deep sense of mystery that is inherent in the human mind has a predilection for certain natures, places, and times.

For thousands of years man struggled against the darkness of the night; for him, the discovery of artificial light must have been the first great scientific victory. In the thick night of winter he at last had the power to resuscitate images and the form of palpable matter, for even though they were sometimes perceptible to his sharp senses and the thousand eyes of his intelligent flesh, at a distance they dissolved into impenetrable opacity.

One day, then, there was the invention of that light, and then, through the centuries, the invention of light able to vanquish a whole night, and our ancestors gradually lost the mysterious contact of twilight, that fantastic hour when daylight is no longer completely daylight and night is not yet night.

The ancients believed that at this time man entered the Other World and acquired magic powers. Their view can be expressed as follows:

At twilight, try to let yourself be consciously infiltrated by the peoples of the Other World, which may be an inner universe. As the insistences of the lighted world cease to reach and penetrate you, the inner radiation of your thought will become aware of new perceptions from the Other World. Do you not close your eyes to find that propitious isolation during the day? Outside will be darkness, opacity; inside will be light that propagates and exalts itself. With a little practice, you may become capable of fully analysing the brief moment when your body, still impregnated with light, exudes a marvellous expansion.

L.G.—14

It is a phenomenon of endosmosis in reverse, an electric phenomenon that is no doubt similar to the action of a battery which ceases to accumulate, then releases its excess energy in a fraction of a second.

Man has lost his memory of the magic moment of time, as he is now losing his sense of orientation and of the geographical predestination of space.

Eleusis-Alesia

Xavier Guichard, former Prefect of the Paris Police, is the author of a curious book titled *Eleusis-Alesia* and described as an 'essay and hypothesis on the geographical positions (latitude and longitude) of cities with a sacred character, founded near a lake or a miraculous spring.'

Guichard tries to prove that these cities 'were established in very ancient times according to immutable astronomical lines, determined first in the sky, then transferred to the earth at regular intervals, each equal to a 360th part of the globe.'

On the basis of this hypothesis, he provides the map of the world with a network of 'Alesian geodesic lines' and 'lines of direction.'

On the Calais-Eze transversal line in France he situates Olizy, Elise, Alaise, Eyzins, Aussois; on the Elsenburg-Alès lines: Aisey, Lisey, Alaise, Lezat, Laiziat.

All the 'Alesias,' says Guichard, occupy sites surrounded by streams of varying sizes which isolate them into peninsulas.

Alesian sites all have a mineral spring and many of them show evidence of having been inhabited in prehistoric times. And Eleusis, Greece, the capital of mysteries, was naturally on an important diagonal.

It is hard to check the cogency of this theory, but it would be interesting to compare it with telluric currents.

Are there areas of beneficial radiation where people, animals, and plants achieve maximum development of their psychic, intellectual, and physical abilities? It is quite likely. (One tradition says that the underground sanctuary of the Agartha is located in Sinkiang, near Urumchin, on a line where telluric currents emerge.)

In these areas the mysterious telluric currents that criss-cross the globe rise to the surface, and people experience their beneficial influence in greater well-being, greater success in their endeavours, and especially an ease of acclimatization.

Such an area may be a whole region, a district, or simply a field; sometimes it is a sacred place where men have erected temples, and sometimes it is a valley near a spring considered to be miraculous – an 'Alesia,' Xavier Guichard would say. It may be only a few square yards, or even a few square feet. Farmers know that there are places where any tree will die soon after it is planted, while everything grows normally only a few feet away.

In a thicket there is often a small patch of land where brambles and shrubs will not grow. Why? No one has yet been able to find the key to that Mysterious Unknown.

There has been some discussion of faults in the earth which cause ionization and electromagnetic disturbances in the atmosphere. The geologist Claude Trouvé believes that certain terrains, notably ancient granitic ones, have harmful radiation, while at the opposite pole are limestone terrains of more recent formation.

The legend of Saint Enimia

In the seventh century Princess Enimia, daughter of Clotaire II and a descendant of Clovis, was the most beautiful girl in the kingdom.

'My child,' her father said to her one day, 'which of the barons of France do you want to marry?'

'I want no other husband than Jesus,' she replied. 'I have sworn to him that I will remain a virgin.'

Legend says that Jesus immediately covered her with hideous leprosy in order to keep her for himself, to the great despair of her family.

Touched by her terrible suffering, God advised her to make a pilgrimage to the spring of Burla, in Gévaudan. Each time she bathed in the water of Burla, it restored her health and her smooth skin, but the leprosy reappeared as soon as she left the spring. Seeing God's will in this, she built a convent at that place and governed it till her death.

Today, pilgrimages are still made to the spring.

Even though they probably come from the same vast underground lake, the waters of other springs nearby do not have the miraculous power attributed to those of the Burla spring. Its geodesic position or the nature of the soil may explain why Saint Enimia could not leave it without losing the effects of its powerful beneficial radiation.

'There are places where knowers will not sleep,' say initiates, which means that a house should not be built on a malignant site, but on one whose beneficial nature has been determined by experience or careful study.

Most ancient cities are in beneficial places, because when a place seems malignant human efforts do not prosper, which causes populations to abandon certain areas.

It is not impossible, however, that the earth's lines of force and the points where telluric currents emerge are subject to geophysical displacements.

Why is a village sometimes rebuilt a hundred yards or a mile away from its former location?

If you sleep well at night, do not worry about these matters, but if you sleep sometimes well and sometimes badly, depending on where you are, place your bed in a north-south direction and you will then find the best possible conditions for sleep. It does not matter whether you lie with your head toward the north or the south; all that matters is being parallel with telluric currents.

Science has not yet answered the questions raised by this realm of the Mysterious Unknown, but, relinquishing the rigour of experiment, it is now venturing toward more or less rational explanations of all these obscure phenomena.

Creating by thought

The atom is still a mystery to scientists, but Lucien Barnier, making himself a spokesman for advanced physicists, has stated that the particles composing it may be something like 'fluid bubbles' that imprison forces in perpetual motion. (We are still far from having identified the constituents of the atom, which are actually mathematical entities.) The atom, in its literal sense (the smallest possible particle or, still better, the beginning of everything), would thus be motion, and this form of energy, like all others – electric, luminous, electromagnetic – would be capable of being converted into light or other systems of waves propagated in space.

If this theory is confirmed, it will open a boundless field to the imagination even before it is given practical application.

Transmuted into light waves, a man could be sent at a speed of 186,000 miles per second to another planet or a star, though there would still be the problem of returning him to his original form. Despite its great speed, however, light cannot conquer infinite space, or even reach a distant star in a human lifetime.

Yet man has a possibility of attaining the near-infinite: by thought, which can instantaneously transport him through space in spirit, to the farthest world of our universe. Since everything is energy-matter, this is actually a journey in space-time.

It is probable that space-time itself is energy-matter. Since the journey is instantaneous, it is practically 'immobile,' which would lead to the negation of motion. This concept of the immobility of time is analogous to the concept of the opacity and immobility of matter. A house seems motionless to us, whereas it is really moving, vibrating, and swirling in all its elements. If, even in thought, we perceived that motion, our world would take on a different appearance: everything would be only vibrations.

In principle, the little 'fluid bubbles' of the atom are constituents of thought-matter; it must therefore be theoretically possible to convert that thought-matter and transport it at 'instantaneous speed' into all of Professor E. Falinki's possible worlds.

This hypothesis is supported by the most ancient cosmologies in sacred writings, notably the Vedas, which say that the universe and its creation are *thoughts* of God.

The magic word

More exactly, God thinks and speaks, and his thought takes on substance in space.

The god Thoth was created by his words, but according to Maspero this is not a divine privilege, since the power of words is greater than that of the gods: 'Creation is the work of the articulate voice.'

The Egyptians even believed that a man's name was like his physical being and that anyone who possessed the name possessed the being. But the secret and all-powerful name had not been formed by chance and only a great initiate could know it. Each of the letters that composed it had its meaning and power, which contributed to the general meaning and power of the whole. If a single letter was displaced or omitted, or if the name was not spoken in the proper tone, the charm either ceased to operate or turned against the person trying to use it.

Occultists deteriorated the secret by combining words difficult to pronounce, as in this magic prayer: 'In the name of the Father, the Son and the Holy Ghost, a single God. We say the names of Our Lord and Saviour Jesus Christ, by which evil spirits and demons are driven away, in the name of the Trinity: Sedrelawi, Badegawai, Kedalolael, Kederufregadigon,' etc.

It was by the power of the Word that Moses killed an Egyptian, that Isaiah escaped from King Ahaz, that David contained the abyss that threatened to ruin his work when he dug the foundations of the altar.

For the Hindus, the Sabda Brahma, or Word of Brahma, is a meditation on the sacred and mysterious monosyllable OUM or OM, which is Brahma himself. The word contains three letters which form only one in writing: O = Brahma; U = Vishnu; M = Siva. The letter that represents OUM is a semicircle with a dot in the middle, called *biudu*, symbol of purely spiritual being. For salvation, one must constantly meditate on this word and repeat it often, concentrating one's thoughts on the dot.

By an extraordinary coincidence, the modern 'fluid bubble' theory of the atom is thus linked to the knowledge of the sages, whose creative thought is said to have had the power of materialization.

Will man some day achieve that creative power, that crossing of the frontier of the Mysterious Unknown? He will surely not achieve it to an unlimited extent, because he would then be able to create or destroy planets and the whole cosmos.

Everything has mass

In magic, materialization is essentially the transfer and transmutation of psychic energy. This theory has a surprising extension that intrigues the imagination.

Since everything is ultimately energy = matter = motion, nothing can exist without being energy, which means that everything must have a certain mass, however slight it may be.

This postulate is not self-evident. If light, for example, has weight, can we say that its intensity, colour, and speed have weight? Does a word have weight? In short, we may as well ask if a thought has weight. It probably does, not in practical physics, but perhaps in mathematics and metaphysics.

Put into another form, the question is: can there exist something which can be without being, be something and nothing, be created by man in a universe already created?

Although it is a function of the mind, thought does not seem to draw its substance from any identified mass of our known universe. If a thought does not exist before it appears spontaneously in a man's mind, is he a creator like God, and can he add to God's work? If he cannot add to divine creation, it means that thought already exists in an unknown form, before it comes into the mind.

Whatever belongs to the created universe also belongs to what we assume to be its original constituent: energy. It therefore seems that thought cannot be anything other than energy in a form that has mass. If so, the process of thinking draws on a Mysterious Unknown of energy, no doubt in man's unknown self, to create in a world that is probably not our material world of three or four dimensions.

And the more thoughts man emits, the more he draws from within himself, lightens himself, and creates, in the Elsewhere, a kind of matter that may be as fleeting as the light of a flash bulb. It may be lost in the plasma of the universe, or it may return to its point of emission.

Does man bear within himself an enormous mass of energy, millions of times greater than his measurable physical mass? Is that mass related to his weight, or is thought drawn from the universal 'plasma' and then dissolved in it again?

We must leave the question unanswered, but a summary of these theories helps us to conceive the problem of the Mysterious Unknown of occultists (God creates the world with a thought; a medium's energy causes materialization), which coincides exactly with the Mysterious Unknown of scientists (creative thought, the mass of all energy).

Thus we see the conjunction of two concepts whose basic magic formulas are both expressed by Einstein's equation: $e = mc^2$ in which e is energy, m is mass and c is the speed of light.

Time travel

In the generally accepted system, no event can reach us, and no action can occur, at a speed greater than that of light.

In metaphysics, thought is an action that is propagated instantaneously and it must obey the universal law of the contraction of time by velocity. By virtue of its infinite speed, then, a thought should have an infinite mass. Furthermore, when it enters time it should 'become younger' as it moves, and go directly into past time; that is, it should necessarily be materialized in the past, and perhaps in the immeasurably remote past of original creation.

On this hypothesis it should be possible in the future to save Joan of Arc from death at the stake, provided we are able to measure the time-penetration of thought, so that it can be directed to the year 1431. The materialization that we could 'think' – for example, a group of paratroopers armed with machine guns and grenades – would be more than adequate to assure the liberation of the French national heroine.

If thought is imprisoned in our brains, it cannot be

propagated at a speed greater than that of light; but if it can be projěcted and sent through space, it may offer a solution to the problem of time travel. In any case, it is either a speculation in the abstract or a projection into the past or the future.

By thought, we experience the martyrdom of Joan of Arc: an imaginary journey. If a wave converter transmuted our thought on its arrival in the year 1431, the journey would become a physical fact. But how could we *first* send a converter and technician to operate it, in order later to transmute a whole fantastic world of thoughts?

The problem seems insoluble, but it is no doubt simpler that we think, because occultists *claim* to be able to travel in time, by means of the astral body, clairvoyance, or radiesthesia. They do not claim, however, that they can explain the mechanism.

No empirical proof

They have never given any proof of their journeys, yet certain unexplained phenomena make rationalists inclined to believe that the Mysterious Unknown is not a delusion. But we must still recognize that there is no proof. There would be proof if, for example, a medium found the Tables of the Law by asking Moses where they were, or the treasure of the Templars by asking Jacques de Molay.

Even though we have no proof of that kind, however, the Unknown still gives us certainty of the existence of invisible forces and worlds by manifestations known as supranormal, which all flow from the mysterious power of man's inner self, or his thought, or his Word. It seems likely that the problem is centred around those three elements, the function of the medium being that of an automatic converter.

The fact that one can project oneself is surely a miracle which, besides the certainty of a human energy potential of great intensity, implies the pre-existence of parallel worlds.

Magic may thus be a superior science, the key to which will be given to us in the future by nuclear physics.

Cosmic isolation

If people of our planet and our visible universe can project themselves in space-time by introspection, it is permissible to think that the process can work in both directions. If so, beings or intelligences from other worlds and other planets may be among us in an electric form – waves or unknown energies – that could theoretically be materialized by converters.

Our radio telescopes, radars, and other receivers of cosmic signs and signals may be registering countless messages that seem meaningless to us only because we do not know how to transmute them. Since the reception of emissions from CTA-102 in April, 1965, astronomers and physicists are increasingly inclined to believe in the reality of such messages. I cannot help thinking that the obstacles which prevent us from understanding them will be overcome in the near future, for the logical reason that our cosmic isolation cannot continue indefinitely.

A few years ago, an unprogrammed television broadcast was received in America. Investigation revealed that it had not come from any station operating at the time, but that it had been transmitted four years earlier by a station that had later shut down. The least unreasonable explanation was that a series of Hertzian waves had wandered off into the cosmos, been reflected countless times by heavenly bodies or held prisoner in a magnetic field, then miraculously returned to the American atmosphere, the earth having travelled hundreds of millions of miles in the meantime.

Scientists give little or no credence to this explanation. If we are to seek an adventurous hypothesis, we may imagine that the broadcast was received by 'space people' living two light-years away from our planet, then sent back to us.

For or against interstellar spacecraft

Our cycle of civilization began thousands of years ago with the arrival of extraterrestrial men. And now the possibility of visits from other extraterrestrials seems to loom in the future like a premonitory sign. Is it only a phantasm, a collective psychosis generated by our fear at the approach of the year 2000?

The Catholic writer Daniel-Rops favours a fantastic explanation. 'With regard to flying saucers,' he wrote in *Ouest-France*, September 13, 1963, 'we twentieth-century people may be in the psychological situation of the first South American Indians who saw firearms, or the first Africans who saw airplanes. ... Those primitive people thought the explanation lay in magic, or hallucinations, or dreams. But is it really inconsistent and inadmissible to grant the possibility that a form of conscious, intelligent life inhabiting another heavenly body may be thousands of years ahead of human science, and may thus have penetrated all the secrets of cybernetics and atomic physics?'

In the opinion of the writer M. Ollivier, unidentified flying objects are not spacecraft: 'Why should those gyrations not come from our spatial, substantial unknown, agitated by waves of all origins, and particularly by our own waves?'

It is an attractive hypothesis and it does not deny a manifestation foreign to our planet. We might extend it and imagine that spatial phenomena come from a parallel Earth, existing in other dimensions. But would that not mean giving too little significance to sacred writings and tradition?

In 1962, NATO radars recorded unidentified images that kept them on the alert for a whole week. (It is well known that radar often registers phantom images, so any well equipped station has three, four, or five screens, and an image is considered valid only if it is registered by several screens.) Something mysterious obviously took place in our sky.

It can now be said that the air forces of all the world's nations take very seriously the possibility of a visit or an attack by interstellar spacecraft.

After a forty-five-minute conversation with General Douglas MacArthur, the Italian General Lauro announced that MacArthur foresaw disturbances coming from space, and that in view of the development of science he felt that all nations on earth should some day unite in order to survive and present a common front to any attack that might be made by peoples from other planets.

What do we know about those other planets? Not much!

The mystery of the cosmos still holds many surprises in store for us.

Luminous craft

On January 9, 1964, strange luminous objects with oval shapes were sighted floating off the coast of Sant Eufemia Marina, Italy. A group of fishermen rowed out to investigate. When one of them touched the largest of the objects with an oar, he received an electric shock that nearly killed him. When a police boat approached the objects, their lights went off and they disappeared.

Were they unknown monsters or small submarines? The mystery has never been cleared up. It is only one of hundreds of reliable observations that pose serious problems.

In Brazil, the police had to deal with the abduction of Rivalino do Manfra da Silva on August 19, 1962, and the theft of seventeen chickens, six pigs, and two cows by 'the crew of a craft presumed to be extraterrestrial.' These events strongly suggested the idea that extraterrestrials were taking samples of Earth's animal life.

Contacting other planets

A conference on 'extraterrestrial civilizations' was held in September, 1964, in the observatory at Yerevan, U.S.S.R. The programme included study of apparently natural signals (emissions of various particles and waves) from outer space.

The star nearest to our solar system is Proxima Centauri. It is 4.3 light-years away, which means that an exchange of signals would take eight and a half years.

The scientific journalist Lucien Barnier, an eminent specialist on the matter, believes that dread of solitude is the dominant trait of our species and that we must try to contact other planets.

'If there is thinking life elsewhere than on Earth,' he

writes, 'it has surely engendered a civilization analogous to ours, tormented by the same anxieties. Perhaps it is carrying on the same quest and trying to reach us, although we have not yet received any signals from it.'

If a dialogue is begun, it may last thousands of years, but who can say what surprises science may give us in the realm of interplanetary exchanges?

A message from Proxima Centauri?

'What I am about to write to you is not a fairy tale or a science-fiction story. The pieces of information that I have been instructed to give you will complete each other and form a homogenous whole, and perhaps only when you have read the last word of my last letter will you become certain that your occasional correspondent has never tried to mislead you.'

That was the beginning of the strange letter I received on March 16, 1964. It came from Mr. N. Y., living in a town near Paris, and described the mission he had been given by beings from a planet in the system of Proxima Centauri. Publication in my earlier book. *One Hundred Thousand Years of Man's Unknown History*, of archaeological discoveries tending to prove the existence of superior ancestors and ancient vanished civilizations had prompted these extraterrestrials to enlighten me on man's real genesis.

What would you have thought in my place? My first feeling (and I beg my informant to forgive me) was that the letter was from a madman, a pathological liar, or a practical joker. I have little belief in flying saucers in our century and I have never concealed that attitude, but Mr. N. Y.'s letter was at least entertaining and I decided to play along with him. I was willing to see what would come of it, but inwardly I had already made up my mind.

However, the documentation I later received (I will quote or summarize the essential parts of it) convinced me that Mr. N. Y. was a perfectly honourable man and that he had unquestionably been given a mission by a group of *terrestrial or extraterrestrial beings* that included first-rate scientists: physicists, chemists, biologists, linguists, archaeologists, etc.

The Baavian speak

The extraterrestrials who fly across our sky in elusive flying saucers explain their intervention in our life as follows:

'We have resolved to spare you the worst, to influence the behaviour of certain leaders who claim to be your masters. Our influence is exerted through "those who know us," who are able to orient the leaders without their realizing it.

'Our initiators have a faculty that enables them to draw from the immobility of their knowing consciousness elements of positive forces more powerful than all your determinisms combined.'

They are worried about the anarchical and dangerous use that we are making of atomic fission. They want to bring us back to the right path, and they probably would not hesitate to destroy us if our reckless experimentation should become an interplanetary threat.

Actively but discreetly, they keep watch on us and maintain communication with their home planet, whose name is Baavi. Their spacecraft, which have the general appearance of flying saucers and are called vaidorges, can move faster than the speed of light. This enables them to 'enter time'; that is, to cover vast distances in a few minutes of positive time or even in negative time, which means that they can reach their destination before their departure.

The vaidorges do not land often in the course of their reconnaissance flights, but they sometimes hover, with the disc rotating, a few feet above the ground. They have a secret base on one of the countless atolls of the Maldive Islands in the Indian Ocean, south of India, probably directly on the equator.

Their occupants have correspondents in most earthly nations. They contact them on fixed dates and collect information that may be useful to the Knowers (leaders) of Baavi.

An alien science

The documentation that has come to me from the Baavian astronauts is extremely detailed and includes a scientific part explaining the principle and mechanism of the vaidorges, a description of Baavian civilization, the grammar and alphabet of the Baavian language, a list of Baavian units of measurement, and a statement of various concepts in physics, chemistry, astronomy, etc.

With Mr. N Y.'s consent, I had the scientific part of the documents appraised by technicians, notably Robert Frédérick, a Doctor of Science. The results were conclusive: everything is either scientifically correct or possible. Nothing can be rejected for theoretical or technical error.

It would be long and tedious to go into detail, but it may be interesting at least to note that on Baavi the unit of time is the tolt, which equals 1.4 seconds, and that public clocks have three hands which mark the eighteen serkaes that make up a sidereal day. The unit of length is the sys, equal to forty-two centimeters (the Egyptian cubit).

Baavian scientists have established physical laws in accordance with the most recent scientific hypotheses, such as 'hypersonic matter,' one cubic centimeter of which would weigh ten billion tons.

After this introduction, we can now go on to the fantastic story of the genesis and invisible history of our time, related on the basis of documents from extraterrestrials who land on our planet every day.

Baavi

Mr. N. Y. refers, as I have done in this book, to the passage in Genesis that mentions the arrival on Earth of 'sons of the gods.' The literal meaning, he says, is 'sons of those who came from above': that is, from the sky, and therefore from a planet other than Earth.

They were tall men who came in interstellar spacecraft from another star in our galaxy: Proxima Centauri, 4.3 light-years from Earth.

The planet Baavi is half again as large as Earth and completes its orbit around Proxima Centauri every 311 days. In Earth time, each of these days has a duration of 27 hours, 12 minutes, and 57.6 seconds.

The temperature of Baavi is remarkably even. Its nights are luminous and in the daytime the sunlight is so bright that it justifies the name by which the inhabitants call themselves: Sons of the Sun.

Men from Earth are now living on Baavi. They are free and have adapted to the life of the Baavians.

Since the great schism that took place ten thousand years ago, the Baavian social structure is no longer based on the family. Because the Baavians are theoretically immortal, strict limitation of births has been necessary. A child is regarded as belonging to the whole population. At birth, a small golden plaque is placed under his scalp, bearing letters and figures known only to the conceivers, and then he is placed in a child-rearing centre where he is given a provisional bracelet with a number on it.

He spends the first five years of his life in this centre, where no one knows his origins. Between the ages of five and ten he goes to an educational centre. At the age of ten his bracelet is taken from him and he is sent back to the conception centre that formed him, where Knowers give him awareness of his psychic power and the practices that enable him to acquire immortality. At a favourable time, chosen by the Knowers, the pupil makes his or her genetic contribution by giving a child to society, then he or she is sterilized.

Before leaving the conception centre, everyone chooses the names he wants to bear and receives official confirmation in the form of a bracelet with a plaque which, in case of verification of identity, can emit a signal to the verification device only if it is synchronized with the figures and letters on the golden plaque under his scalp.

The adult thus created goes to a university where he is trained in the occupation he has chosen: astronaut, social hostess, manager of a national farm, and so on.

If an individual eventually decides that he has lived long enough, he goes to the conception centre and voluntarily liberates his spiritual ego by separating his astral body from his physical body. The latter belongs to the Knowers, and the ordinary inhabitants of the planet do not know what they do with it.

The mystery of the Yetis

Besides the highly developed inhabitants of Baavi, there are also ten-foot giants of the type known on Earth as Yetis (or abominable snowmen). They are extremely gentle, but their intellectual level is that of a child from five to eight years of age. They are employed on the national farms and treated with great kindness.

These Yetis live and procreate as they wish; the general laws of the planet do not apply to them. They do not have sexual relations with the other inhabitants, and if they did, their relations would be sterile, which leads the Baavians to believe that the two races do not have the same origin.

The Yetis are considered to be the common ancestors of most men in the universe. Some of them live in a wild state on all inhabited planets. On Earth, they have been reported in the Himalayas and the Andes, apprehensively avoiding contact with other men.

The base at Baalbek

Baavian spacecraft use a system of gravitational appropriation that has nothing in common with our primitive rockets.

The ancient Baavians first used photonic, then ionic propulsion, outside planetary fields of gravity, to give their craft an acceleration that could reach a speed of 170,000 miles per second. Escape velocity was obtained by anti-gravitation.

Fifteen thousand years ago, in the course of their reconnaissance flights, they built their base on Earth at Baalbek, in what is now Lebanon, where the enormous stone slabs, that formed the landing area still remain. The world's largest cut stone, known as the Hadjar el Gouble, was left in place by the Baavians as testimony to their sojourn on Earth and their knowledge of levitation.

From Mars to Earth

The wanderings of the Baavian astronauts took them to all the inhabitable planets of our galaxy, including Mars.

Mr. N. Y. writes as follows:

Before coming to our planet, and before the Baavian Charter was established, the Sons of the Sun had already sent many expeditions to Mars, which is smaller than Earth and has a gravity only two-thirds as strong, which favoured the landing of spacecraft.

Mars is a vast plain or reddish sandstone rich in oxides, with countless canyons between fifty feet and more than six miles in width, most of them running in a north-south direction. At the bottoms of these canyons are a few shrubby trees no more than ten feet high, standing on both sides of a narrow stream. On the banks of these streams grows a lichenlike moss.

This moss was providential for the Martians because it has the property of storing infrared rays during the daylight hours and then gradually releasing them during the night. As a result, when the temperature on the Martian plateau is from sixty to a hundred degrees below zero, in the canyons, fifteen to twenty feet below ground level, it is close to zero, and near the moss it may be as high as forty or fifty degrees above zero.

The oxygen of the air is largely fixed by the ground under an atmospheric pressure only a tenth that of Earth. During the daytime there is a forty-degree temperature difference between the air and the ground, so that one could walk barefoot in the sunlight and, at the same time, freeze one's nose and ears. This explains why only the bottoms of certain canyons have enough oxygen to maintain a 'monad' of little Martians with robust vitality.

The mammals of Mars are rodents with thick white fur, comparable to large hares. They feed on roots, larvae and the eggs of the big lizards that live among the low rocks of canyon walls.

In deep hollows, water forms marshes in which crustaceans proliferate.

The Baavian astronauts fraternized with the inhabitants of Mars.

It is important to note that their spacecraft were not yet capable of exceeding the speed of light. Since the journey from Baavi to Mars took more than six terrestrial weeks, it is easy to understand why the astronauts quickly had sexual relations with the yellow-skinned little Martian women belonging to the 'Mongol monad.' Furthermore, it was a good chance to escape from the stern regulations of Baavi by founding a lineage of halfbreeds with traits inherited from the giant Sons of the Sun and their small wives.

About twelve thousand years ago, life-sustaining conditions on Mars deteriorated to the point where it became urgent to evacuate the inhabitants. Earth was naturally chosen as the new residence.

This titanic emigration took thirty years of coming and going between the red planet Mars and the blue planet Earth. It was in Tibet, on the high plateaus resembling those of their homeland, that the Martian Mongols chose to settle, and it was here that they procreated with terrestrial women.

Such was the origin of the extraterrestrial strain in all the yellow peoples of Earth; more specifically, the direct ancestors of the Chinese, Japanese, Mois and Koreans, and also the Mayas of South America, whose Mongol forebears migrated there by way of the Bering Strait.

Gratifying amorous experiences with Martian and terrestrial women gradually changed the psychological attitudes of the Baavian astronauts. The social system of their home planet (particularly the elimination of passionate love in favour of planetary love) finally appeared to them as it really was, barren and monstrous.

When they returned to Baavi with these feelings, they soon rebelled openly against the 'Immutable Order' of the Knowers, and they were supported by large numbers of idealists.

It was tacitly agreed between the two opposing sides that the rebels and those who had opted for their ideology

*– all males – would leave Baavi forever. The expatriation
took place ten thousand years ago and was spread over
ten years because the emigrants who included many astronauts, university professors and eminent scientists, numbered 827,600.*

*It was these extraterrestrials who became the superior
ancestors of the people of Earth.*

Such is our unknown genesis, revealed by astranouts of
our time, all Sons of the Sun who have remained faithful
to the inhuman laws of Baavi.

We have now been initiated into the terrestrial and
extraterrestrial life and adventures of our mysterious correspondents, but perhaps you would like to know more
about their antigravitational spacecraft, which undoubtedly foreshadow our future technology.

The secret of antigravitation

Matter is a condensation of motion; that is, an energy
which engenders waves, each with its own frequency. A
material body is therefore nothing but a centre of vibrations with certain characteristics.

Gravity is a pressure resulting from a reaction of surrounding space deformed by the presence of the earth.
Inside the space under consideration is a gravitational
field in which all bodies tend to be pressed against the
ground, in accordance with a law common to gravitational electric, and magnetic phenomena.

To maintain a massive body in levitation close to the
ground, the vibratory frequency of that body must be altered in such a way that it opposes the frequency of the
gravitational field. To do this, the frequency of the body
must be raised to a very high potential (forty-five million
volts for each stone slab at Baalbek).

Vaidorges

Vaidorges are not based on the outmoded principles of
our rockets, which senselessly struggle against opposing
forces steadily increasing toward a limit that will necessarily be reached sooner or later.

The vaidorges of Baavi are antigravitational machines which utilize those forces. They have neutrinic hulls with negative weight. They enter into resonance with gravitational waves which are propagated at a speed greater than that of light, and penetrate everywhere. This entrance into resonance produces an energy that opposes the effects of mass if the spacecraft is already in an environment of negative weight and autonomous gravitational force.

After twenty pages in which he explains the whole scientific process of travel in time and space, Mr. N. Y. comes to the critical moment when the vaidorge, having reached the frontier of gravitational speed, plunges into antitime, or the antiuniverse, without being disintegrated. In this connection, he says, we must not confuse the 'universe of negative time' (known as antitime) with the negative particles of the expanding universe (our universe) which constitute antiworlds. An antiworld is only another galaxy whose matter is antimatter for our galaxy. The universe of negative time flows in the direction opposite to ours: it is the contracting universe.

You now know the essential elements of what Mr. N. Y. writes about the mystery of interstellar spacecraft and the secret masters of our planet. It still remains to be seen whether his account is a remarkably constructed hoax or the greatest revelation of the century.

Also by Robert Charroux in Sphere Books

Masters of the World

'Enigmatic objects fly across our sky; monuments whose
purpose is unknown to us stand on the surface of our land,
and beneath it are buried structures belonging to no
known civilization. Mystery is all around us and neither
our science nor our history can give an answer to it. In
spite of everything, and in the face of opposition, silence or
disapproval from those who do not want the veil to be
lifted, Man tries to break open the door that leads to
knowledge. Documents are speaking, initiates are breaking
the seals of tablets hidden in sanctuaries – Man will soon
know much more about his unknown past . . .'   Robert
Charroux in MASTERS OF THE WORLD

Among Charroux's shaking disclosures are:

* Proof that a Universal Deluge – with waves of six
  thousand feet – did indeed occur in ancient times
* The true facts behind the Miracle at Fatima
* The fascinating history of the Rosicrucians, for many
  centuries the most carefully guarded secret society in
  the world
* The secret powers of jade – and the enigma of The
  Man in the Jade Mask . . .
* The strange stone discs of Tibet with their awesome
  message of spacecraft visiting Earth in remote
  prehistory

These and many more such revelations will make you
change the way you think about history – and your own
lives . . .

0 7221 2271 3   COSMOLOGY   £1.25

And also from the Non-Fiction lists

UFO Magic in Motion

ARTHUR SHUTTLEWOOD

Shimmering spheroids hovering over the British Isles
Strange lifeforms beneath the Antarctic
Extraterrestrials with a message for mankind

UFO MAGIC IN MOTION is Arthur Shuttlewood's most
penetrating study yet of a phenomenon which has
captured the imagination of millions of people. Mr
Shuttlewood examines innumerable eye-witness accounts
of close encounters of the first, second and third kind
which provide strong evidence for the existence of
extraterrestrial life. He raises the issue of whether these
lifeforms are friendly or aggressive, and what their
purpose is in appearing to us in their mysterious
spaceships:

* Could it be that these creatures are responsible for the
slowing down of the earth which is currently taking place?
* Are they connected with the sun-spots which affect our
planet's weather patterns so drastically?

These and many other questions are answered by Mr
Shuttlewood in his latest contribution to the study of
Unidentified Flying Objects –

UFO MAGIC IN MOTION

0 7221 7808 5   COSMOLOGY   £1.10

Alternative 3

WATKINS, AMBROSE AND MILES

THE MOST ASTOUNDING AND FRIGHTENING CONSPIRACY EVER

Research for what was originally intended as a straightforward TV documentary on the scientific 'Brain Drain' from Britain revealed some extremely disturbing things:

* Many people joining the Brain Drain are vanishing off the face of the Earth – literally
* Earth will soon be unable to support life: our climate's recent strange behaviour is only a warm-up for the cataclysms to come
* The super-powers have been working secretly together in space for *decades*
* Government agencies are kidnapping ordinary people and turning them into mindless slaves by advanced brainwashing methods
* Astronauts' reports of strange things they saw on the Moon have been suppressed
* Ultra-secret joint US/USSR conferences are held each month in a submarine beneath the Arctic ice-cap

And this was just the tip of the iceberg. Behind these and many more sinister features lurks the top secret operation known as ALTERNATIVE 3 – an international government conspiracy so monstrous that the human mind can scarcely grasp its true enormity. This courageous book goes beyond even the ground-breaking TV exposé to reveal the full awesome horror of ALTERNATIVE 3 . . .

0 7221 1145 2   OCCULT/COSMOLOGY   95p